SLEEPING BEAUTIES, AWAKENED WOMEN

DR. TIM JORDAN, M.D.

Permission to quote in critical reviews with citation:
Sleeping Beauties, Awakened Women
By Dr. Tim Jordan, M.D.

Print ISBN 978-0-9884613-6-9
E-book ISBN 978-0-9884613-7-6

www.dunrobin.us

ACKNOWLEDGMENTS

First, and most importantly, I am so grateful to all the girls I have sat with in my office, my retreats and camps, and in schools for all that they have taught me. So much of my education about girls has come from sitting on the carpet listening to their stories. I appreciate the courage it took to be so open, vulnerable, real, and honest. And your stories inspired me to write this book, so I am forever grateful. You rock!

My wife, Anne, is happy to, in her words: "be getting her husband back!" She truly is the best mom I have ever met, and I am thankful for all the ways she contributed to this book: typing out my scribbles, editing, suggestions, facilitating camps and mother-daughter and father-daughter retreats with me, and giving presentations around the world together. Anne has always supported me when I have started off on new adventures, this book being the latest in a long line. And she has been an incredible role model to so many female campers and staff about what a balanced, whole woman can be.

When people ask me why I have such a passion for working with girls, I often reply that my interest in girls started with being the older brother to 5 younger sisters growing up. Lynn, Molly, Julie, Barbara, and Jenny all helped me to become both comfortable with girls and also to be safe for girls to be around and talk to. So thank you for giving me my earliest education on girls.

I also tell people that one of the happiest days of my life was when our first child was delivered and it was a girl! I have wanted to be a dad since I was a kid, and my daughter Kelly started me out on that path. We spent so much time together reading, playing with her dolls and having tea parties, doing imaginary pretend games; she taught me a ton about girls and about the role of parents in raising daughters. My two sons TJ and John were blessings and a blast as well, just in a different way. Raising children with Anne has without a doubt been the most fun and valuable thing I have ever done.

Next up is Barb Kaste, who for some reason took on the task of typing out each chapter from my hand-written notes. As a physician, I have so many abbreviations and a sort of half-print/half-cursive handwriting style that it was a monumental task for her to undertake. She is one of our stalwart camp counselors too, so her heart was really full force into this book. Thanks for all the time and love you poured onto the pages for me.

I also want to thank several people who read chapters and gave feedback along the way. So my heartfelt thanks to Beth Knight, Leilani Long, Liz Fuchs, Gail Strubberg, my son TJ Jordan, Anna Marie Bushlack, Savannah McCord, Pamela Dunn, our camp director Gretchen Long, and my sister Jenny Harrell.

A huge shout-out also to my group of dear friends, Gail and John Strubberg and Liz and Dave Fuchs for their undying support of me and my adventures. I have learned so much from all the deep discussions we have had over the years. Your ideas and feedback have for many years been instrumental in my thinking and perspectives. This book would have been less rich without your love and support.

There are several people who have jumped on board over the past months to help me get this book published, marketed and read. They include Brian Cross, Mark Sutherland, Amy Burger, Kelly Ganz, and Courtney Rothman and of course, Dunrobin Publishing. I appreciate that they understood the value of what I wanted to say, and their expertise and enthusiasm was extremely beneficial.

Finally, I wish to acknowledge the many authors whose books I have devoured over the years. I love to read, and I love to learn new things. When I get into the flow, I grab ideas from all over the place, many of which came from past readings or lectures. I love to put ideas from various sources together into new ways of looking at issues. I would not have been able to accomplish this without the ideas put forth in the books in my bibliography.

Warmest thanks to all…

~ Dr. Tim

TABLE OF CONTENTS

INTRODUCTION

ONCE UPON A TIME...

How should we be able to forget those ancient myths that are at the beginning of all peoples, the myths about dragons that at the last moment turn into princesses; perhaps all the dragons of our lives are princesses who are only waiting for us to see them as beautiful and brave.

"Perhaps everything terrible is in its deepest being something helpless that wants help from us." Ranier M. Rilke

I don't believe our girls are as troubled and whacked out as the media has made them out to be for the past 40 plus years. Have we experienced more bullying and aggressive, violent behaviors with adolescent girls in the past twenty years? Yes. Are we seeing relational aggression behaviors once thought to be the privy of middle school and high school girls in younger and younger girls? Yes. Have we seen a disproportionate rise in depression, anxiety, self-mutilation and eating disorders in girls? Yes.

But what if the real problem isn't these issues, but how we have framed them?

For over 40 years we've heard the mantra that starting in middle school, girl's self esteem plummets and doesn't recover for years.

What if we've gotten it all wrong?

Depression, anxiety, cutting, and eating disorders on the rise...

Sleeping Beauties, Awakened Women

What if we are missing the forest for the trees?

You see, I choose to view these behaviors as symptoms of a deeper need in girls. As the Ranier quote indicates, I see these issues as a cry for help from girls. They are suffering and struggling through the normal transformation from girl to woman, from maiden to matron, but they are not getting the knowledge and support they need from adults.

"The only journey is the one within." Ranier M. Rilke

The myths, fairy tales, and time-honored stories from past times were actually told to adolescent girls and boys to impart lessons about their metamorphosis to adulthood. They taught us that the Heroine's Journey is an inward one, where a girl, through overcoming hardships and challenges, becomes a loving, wise, powerful woman ready to rule her kingdom.

That story is still alive and well and essential for girls in the 21st century. But the path of transformation has been clouded over by more pressing needs and issues today: materialism; look-ism; perfectionism; early sexualization and objectification; earlier onset of puberty; technology. Girls today are so busy, distracted and stressed out that they have lost sight of what's truly important, the Heroine's Journey.

Transformation for girls is a different animal than it is for boys. The Hero's Journey has always been a more external experience. Men leave home to slay dragons, go on quests to discover the fountain of youth, capture the Holy Grail, or join the Starfleet. Men long for victories and adventure and domination, with little or no time for relationships. It's about fighting to the death, and with regards to aging, it's even about fighting death to the death.

The Heroine's journey is more inward, often involving some pain and struggle. It's more of an internal struggle, in the end resulting in a raised level of consciousness and a higher sense of self. Transformation is the Heroines work, and it requires a period of darkness and solitude. The best metaphors that illustrate this journey lie in fairy tales, both old and modern.

> *"It seems to me that almost all our sadnesses are moments of tension, which we feel as paralysis because we no longer hear our astonished emotions living; because we are alone in the unfamiliar presence that has entered us, because everything we trusted and are used to is for a moment taken away from us; because we stand in the midst of a transition where we cannot remain standing."*
>
> Ranier M. Rilke

I spent a year of fellowship training with Dr. T. Berry Brazelton at the Harvard Child Development Center in Boston, where he taught us his beautiful Touchpoints model. I will go into more detail about how this model fits preadolescent and adolescent girls in Chapter 2, but for now allow me to summarize.

"You must go into the dark to bring forth your light." Debbie Ford

Whenever kids, teens, or adults go through an important emotional, psychological leap in growth, it is always accompanied by a period of disruption. People feel out-of-sorts, moody, and ambivalent about their growth; think 5 year olds, high school and college seniors, midlife crises, and empty nest for points of reference.

Starting at about age ten to twelve, girls need to undergo a touchpoint that will to a large degree define who they become as adult women. And like Cinderella, Snow White, Sleeping Beauty, Rapunzel, and all the other fairy tale heroines from past times, this touchpoint involves hard work, suffering, pain, metaphorical sleeping (solitude and going inward and downward), and overcoming challenges that allow girls to transform from an innocent young girl into a princess or queen. The depth and importance of this normal developmental stage is matched by the disruptions girls experience emotionally, socially, psychologically, and biologically.

"Embrace your solitude and love it. Endure the pain it causes, and try to sing out with it." Ranier M. Rilke

It takes a lot of quiet, reflective, alone time for girls to discover what's going on inside of them; to know and understand what they are feeling; to know what they need; to figure out who they are and who they aspire to become.

Cinderella toiled for years, becoming more independent and self-reliant. Sleeping Beauty and Snow White spent time 'sleeping' at this crucial stage of development, in essence withdrawing from the external world and connecting more deeply within themselves. Rapunzel roamed the desert taking care of her twin children for seven years on her own.

Fairy tales teach us that real growth and transformation require time, patience, sometimes pain and suffering, and focus. It's a process, and at times it can look messy. Just ask Snow White, Jane Eyre, Scarlet O'Hara and Eleanor Roosevelt. Better yet, have girls ask their mothers, grandmothers, and aunts what sort of 'sleep' they underwent during their adolescent years, and what 'woke them up.'

"All of mans miseries derive from not being able to sit quietly in a room alone." Blaise Pascal, French philosopher

I worry that most girls today are not focused on this inner growth and development. They are too busy striving for straight A's and spots on select sports teams and vying for seats at ivy-league colleges.

They are distracted by all the screens and technology that shriek at them 24/7, and by all the images and information that overwhelms their senses.

"Why should we be in such desperate haste to succeed and in such desperate enterprises? If a man does not keep pace with his companions, perhaps it is because he hears a different drummer. Let him step to the music he hears, however measured or far away." Thoreau

And so the 'sleeping' today's girls are experiencing is unhealthy: feeling numbed out; disconnected from themselves and others; depressed and anxious; feeling lost and stressed and empty. This kind of sleep doesn't allow girls to evolve to higher levels of consciousness. It keeps them feeling stuck, powerless and out-of-control.

This book will provide you with ideas about helping girls to:

- Become aware of what's going on internally with their brain wiring and hormones, i.e. the biological component of their touchpoint.
- Learn how to slow down, become quiet, reflect, and soul-search. Girls need these skills in self-calming, mindfulness, and living in the present moment.
- Learn how to recognize, understand and express all of their emotions in healthy ways. They also need to learn how to suppress their emotions sometimes when it is required.
- Create sacred spaces where they can learn about themselves, be real and honest, share their stories with girls and women of all ages, question everything, and learn that they are not crazy or alone with what they are feeling and experiencing.

- Acquire skills to handle their conflicts directly and effectively, speak their truth with authority, assert themselves, redirect negative self-talk, and get their needs met.
- Learn how to become more media savvy and scrutinize all the images bombarding them every waking moment of every day.
- Develop and become fully engaged in their interests and passions.
- Focus on and develop their "inner resumes."

I will be using many stories throughout this book to illustrate points about girls and what they are experiencing today. I have changed the names and details for confidentiality purposes, but these stories are real ones, from real girls. I am so grateful for the courage they have shown in being so vulnerable, real, and honest. Most adults have never bared their souls in these kinds of settings, but these girls did. I am so proud of them for teaching us all so much about their lives and needs.

After 30 years of working with girls of all ages in my counseling practice, support groups, personal growth/leadership weekend retreats and summer camps, and with classrooms of girls in my Strong Girls, Strong World Program, it is still amazing to me to discover how little girls know about the female brain and the normal hormonal changes and effects of their menstrual cycles. In the past ten years, girls are finding it harder and harder to identifying what they are feeling. And I am saddened that ninety-five percent of the high school girls I work with don't put aside any moments to be alone, quiet, and to reflect because "There's no time!"

Well, I think it's time we shake up the system and start teaching girls to grow up in a more conscious way. It's vital that they understand and focus on the Heroine's Journey that every one of them must undertake. And it is imperative that adults give them the time, opportunity, information, guidance, and personal stories to guide them at this critical stage of development.

That's why I wrote this book!

CHAPTER 1

SLEEPING BEAUTIES

The versions of Sleeping Beauty written by the Grimm brothers and Charles Perrault in the late 1700's, and in the older folk tales they based their stories on, communicated a much different message than our modern Disney versions. The stories even had a different title, *Brier Rose.* Let me summarize these original tales here.

A king and queen tried for years to have children, but to no avail. Then, magically, the queen became pregnant. After the birth of Rose, the King gave a great feast to celebrate. He had only 12 golden plates, so he invited only 12 of the 13 wise women in the kingdom. The first 11 guests stepped forward and gave their gifts to the baby, when suddenly the uninvited wise woman appeared and, angry at being snubbed, she put an evil curse on the baby.

"When she is 15, the princess will prick her finger on a spindle and fall down dead."

Luckily, the 12th wise woman had yet to bequeath her magical gift.

"The princess will not die, but only fall into a deep, 100-year sleep."

The king had every spindle in the kingdom destroyed to protect his daughter. She grew to be beautiful and kind, but as she got older, she started to feel stifled and constrained due to her parents' overprotection. Rose longed for some adventure. On the day she turned 15, her parents were away for a short while, leaving Rose alone. She climbed an old tower in the castle, coming to an old door with a rusty key in the lock. She opened this door and saw an old woman spinning flax.

"What are you doing?" she asked.

"I'm spinning, want to try?"

Rose took hold of the spindle, and the magic curse was realized as she pricked her finger, drawing blood. She fell down onto a bed, and a deep sleep overtook her. Her sleep spread to the entire palace, casting everyone and everything, including the just-returned king and queen into a deep, heavy slumber. All around the castle, a brier hedge began to grow until it surrounded and covered the entire castle. All that was left was the tale of Brier Rose, the sleeping princess. From time to time, a prince, upon hearing this story, would attempt to pass through the hedge, but none succeeded, and they all died a horrible death.

The 100 years passed, and the day came for Rose to wake up. It so happened that a young prince arrived in this town on that very day, and after hearing the story, he resolved to try his hand at seeing the sleeping princess. As he approached the hedge, the briers turned into big beautiful flowers, which let the prince through, then quickly closed behind him, becoming the hedge once again. He wandered through the castle until he found the room where the princess lay asleep.

In the old folk tale and the Perrault versions, the prince found Rose already awake, and they sat and talked for hours, after which they got married and lived happily ever after. The Grimm ending was a little different: The prince bent down and kissed her, and as soon as his lips touched hers, Rose opened her eyes and smiled. They walked downstairs together to find the king and queen and the whole palace awakened.

A great feast was held to celebrate. And the prince and Rose were married in splendor and lived happily to the end of their lives. But what are we, and our daughters, supposed to make of this story?

Many of its symbols appear over and over in other traditional fairy tales and myths. Let me explain the metaphors here.

Girls and women fall asleep when they face fears their parents can't protect them from and they feel unprepared to face. One prominent time in a girl's life this occurs is puberty. And what does an adolescent girl fear? Many things. They feel overwhelmed with all the changes occurring within their bodies, including the upcoming first period. They don't feel ready to face and handle their own sexual desires, nor the desires of boys. Girls at this age don't feel ready for sex and the threat of getting pregnant and motherhood. And today, we can add STDs, the pressures described in Chapter 3, sexual abuse, and other fears to the challenges girls must face.

Adolescent girls are also experiencing changes in their friendships, their values, their perceptions of the world, their relationship with parents, and their interests and passions. Girls become overwhelmed with their feelings, stresses and pressures in their lives, and the looming responsibilities of adulthood. It is the immense specter of all this that creates the need for girls to retreat at times, to withdraw and gather themselves.

What girls need at this stage is not continuous and unrelenting connections and busyness via technology and activities. They require space, solitude, and times when they can be alone and quiet—and unreachable. In this day and age that may sound impossible, but we all must rethink what our girls need.

The king does his best to protect his daughter, destroying spindles and keeping her locked away in the castle. At 15, she's starting puberty, she begins to feel smothered, and she wants some adventure. The king and queen leaving the castle represent the need for Rose to explore and understand the world on her own now. She needs some distance from her parents. Rose asking the old woman, "What are you doing?" is her way of saying, "What's going on with my new body and feelings and desires?" Pricking her finger and drawing blood is considered signs of her first period or even her first intercourse, also represented by the rusty key in the lock.

Girls today are pushed to be sexual and grown up and into boys before they are emotionally mature and powerful enough to handle it. Their bodies are ready for it at earlier and earlier ages, but they are not emotionally or psychologically ready for it. They have been experiencing subtle and not so subtle messages of sexualization and objectification since they were little girls, so that by adolescence they have numbly accepted it as gospel. Most girls no longer question these cultural messages, if they ever did. Thus, it's hard not to act these messages out. Without the benefit of the acquired wisdom and strength that comes through a conscious transformation, girls end up having to find ways to withdraw, often unhealthy ways: numbing their feelings, depression, anxiety, alcohol and drugs, hook-ups, driving themselves to be the best student, athlete or career woman. They literally 'lose themselves' in their activities and work.

The 'sleep' girls require is not total withdrawal from the world for 100 years. It calls for a balance of factors:
- Times to be in sacred spaces, times of solitude and reflection and soul searching, time spent with girlfriends and family where they feel safe to be themselves.
- Times they engage in their passions, discovering strengths and weaknesses, discovering what they like and need, moments to

feel deeply and express emotions in healthy ways, and periods when adults /mentors work with girls in ways that allow them to see their highest self. They need time to experiment and attempt new things and stretch themselves out of their comfort zones.

So it's a kind of dance where they withdraw to collect themselves, in addition to engaging in activities that enlarge them as people and help them define themselves and their life's purpose. The prince didn't transform Brier Rose. She spent 100 years, metaphorically, outgrowing her fears and gaining wisdom, strength and confidence. On the contrary, in Disney's version, when the prince awakens her with a kiss, she's no different than when she fell asleep. Brier Rose in the original versions awakens as a new person, transformed to a higher level of awareness. Metaphorically, it's not a prince's kiss that awakens women; it is having discovered who they are and embracing their magnificence and passions. Girls are transformed, not rescued!

In The Wizard of Oz, when Dorothy was lost on the yellow brick road, the scarecrow appeared to guide her. Girls at this stage need mentors who can provide information and be sounding boards. But the scarecrow also represented Dorothy's own, inner knowing. She needed some quiet time to tap into her inner voice and to know which direction to take in her life. The same applies for women during their senior years of high school and college, and at other significant crossroads in their lives.

Julia Roberts' character in the movie *Runaway Bride* docked her boat. After leaving Richard Gere's character at the altar, she stopped rebounding from guy to guy and spent the next year focused on her own growth. As described in more detail in chapter 9, Julia engages in self-discovery that year through many avenues, including finally following her dream of making decorative lamps. At the end of the year she is a different person. Her year of transformation involved both quiet times and action. She became whole and finally ready for a committed relationship, but on her terms. I suggest you watch this movie with these metaphors in mind.

In the tales about Sleeping Beauty, Cinderella, Snow White, Rapunzel, Jane Eyre, Dorothy and *Runaway Bride*, the woman herself is the agent of change, not a man. The marriage of the princess and prince, or king and queen, is symbolic of the marriage of a woman's feminine and masculine energies. With this balance, the woman feels whole, and is then ready to rule her kingdom.

These are the versions that ring true for me.

CHAPTER 2

TOUCHPOINTS

Six-year-old Fae had always been a pretty easygoing child. She had two siblings, a 9-year-old sister and a 2-year-old brother. She had started preschool at 2 years old, with some mild separation issues that resolved after a few weeks. Afterward, she coasted through three more years of preschool uneventfully.

And then, two weeks before kindergarten began, the stuff hit the fan. Suddenly this cute little kid had turned into a whiny monster. There were fits about getting dressed in the morning; there were fits about going to bed at night. She complained loudly about how much easier her parents were on her younger brother, and how it wasn't fair that her older brother got more freedom and privileges. And most disturbing was her newfound anxiety. Fae wanted, no demanded, that a parent or sibling be with her wherever she was in the house. She threw fits whenever her parents tried to go out and leave the kids with a sitter, to the point that they usually gave in and stayed home.

They called my office for an appointment after Fae's first tumultuous week in kindergarten. She didn't want to go. There had been major tears, whining and screaming all week long. She worried about going to school every evening, threw a tantrum all the way to school, and even threw a few fits in the school hallways when her mom tried to leave her. Her parents were perplexed; this was so unlike her. I took an extensive history, then described to Fae's parents my thoughts on what was going on. At the top of my list was the likelihood that Fae was going through a normal touchpoint.

Back in the mid-1980s, I did a year of fellowship training in Developmental Behavioral Pediatrics with acclaimed pediatric authority Dr. T. Berry Brazelton. Of all the myriad lessons I learned from Dr. Brazelton, his touchpoints model may have affected my thinking and practice more than anything else. For an in-depth read on this subject, I suggest his books, *Touchpoints Birth to Three* and *Touchpoints Three to Six*.

In essence, touchpoints are times in children's lives when they undergo important stages. Children's development isn't linear; it's jagged with periods of intense growth followed by periods of homeostasis where kids internalize and practice their new skills. By growth here I don't mean physically, I mean emotional, social and psychological growth. Just prior to and during these intense phases, kids tend to fall apart. They become moodier, more out of sorts and crabbier. They also may regress somewhat from their latest new skill acquisition. It's as though their whole system is gearing up and gathering energy for the next big leap in development.

Once they've achieved the new growth, i.e. learned to walk, become more autonomous, learned to use their words to get their needs met, etc., they settle back down and practice their new skill. But their nervous system and spirit are constantly pushing them onto the next developmental challenge.

Dr. Brazelton named these periods "touchpoints" because he saw them as opportunities for pediatricians and professionals working with children to 'touch' into the family system and make a difference. At well-child visits, pediatricians could anticipate with parents the next stages coming up and give them developmental information on what to expect and why. By normalizing what was to come, pediatricians could prevent parents from freaking out and overreacting to their child's new behaviors. And it works.

When I practiced general pediatrics for three years after my fellowship training, I used the touchpoint model at my well-child visits, and I know it gave parents much more confidence to deal with their children's upheavals. They could remain more emotionally detached when their child was losing it, and could become the calming influence their children so desperately needed during intense stages.

Back to Fae. There is an important growing-up stage that children experience somewhere between 5 and 7 years of age. The end result is that kids grow more independent and confident in themselves and their ability to master challenges. They learn to overcome the normal fears of this age and assume much more responsibility for taking care of themselves in every way. But first there is the upheaval, as Fae was demonstrating. What most parents of 5- to 7-year-olds will describe is a child who in one moment acts or speaks like a 10-year-old and then in the next moment acts like a 3 year-old. Parents often see a lot of regressive behaviors such as thumb-sucking, baby talk and separation anxiety. Siblings can have a big effect here, too.

Older siblings tend to pull younger ones in their direction, making the younger one desire to act like the older, and be treated the same as well. Conversely, younger siblings tend to draw out more regressive behaviors, pulling older ones backward. It's as though they have a foot in both worlds, and it reflects the child's ambivalence about growing up. What kids are saying in essence is, *I want to grow up, but I don't!* I've had kids in my counseling practice look me in the eyes and flatly declare, *"I don't want to grow up!"* Kids have told me, *"I like being a baby,"* and, *"I like being at home."*

All of these ambivalent feelings end up looking like temper tantrums, whining and power struggles. If parents focus too much energy on the regressions, engage in the struggles, and add their own emotions to the child's, the situation becomes unmanageable. That's when I got the phone calls.

What parents need first and foremost is developmental information to help them normalize their child's behaviors. With that information in hand, it's easier to take a step back and stay detached from their child's emotional upheavals and regressions. They can devote a lot less time and energy to regressive behaviors, and they can look for opportunities to nudge their children forward, i.e. with privileges and responsibilities or appropriate ways to help them feel powerful. For more details about this stage, see my book *Food Fights and Bedtime Battles*.

Fae was in the midst of this stage, and there were a few other factors adding to the chaos. Her mom had quit her job that June and spent the summer at home with the kids, and her 2-year-old brother was going to preschool only two mornings a week. So it was doubly hard for Fae to go to school while her brother got Mom to himself all day in the comfort of home. Plus, her dad's business had taken off, so he was home less, and when he was around, he was extremely tired and distracted.

I encouraged Fae's parents to carve out some special one-on-one time with her, especially out of the house so that their 'dates' really were focused on her, away from all the distractions of home life. Some of her behaviors came from feeling left out, so I advised her parents to teach her to tell them when she felt this and to ask for some special time with them. *"Dad, I've been feeling sad lately because we haven't had time to do much together and you've been working late. What I want is for us to go to the park Saturday morning and practice my soccer."*

Fae's parents learned how to avoid adding their emotions to hers, and to stay calm when she started to unravel. They negotiated some new freedoms and responsibilities with her, and that made Fae feel more grown-up and empowered. Within a few weeks, their home had settled down appreciably. A month later it was all just a memory as Fae had progressed through the phase and became well ensconced in her new school.

Dig into yourself. Go into yourself and find out how deep is the place from which life springs; at its source you will find the answer to your question. Rilke

Let's talk now about the touchpoint girls experience during the middle and high school years.

Fairy tales and myths show us a different way of understanding touchpoints, especially the ones for adolescent girls. And the original versions of our favorite tales, in particular, give us valuable perspective on girls. The girls in stories like Sleeping Beauty and Snow White spend much of their adolescent years in a deep sleep. Why would these myths require an adolescent girl to sleep? Because they were not ready to face the heavy demands life was presenting to them. In her book *Spinning Straw Into Gold*, Joan Gould shows that for girls in the 1600s, it was fears of abusive men, sexuality, marriage, menses, childbirth, motherhood, death of their children and their own deaths at young ages. About two in 100 women died of childbirth, a quarter of children died before the age of 1, and half of all children were dead by 10 years of age. That's a scary proposition.

Today, girls approaching puberty and adolescence also have things they fear and want to avoid: early puberty, body changes and periods; early sexualization, objectification and sexual feelings; being harassed and desired by boys; sexually transmitted diseases, teen pregnancy and sexual abuse; pressure to balance career and family; high expectations in school and getting into 'the best colleges'; pressures to succeed by parents, teachers and coaches. Whether consciously or unconsciously, girls don't feel ready for sexuality and being desired by boys, the changes in their bodies, and their feelings. They get exhausted from the pressures of having to be perfect and 'good girls.'

When teen boys go through puberty, their bodies grow bigger and stronger, but they don't feel like they are changing that much. Girls, on the other hand, undergo tremendous changes at puberty. The bleeding from menstruation is scary and mysterious. Their bodies after puberty look a lot different, with breasts and hips and curves where there once were none. They can actually get pregnant! There are also many more taboos and judgments related to girls when it comes to sexuality. Boys who have multiple sex partners aren't called sluts, and even today can gain elevated social status because of it. Not so for girls.

Teen girls also sense that in the eyes of our culture and the media and men, they are at the height of their value. This value, of course, is measured by their looks: beauty, sensuality, hotness and desirability. And this occurs at a time in their lives when girls are the most self-conscious, the most vulnerable and the least confident. On the one hand, it feels good to be attractive and desirable and wanted. But, on the other hand, girls also know at some level that it is very superficial, and it is not intimacy.

Many girls have demonstrated a wish to get rid of their body that has so complicated their lives and brought on so much fear and stress. Or they may give into the pressures and hook-up or sext, or dress and act provocatively because to allow themselves to be objectified, i.e. treated like an object, means there are no emotional strings attached. They get to be numb to the pain and fears. Combine this with all the challenges I describe in chapter 3, and it's easy to see why girls need to retreat from the world until they can gather the wisdom and strength to face these daunting pressures and demands. It also makes sense why they get so out-of-sorts, so moody, and regress. Many girls have told me they wish they could just fall asleep after fifth grade and not wake up until they are in college. That way they could avoid all the 'mean girl' dramas, harassment from boys, dating, pressures of grades, sports and activities, the acne and braces. They could just awaken as a woman with all her ducks in a row.

As a result, I hate Walt Disney! Well, not really him, just the messages about girls in his movies. My love of Disney movies like Cinderella and Sleeping Beauty was shattered once I read the original versions of these stories, written in the late 1600s by the Grimm Brothers and Charles Perrault. The original stories were truly about the heroine's journey, the transformation of young girls to princesses, queens and mature women. Disney bastardized the message into a hero's tale, with the victim girl needing to be rescued by a handsome prince. The girl was no longer the object of change; the boy took on that role.

Joan Gould's book, *Spinning Straw into Gold*, turned me onto reading the original versions of stories like Cinderella, Sleeping Beauty, Snow White, Rapunzel, and Beauty and the Beast. These stories were written for adolescent girls and boys as a way to guide them through their teen years. Disney made them into love stories aimed at younger children, and brought the patriarchal perspective of his time into the narratives.

Here are a few snapshots of those earlier versions of fairy tales:
- At the age of 15, an innocent and well-protected Sleeping Beauty is left alone one day and, just as predicted by a curse on the day she was born, she pricks her finger on a spindle and falls into a deep sleep.
- Snow White has been hiding in the forest for years, taking care of seven dwarfs. She bites into an apple poisoned by her jealous stepmother, and she too falls into a deep sleep. She is laid in glass coffin where she slumbers for several years.

- Cinderella is forced to work alone, day and night, for years in her stepmother's home. She is ignored or teased by her two stepsisters, and spends her adolescence alone, without friends, slaving away.

- Rapunzel is taken from her parents by a witch and locked in a tower as a child. When the witch discovers that a prince has been climbing up her long hair to visit with her as a blossoming teenager, she sends a pregnant Rapunzel off into the desert where she is forced to take care of her twin children alone.

The common thread in these original stories is that at the time of puberty, girls require a time of growth and transformation. 'Sleep' for Snow White and Sleeping Beauty is a metaphor for going inward, retreating from the pressures and challenges of the real world as described in chapter three. They don't awaken until they have developed the confidence and knowledge to face their fears and challenges. They go to sleep as young girls and awaken as mature women. Cinderella uses her years of servitude to learn how to be independent, rely on herself, work hard, endure suffering and loss, and gain self-efficacy. When the ball to find a wife for the prince occurs, she is ready to meet the world on her terms. She is confident and powerful, and this energy is what radiates outward from her and attracts the prince. She has connected with the princess within her, and she's ready for a man, but on her terms. Rapunzel's seven years wandering the desert, taking care of two children, is her time to grow in strength and confidence. When the blinded, weakened prince finds her, it is her tears that heal his eyes and return his sight.

But what insight do these stories give us into what girls need today? They give us a huge amount.

This touchpoint requires girls to have some quiet, alone time to connect with themselves: time to know and understand their feelings, needs and desires; time to soul search and daydream. It requires sacred space where they can fully engage in their interests and passions, leading to a sense of fulfillment and discovering their life's purpose and work. They need to 'sleep' metaphorically. The evolution from girl to woman also may involve some suffering, sacrifice, loss and pain. Overcoming these feelings and experiences is grist for the mill; it strengthens girls and creates resiliency, confidence, and grit.

I see girls in middle and high school whose moods and confidence fluctuate daily, even hourly, depending on what's going on in their world. One minute they are on top of the world because a boy noticed them or a popular girl included them. The next moment they are totally devastated because a boy they like is talking with their best friend, or two friends don't invite her to a sleepover. But don't equate this with poor self-esteem! When I watch girls this age at my retreats, I am so impressed with their vitality and spirit. Their core seems fine to me. The hourly fluctuations are part hormones, part drama, and part lack of coping skills. Everything is in flux with them: their bodies and feelings, their friendships, and their relationship with their parents.

It may be hard to see the princess beneath the layers of emotion, drama and mood swings, but she is there, intact, just sleeping! Withdrawal is a protection from feeling overwhelmed by pressures, boys and all the fears she's facing, real or imagined. Girls need time to retreat, and they need safe places to relax and let their hair down and just be kids. My retreats and camps have become that safe place for the girls who attend, and because they feel safe, we can see their best selves come out and play. Not recognizing the importance and needs of this transformative touchpoint leaves girls feeling out of control, overwhelmed and unsupported. That is why things like depression, anxiety and self-mutilation start to emerge. These are signs of being overwhelmed.

Sleeping Beauties, Awakened Women

There will be other times when women need a healthy balance between 'sleeping' and 'engaging' as I described in chapter 1. High school and college seniors find themselves at a crossroads, a touchpoint. They need to make some important choices that will have a huge impact on their lives. Like in other touchpoints, girls tend to be out of sorts during these transition years too. I see many high school girls in my counseling practice during the spring of their senior year because of intense power struggles with their parents, especially their mothers. They experience more meltdowns and often feel overwhelmed with all they have to do.

One unhealthy way girls 'sleep' during the senior year is by procrastinating and appearing apathetic. Parents complain throughout the senior year that their daughter is behind on applications and letters and school visits. This is another example of a detrimental way girls can deal with their fears and other feelings: by avoiding them. And it's another opportunity for parents to see this touchpoint for what it is and to provide the appropriate support their daughter needs. Future touchpoints occur during the months before women get married, during the nine months of pregnancy with a first baby, and during the empty nest. Other awakening periods can occur at the death of her parents or another big loss, including divorce, or because of cancer or some life-threatening illness. At these transformative times, women need opportunities for solitude to go inward and know what's right for them. They need to 'dock their boats' instead of sailing here and there, rudderless.

One last aspect of the touchpoints model parents should understand is balancing female and male energies. Robert Johnson, in his 1983 book *WE: Understanding the Psychology of Romantic Love*, brings his Jungian training to the table to describe this process.

"The psyche sees our capacity for relatedness and love as a 'feminine' 'quality, emanating from the feminine side of our psyche.

By contrast it views the ability to wield power, control situations, and defend territory as strengths that we find in the 'masculine' department of the psyche. To become a complete man or woman, each of us must develop both sides of our psyche. We must be able both to handle power and to love, both to exert control and to flow spontaneously with fate – each value in its season. "

Johnson has written many books, most of them in the 1980's, on the topic of archetypes and male and female energies. I encourage you to read his books: *She: Understanding Feminine Psychology, He: Understanding Masculine Psychology*, and *We: Understanding the Psychology of Romantic Love*. The following information about male and female energies was derived from his works and other authors you can find in the bibliography.

Feminine energy is usually described in myths and fairy tales as being about growth and evolution, being still and receptive. It guides one toward intimacy, relationships, feelings, introspection, intuition and love. Myths show us that the feminine qualities give life meaning, i.e. relationships, love, beauty, creativity and inner wisdom. Feminine energy is also the ability to give up control and hand over challenges to fate, to trust the universe. Masculine energy is more about the pursuit of power and hierarchy, defending territory and family, accomplishing great things, competition, being the best, notoriety, getting ahead and aggression. Mythical males went on quests and journeys slaying dragons and hunting for treasures like the Holy Grail and the one ring to bind them all in *The Lord of the Rings*.

For a long time, our society has been patriarchal, with masculine values overriding feminine ones. Feminine qualities like relationship, love and collaboration have been shoved aside for the much more valued masculine qualities of striving to be the best at all costs, of achieving power. Thirty years later, I see girls struggling mightily in trying to achieve this balance. Our culture, and in some ways even the feminist movement, has so overvalued prestige, achievement and competition that the other parts of their psyche get little time, attention or affirmation. If a 25-year-old woman says she wants to stay home and raise her children, a lot of eyebrows are raised. Many people, and often women, will judge her as settling or throwing away her career and potential. The masculine qualities of ambition and the acquisition of power and prestige has driven out feminine qualities, or at least pushed them into the back seat.

I think that's why so many young women I know in their twenties and early thirties feel unfulfilled and unhappy. They are out of balance. The money they earn from their careers and the short-term thrills from going to clubs and hooking up don't really fulfill them. There is a palpable lack of contentment in these women, and they tell me their lives lack meaning. Most fairy tales and myths show both the feminine and masculine sides: there is usually a princess and a prince, a queen and a king, a goddess and a god. And the girls in the stories exhibit qualities of both the heroine and the hero. Once their balance is complete and they are whole, then and only then can they live happily ever after.

In order for girls to successfully traverse this touchpoint, they need all kinds of support from adults. I liken it to what is necessary for successful gardening.

Springtime is an opportunity for renewal and rebirth, just like the adolescent touchpoint. Before planting seeds, the soil must be prepared, by adding fertilizers and nutrients, and by tilling. Old layers of soil must be turned over in order for new levels to emerge and prosper. Then, and only then, is it time for the seeds to be planted. Much care is taken to plant flowers and vegetables only in places that are optimal for their growth. There has to be just the right amount of sunshine and shade, and soil that is conducive for that plant. Even the hardiest plant will suffer in the wrong environment. I have read that it is better for plants in the long run if there is less rain in the spring, because it forces young plants to develop deeper root systems. During the dog days of summer, when there is little rain, these plants can survive because of these deeper roots. Too much early spring rain creates plants with shallow root systems that later on are unable to survive drought conditions; they are less resilient.

As the flowers and vegetables grow, they need tending by vigilant gardeners. They need watering, pruning off of dead leaves and limbs, occasional food, and sometimes support from trellises. When the plant is ready, at their unique time, they bloom, ripen and bear fruit. And even then, they still need some continued support. Guiding girls through their adolescent transformation is kind of like that.

The adolescence touchpoint is a time for growth and transformation. Girls need guidance, information, skills, and support from many caring adults. They need to be allowed to make their own choices and decisions and then face the consequences of their choices. They need to make mistakes and learn from them, take risks and stretch, fall down and pick themselves up, and handle the normal ups and downs of this stage. These experiences help girls develop the resiliency and self-efficacy, the deep roots if you will, that will carry them through the tough times and challenges involved in adolescence. It helps if girls are able to spend time in environments where they can bloom. These are the sacred spaces I will discuss in chapter 10. And it also involves surrounding them with adult mentors who can guide them when their parents can't or aren't invited by their daughters.

I like this metaphor a lot. We do plant seeds in our daughters as they are growing up; seeds of wisdom, modeling, perspective, and our stories and experiences. And this touchpoint is a time that involves germinating, seasoning, pruning old unhealthy beliefs and relationships, new growth and awareness, ripening, and blooming. Whether through fairy tales or discussions, we need to educate girls about this transformational touchpoint they are undergoing, and why they feel out of sorts. They need to hear stories from their mothers, grandmothers and other important women in their lives about their own journeys and how they got to the other side. Let them know how and when you bloomed. They can find solace in reading biographies as well.

Information and stories let girls know they aren't crazy, that what they are going through is normal even if it doesn't always feel that way. They would better understand that they aren't the only ones experiencing all this, and that they are not alone. Knowing there is light at the end of the tunnel gives girls courage and hope.

CHAPTER 3

CHALLENGES

Girls today face some unique pressures and challenges during their transformative teen years. The information in this chapter has been drawn from many sources, first and foremost from my more than 30 years of working with girls in personal growth weekend retreats and summer camps, school programs and group therapy. I also owe a great debt to many authors from whom I have learned so much over the years. A list of my favorite books on this topic can be found at the end of this book. It's hard for me sometimes to pinpoint exactly where my ideas originated, they are such an amalgamation of thoughts and experiences. But I will refer to specific authors and books when I can, and I encourage you to read the books listed to deepen your understanding of these important girls issues.

One challenge girls face today is the early onset of puberty. The average age for a first period is around 11 or 11 1/2, which means bodies start changing in the fourth and fifth grade. There is a huge difference between dealing with puberty in fifth grade versus ninth or 10th grade, like most girls did a generation ago. And, as I will discuss in more depth in Chapter 4, most girls don't know the first thing about how their brains are wired or about hormonal changes and their effects during puberty. No one has ever explained to them why their emotions shift so much during menstrual cycles, or why the shape of their body changes like it does, or even why they gain weight or inches where they do. Compound their lack of information with the barrage of sexual imagery and messages girls experience, not to mention the unhealthy conditioning girls experience about body image at such early ages, and it's no wonder girls feel so confused and overwhelmed about their bodies.

We are not educating our girls nearly enough about the normal physiological, physical, hormonal changes they are undergoing. And this causes girls to feel more stress and pressure than they need to.

A second challenge girls face today is what Dr. Stephen Hinshaw describes as *The Triple Bind*, which is the title of his interesting book. There he describes in detail what girls in the past 10 years have been telling me about the pressures they are facing. The first leg of Hinshaw's triple bind is that girls today are still expected to be really good at all the traditional 'girl things.' They know they are supposed to be pretty, sexy, thin, hot, good at all relationship skills, empathetic, verbal, organized multi-taskers, nurturing and willing to put other people's needs first. These are qualities ascribed to having 'female energy' and female archetypes. What is new today is that girls also feel tremendous pressure to be good at the traditional 'boy things.' That's the second leg of the triple bind. Boy qualities consist of: having straight A's; being a super athlete; going to a top-tier college on an academic or athletic scholarship; being super assertive, aggressive, driven, ambitious, and competitive with a 'willing-to-step-on-others-to-get-to-the-top' attitude; and willing to have superficial 'hook-up' relationships. These are qualities ascribed to 'male energy' and male archetypes.

The third leg of the triple bind is that girls feel pressured to live up to a very narrow, unrealistic set of standards when they become adult women: be the perfect wife with a perfect, hot husband and 2.5 perfect children for whom you are the perfect mother, while at the same time climbing to the top of her career ladder making a boatload of money. All the while she should maintain and nurture all the relationships in her life (parents, spouse's parents, the parents of her children's friends, neighbors, both sets of relatives, etc.), and do all this while still staying pretty, thin, sexy and hot. And she must succeed in all these endeavors both easily and effortlessly. Whew! In my groups, retreats and camps, girls describe these pressures in detail. They really feel them and have bought into the lies.

I have been doing an exercise for years with middle school girls in retreats and camps and at mother-daughter and father-daughter retreats that will give you a peek at how girls are being conditioned in this way. I ask them to brainstorm ideas and then draw a picture of the ideal woman at 25 to 30 years of age showing what she's like, what she's doing, and what kind of person she is. The following are actual drawings from the girls, and typical of what I have gotten from them over the past 10 years.

I usually give them 10 minutes to complete this task so they don't over-think it. As you can see, much of the girls' focus is on appearance. They obsess over her full lips, blonde-streaked hair, makeup, large eyes, small waist and ample breasts, and her clothes. Most drawings show the ideal woman holding shopping bags from expensive stores, and her most common occupations are model or actress. And she has never been married, and usually does not have a boyfriend. The ideal woman's height and especially weight should jump out at all of us, usually a tall 5'8" to 5'10" with a weight around 110 to 120 pounds. Equally distressing are some of the common descriptive words like rich, likes shopping, tan, popular, no acne, nice, big mansion, nice clothes, lots of makeup, tall and long, sexy,

Ivy League college, perfect teeth and skin, big boobs, likes boys, skinny, 'hot,' great job, sassy, good attitude, graduated top of class, perfect, all the boys like her. You can see and feel the triple bind messages in their words and pictures.

At my mother-daughter and father-daughter retreats with middle school girls, I have the parents make a drawing of their 'ideal daughter' at age 25 to 30 and then compare theirs with the drawings by the girls. It creates a lot of laughter and giggles from the girls and some shock, surprise and sadness from the parents.

Girls' Drawing   Parents' Drawing

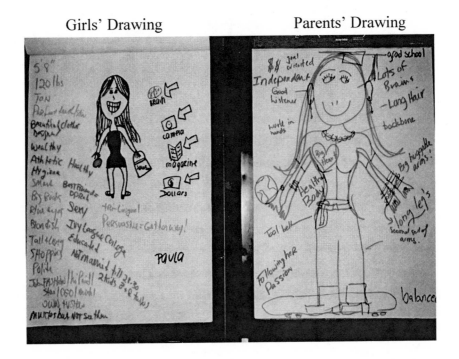

While the girls focus on all the previously listed attributes, the parents have a much different view. Independent, brains, healthy body, following her passion, balanced, respect, spiritual and mature are familiar terms on the parents' drawings.

Girls Drawing   Parents Drawing

We have them all brainstorm a list of where the girls might have gotten the messages about their ideal woman, and the list is usually fairly lengthy: TV, movies, books, the computer, billboards, magazines, commercials, mall displays, teachers, coaches, parents and friends. Those last two don't get the attention they deserve, as it's easier to criticize the media and people removed from us. But girls always share remarks they've heard from their moms or grandparents about weight or body image or about being popular and fitting in. And their friends have a tremendous influence on them as well, which will be discussed in later chapters.

Another big challenge confronting girls is the pressure to be a 'good girl.' Despite the fact that it is the 21st century and we are 50-plus years into the women's movement, girls still feel the conditioning about being 'good.' I have done another exercise with girls in fifth grade, middle school and high school where I have them make lists of the qualities of good girls, bad girls, and real girls. I got the idea from the book, *The Curse of the Good Girl* by Rachel Simmons, and tweaked it to fit the different ages of girls I work with.

I tell them good girls are the kind of girls all parents and teachers and coaches want you to be like. Bad girls are the girls who are, well, naughty or at least have reputations for not being good girls. Real girls are who they really are, their authentic selves or the person they want to become.

According to the girls I have asked over the past 10 years the characteristics of good girls include: being nice to everyone, always; putting other people's needs first; making everyone happy; following the rules; waiting your turn; not speaking up; always being happy, cheerful, passive, sweet and obedient; cheerleader; having only positive feelings; dress appropriately; having friendships that are conflict-free with no disagreements; not standing out, arguing or making waves; being a leader (but not too powerful or out there); not having strong sexual feelings (and being able to control any that might arise). The triple bind finds its way into these lists with descriptions like straight A's, smart, perfect, obedient, nice to teachers, good grades, try your best, and good at everything.

The good girl words that most worry me are ones like: nice to everybody, obedient, boring, not talk too much, always peppy and happy, no bad emotions, people pleaser, follows the rules, sweet and nice. I always have the girls go back over the list and underline words that might be unrealistic or not healthy for them. They are usually the same words I was concerned about.

Girls are still getting the message to be not too big, too loud, too powerful, too outspoken, too out-there. Girls who are powerful and put it out there are still labeled as being 'all that,' a not so subtle attempt to knock them down a peg. My middle school girl support group told me recently that the other way they describe these powerful girls is by using any curse word that comes to mind in that moment. How nice! And of course, like the unrealistic standards mentioned with the third leg of the triple bind, it's unrealistic to always be nice and happy and not be angry or resentful or jealous.

I do the same thing with the bad girls lists, having them underline qualities that actually might be good to have. These beneficial traits include: not be boring; be assertive; don't care what others think; be noticed, independent and not clingy; show off; don't always follow rules; stubborn; be bossy, sassy, have attitude. I guide girls to see how constrained they sometimes feel and that it's OK to bust out some, stretch, take risks and question rules. Girls need permission to stretch in these ways, and not to unconsciously follow the good girl script that's been laid out for them. I love their real girls lists, with qualities like: make mistakes and learn from them; be independent, assertive and don't care what other people think; be willing to take risks; be street smart; conscious of who she wants to be; stands up for others; comfortable with their feelings; takes care of herself; and follows her heart. Girls need to hear these qualities discussed and affirmed and modeled for them. Because the pressures to be a good girl are rampant, but subtle and hidden, it's truly a challenge to awaken girls to their presence and their effects.

Another way girls are challenged today is in managing the ins and outs of their friendships, as described in Chapter 12. Girls are wired to connect and to form close bonds with other girls. And having friends and a group become uber important from grade school on up, setting them up for a wild ride of fluctuating relationships and emotions. The following are tensions girls experience within their friendships:

1. Longing for connection while protecting yourself from loss, pain, and rejection.
2. Needing to be liked for you vs. needing to please, fit in.
3. How can I say what I think and do what I want and still be accepted?

4. Preserving my authenticity vs. doing anything for my friend's acceptance.

5. If I show friends my true self and they disapprove, will I be able to cope?

6. Protecting self by not revealing too much but then being lonely because no one really knows you or your true feelings.

7. Show only a false self but feeling ashamed and worried about being found out.

8. Being loyal and not betraying a friend's trust vs. being included and in the loop.

9. Needing friends to really understand me vs. needing privacy and trust.

10. Longing to be like an "idealized" friend vs. being myself and being aware of that friend's limitations.

11. Reaching out to anyone to not be alone vs. only reaching out to friends who are good for you and to you.

12. Socialized to be a "good girl" vs. expected to be independent, ambitious, competitive and aggressive.

13. Working hard to be popular: 24/7 job with no vacation!

14. Feeling bad for excluded girls but being unpopular is a "communicable disease" so can't associate or hang with them.

15. I forget what it feels like to be me, but I don't want to remember because it hurts more than being fake.

Girls feel torn between these tensions, causing them to feel stressed, confused, guilty, frustrated, worried and out of control. They feel stressed and confused because they can't decide which direction to take. It can feel like they are damned if they do and damned if they don't. Their heart and intuition are telling them one thing, but the culture and their peers are saying something else. Guilt comes when they make choices they know are out of sync with who they are, their values, and what they intuit is right. Guilt also can come up when they feel that boundaries they set may hurt someone's feelings, as the good girl part of them struggles with the notion that taking care of yourself is okay and healthy. Girls become extremely frustrated as they try to figure out how to make it in their friendship circles. Who's happy or who's mad fluctuates minute by minute, and it's hard to know where you stand. You think you've done everything right and covered all the bases, and wham! Another unexpected drama erupts and you have no clue why.

The worry is a non-stop, 24/7 feeling. Girls worry every night about their behaviors of that day: *Was I too strong with Allison? Was Kay mad at me? Did I flirt too much with my friend's boyfriend? Who's going to sit with me at lunch tomorrow? Will I see any inviting faces when I walk into the commons area tomorrow morning?*

The following are questions girls ask themselves as they fret over their appearance and friendships:

1. Am I okay? Am I good enough?
2. Am I pretty enough to deserve friends or a boy friend?
3. Will I be left out and alone? Bullied, teased or rejected?
4. Who will I sit with at lunch or play with at recess?
5. Who will talk to me when I walk into school, in the hallways between classes, and in class?
6. Middle school and high school are harder; will I make it? Do good enough?
7. Will I disappoint my parents if I don't get perfect grades or not do the activities they want me to do or hang with who they want?
8. Why don't people call me to do stuff on the weekends? Why do I always have to call them first?
9. What would happen if I let everyone in on my secret i.e....who I *really* am?
10. Should I be someone I don't want to be (me) or someone nobody wants or likes?

11. Why don't boys notice me like they do the other girls?
12. Do other people think I'm as ugly as I think I am?
13. Will I ever have the courage to be true to myself?
14. Does anyone understand what I am going through?
15. Am I the only one???

I have met countless numbers of girls in grade school through high school who have these types of questions rattling around in their heads all day long. It's disturbing, confusing, discouraging and exhausting. Out-of-control feelings also seem to be with girls a lot at these ages. Their bodily changes, what other people say and don't say, do or don't do, their up and down emotions, and their intense thoughts all seem to have a mind of their own. It feels like everything is happening to them, and there seems to be very little they can do about it.

Remember, too, that good girls are supposed to have friendships without disagreements or conflict, which of course is unrealistic. And when conflicts do arise, girls are ill equipped to handle them. Their female brains are wired to avoid conflict and maintain social harmony at all costs. So girls are programmed with an aversion to conflict, and also with a fear of loss of relationships. That's the biologic reason some girls are willing to put up with disrespect and abuse from friends: the wiring and urge to connect, gain approval and be nurtured is really strong. And whether you are talking about fourth-grade girls or adult women in the workforce, it is not safe to handle conflicts directly because girls haven't been taught the skills to do so. Feelings get stuffed and girls apologize even though they've done nothing wrong. They'll smile at each other and say, *"No problem,"* when it really is a problem. They'll talk to other friends and get them involved and on their side, even if it creates a ton of drama and gossip. But since they don't handle conflicts directly with the involved person, nothing really gets settled, and girls carry battle scars and festering emotions around with them for months and years.

And this is the source of some of the intense emotions girls suppress as discussed in Chapters 5 and 11.

Girls also are challenged today in the realm of feelings, meaning they have a hard time knowing, understanding and expressing their emotions in healthy ways. I'll discuss emotions in depth in Chapter 5, but for now here are some thoughts on why this area has become such a struggle for girls.

First, they have been conditioned to believe that good girls should have only good feelings, like being happy, excited and proud. Good girls shouldn't feel angry, jealous, resentful or frustrated. So these normal emotions are suppressed and build up inside. Second, girls today are extremely busy and distracted, with no time to be alone and quiet. They have learned to use their distractions, such as homework, activities, texting, social network sites, video games, and TV, to avoid having to think about or experience their emotions. So again, feelings get stuffed, and girls become disconnected from what is going on internally within them. They have little awareness of how they are feeling or how to label or express them verbally. It is so unhealthy for them. Third, they are living during a time when schools are going through another intensification movement that was amped up by the federal government's No Child Left Behind program. What it has meant is that in most schools there is little or no time spent on social-emotional learning. Getting schools to commit to my Strong Girls Strong World program is like pulling teeth because, once again, *"There's just no time!"* Chasing elusive international test scores in the three R's has totally obliterated any interest in or commitment to spending class time working on building community, enhancing relationships, or working through conflicts. And our kids, especially our girls, suffer because of it.

We also can't ignore the issue of divorce. By 18 years of age, somewhere in the vicinity of 40 percent of children will have experienced a divorce and all its effects. That means a lot of girls have been exposed to parental fighting, separations and the dissolution of their families. For many girls it means little or no time with their dads, and stressed moms who work a lot. And it adds a whole plethora of feelings like sad, hurt, confused, angry, disappointed, alone, worried, scared, guilty, shame, and feeling pulled or pressured. And these are yet more feelings they don't handle well, or at all.

Girls today are living with parents who are as distracted and busy as they are. Parents are working more hours. Dad and Mom bring their work along during car rides, at dinner tables, in the evenings and weekends, and on vacations. Parents are distracted with their phones, emails, texts, pads and even social networking sites. You can't go to a restaurant, airport, or even walk through a mall without seeing parents plugged into their phones while their children either stare blankly ahead or plug into their own technology.

Melissa is a 14-year-old whose parents divorced four years ago. She sees her dad every other weekend and occasionally on Wednesday evenings for dinner. Her dad lives with his new girlfriend and her 2-year-old son, so when Melissa spends the weekend with him, he is distracted by his new family. She cried some hurt and bitter tears in my office, telling me, *"I don't even know why I go out there. He works all day Saturday, and he works on his computer at night. I've tried to tell him that, but he just says he's got to work extra hard to pay child support, blah, blah. He promises to spend more time with me, but it doesn't happen. I hate going over there!"*

Twelve-year-old Sammi's parents both work until 5:30, so she's home with her 9-year-old brother after school until her parents get home around 6 p.m. After a rushed dinner, the family settles into their usual patterns. *"My dad lays down on the couch and watches TV until he falls asleep, about 8 o'clock. My mom's always on the computer paying bills and doing stuff for work. My brother plays video games all night. It's like we're all there but we're not there. It's annoying! I wish we'd do more stuff together."*

Rhianna is a fifth-grader whose parents were never married, and her dad split when she was around 2 years old. He moved back from out-of-state a year ago and wanted to start seeing Rhianna. He took her mom to court, a lengthy and testy custody struggle ensued, and her dad won the right to have Rhianna every other weekend. *"At first I was excited to go over there, because I wanted to have a dad, like all my friends. But he never spends any time with me. He's always downstairs working on his computer or talking to his girlfriend. Sometimes he makes dinner for us, but he takes his down to the computer room so I eat by myself. I think he wants me to come over because he's mad at my mom for making him send her money. I don't think he really wants to be with me."*

I hear stories like these from girls every day. It still amazes me what complicated lives so many children are living. And it creates more stress and more emotions for them to deal with.

Last on my challenges list are all the mixed messages I hear girls trying to struggle through. The following are the ones I hear most:

1. Be nice versus be competitive.
2. Be assertive but not too assertive.
3. Be successful but not 'all that' (successful).
4. Be hot and sexy but not sexual.
5. Be a leader but lead mostly from behind the scenes and quietly.
6. Be confident but don't speak too openly.
7. Be willing to step on others to get to the top but also be close to other girls.
8. Be authentic but try to fit in.
9. Take care of yourself but put other people's needs first.

10. Be a loyal friend, but you are out of the loop if you don't gossip and talk about others behind their backs.
11. Stand up for yourself but you desperately want to be included and have friends.

It's sad that girls today are still absorbing messages of "not too high," "not too loud," "not too out there," not too a lot of things. Especially since they are also feeling pressured to be perfect at everything and on top of their game 24/7. Girls hear the mantra, "You can be whatever you want to be," i.e. you can be president of the United States, CEO of Fortune 500 companies, neurosurgeons, astronauts and world-class athletes. But you still can't be yourself! You are still being conditioned to fit into a mold that entails unrealistic expectations: that third leg of the triple bind. So you can't just be a World Cup soccer team member; you have to be a 'hot' World Cup soccer player. You can't just be a racecar driver or presidential candidate, you have to be good looking and sexy too. It's just never enough to be who you are. Our culture has a prescription or menu that is all-inclusive, narrow, and constraining. Girls and women have many more choices and opportunities today, yet they are suffering more, they feel more out of balance and less fulfilled.

We saw it earlier in their drawings of the ideal woman. They've bought the lie, hook, line and sinker, even by middle school, when their important touchpoint is starting. And it makes for a rocky transformation.

Seventeen-year-old Taylor described these feelings well when I had her in to talk with the master's level class I do for teachers. And, for the record, she is a straight A student and captain of her Lacrosse team, i.e. a 'good girl'. *"School is a game. When I'm in class, all I listen for is what's going to be on the test. It's not about learning or pursuing things that interest me. It's about figuring out what the teachers want, learning what they tell me to learn. I hate it, but I know if I want to get into a good college that's what I've got to do."*

Can you sense the frustration and longing in her voice? I hear it all the time in girls, especially girls in high school. And I also hear and feel the stress and pressure on them because of the cumulative effects of all these challenges they face. And, unfortunately, they are facing these challenges without the necessary awareness, knowledge, and skills required to successfully navigate this tumultuous stage.

CHAPTER 4

THE FEMALE BRAIN AND HORMONES

There are a myriad of changes that all girls undergo during their adolescence. Some are external and easy to see, while others are internal and more hidden. And it is these internal changes that I will discuss in this chapter.

Exactly what changes are occurring during adolescence? By about 12 years of age, girls' brains go through a growth spurt, with more neurons in the most-used areas, along with pruning of the areas not used. There are also changes in brain chemistry and hormones, along with the advent of their monthly cycle. These changes result in higher levels of cognition and abstract thinking. And they also produce a plethora of behavioral changes that disrupt the adolescent girl and all those she interacts with.

I will summarize some information I have gathered over the years from my medical training, journal articles and several books. The three references I've most incorporated into my approach with adolescent girls are *The Female Brain* and *The Male Brain* by Louann Brizendine M.D. and *The Wonder of Girls* by Michael Gurian. I strongly encourage you to read these yourself; they are fun and interesting and will help you understand what you're dealing with. When I talk to groups of girls about this information, I use a mishmash of all three, summing up their work on the female brain, female hormones and menstrual cycles. Many of the ideas that follow here came directly from these books, and I am grateful for the information they have provided.

I start by reminding girls that 99 percent of our history as human beings was lived in primitive conditions, so our brains are really wired for prehistoric times, not the 21st century. And in prehistoric times, survival and reproduction were of prime importance. Many aspects of the female brain developed to allow women to survive in harsh, dangerous environments with bigger men. For women, connection became their best ticket for survival.

The female brain, compared to the male brain, has larger areas for hearing, language and observing emotions in other people. This allowed females to have greater verbal abilities and the skills to read faces and voice tones for emotions and clues about what other people are thinking. So girls are primed for communication, connection, emotional sensitivity and responsiveness. How did this serve girls? It allowed them as mothers to be more in tune to their babies' needs and cries, and also to the intentions of the larger males. For prehistoric women, being left out meant death, while close connections meant survival. The neurochemicals and hormones that flood a girl's brain, especially at adolescence, pushed her to connect with other women, because in groups they were more protected. Women relied on these groups, these prehistoric cliques, to protect not only them but their dependent children as well.

When males sense danger, their brain and hormones, testosterone in particular, create the 'fight or flight' reaction; for females, with their higher levels of estrogen, it's different. Dr. Brizendine describes women's reaction to danger or stress as tend and befriend. And women are also wired to have an aversion to conflict, because conflict could result in fractured relationships, and that could lead to death. So girls have been programmed to maintain connections and social harmony, in contrast with men's programming for aggression, provision and protection.

The female brain is also wired differently when it comes to emotions. The corpus callosum in girls is larger; they use both sides of their brain to process emotions, and the connections between their emotional centers are more extensive and active than in males. A study out of Stanford University had females and males view emotional images while their brains were being scanned. When women looked at these images, nine different parts of their brains lit up, on both sides, versus two parts on only one side for men. Girls retain memories better and with more detail, especially if the experience has important feelings attached. If you ask a man how he and his wife met, he may stutter and mutter something about meeting at a bar one night. The wife, on the other hand, will tell you, in rich detail, every aspect of that evening.

The female brain also activates more in anticipation of fear, danger or pain, making it harder for girls to suppress their fears and worries. This is especially true before their brains fully develop at age 19 to 20. A substance called myelin coats the nerve connections between the emotional centers in the amygdala and the emotion control centers in the prefrontal cortex (PFC). Myelin's job is to quicken the conduction of impulses and information between different parts of the brain. But during the middle and high school years, the connections are poorly myelinated, causing girls to get overwhelmed with their feelings and be more reactive and impulsive. By about age 20, myelination has finished, conduction is faster and girls can better handle their emotions.

The higher activation in anticipation of fear and pain also sets girls up to have more anxiety than boys. In fact, anxiety is four times higher in girls by the middle school years. Dr. Brizendine points to theories from psychologists who postulate this anxious anticipation pattern allowed our stone-aged women to respond quicker in defense of their children and friends. It kept them alert and on guard.

Another interesting fact from *The Female Brain* is that for girls, feelings are initially felt in their emotional center, and then channeled through two main circuits. One is the verbal center of the brain, which explains why girls and women want to talk about feelings and issues over and over again. That is much different than the male response. The second area emotions are channeled is to the prefrontal cortex (PFC), causing girls to want to think about issues or feelings over and over and over. The word I use is ruminate, which means to chew, or in this case 'to chew on your thoughts.' Many girls and women are guilty of this.

If something happens at school such as a friend's eye roll, being left out of an after-school get together, a boy ignoring her, all day at school a girl might be distracted by her thoughts, many of those negative. *Why didn't they invite me over? Do they not like me anymore. Did I do something wrong? OMG, I can't lose these friends, I'll be so alone!* When this girl goes home, she'll march straight to her room to ruminate some more. She might text people to talk about it, or she'll scour Facebook to pick up any clues. And it's hard for girls to let these thoughts go. For more on rumination in girls, see chapter 13 on Stinking Thinking.

Boys and men stereotypically experience something differently. They'll confront the other guy, they might whack each other a bit and then they move on. They don't seem to hold grudges like girls do. But girls have several things that make letting go harder. Because they are more in- tune to people's feelings, tone of voice and body language, they absorb more. They retain more vivid and detailed memories of these events. Ruminating keeps them stuck. I will discuss in the Stinking Thinking chapter how girls can redirect this pattern. On the positive side, psychologists believe ruminating served a purpose back in the day. It allowed women to pause before they responded to cavemen who were bothering them. And talking to girlfriends served the same purpose. This response delay allowed a woman not to react with anger in retaliation to a larger, dangerous man, thus protecting her.

During the first six months of life, an infant's brain undergoes tremendous growth. And my old mentor, Dr. T. Berry Brazelton, and other researchers believed that the proliferation of neurons and synoptic connections was one of the main reasons for a baby having colic. Their external behaviors of fussiness, irritability and inconsolability were a reflection of all the changes internally in their central nervous system. I wonder if this is also one of the reasons girls during puberty become more emotional and out-of-sorts. Their brains are undergoing similar construction: more brain matter, pruning off some connections and adding others. It caused infant brains to become more hypersensitive, why not adolescent girls?

Brain growth and reorganization also causes changes in how girls think and process information and experiences. During and after puberty, girls can think more abstractly, and thus they strive to think for themselves more and to have their own thoughts, opinions and values. They like to argue and take contrary positions. They also become even more sensitive to other people's feelings and thoughts. They compare themselves more and judge their standing in the social hierarchy endlessly. They are more impulsive and tend to experiment more and push the envelope. I have seen hundreds of intense, strong-minded teen girls over the years who butt heads with their parents and authoritative teachers at every opportunity. The way I like to describe them is like wild young horses locked up in a corral. The more parents discipline them or don't listen to them, the angrier they get and the more it feels like the corral is closing in on them. So what do they do? They rear up and kick at the slats, trying to fight their way to more independence. Sound familiar?

Estrogen is the wonder hormone that orchestrates the process of puberty, and it is instrumental in the release of several important hormones: progesterone, oxytocin, dopamine and serotonin. These neurotransmitters have a huge influence on mood stability, memory, the desire to connect, sex drive, anxiety and how girls process information. Estrogen and her merry band of hormones affect how girls relate to others, their ambition and competitiveness, their emotions, and their mental clarity. The increased estrogen at puberty makes brain circuits even more sensitive to social-emotional nuances like disapproval and rejection. The wiring laid down in utero and in infancy, and the behaviors the female brain has been programmed to perform, all become enhanced at puberty. This includes a girl's desires to connect, be intimate, maintain social harmony, and to be part of her group.

Let's talk a little about menstrual cycles, the hormonal changes involved, and their effects on a girl's moods and thought processes. In the first two weeks of the cycle, the estrogen level rises dramatically. High estrogen levels cause many changes: girls think more clearly, feel more relaxed, have their emotions under control, and feel less stressed. Estrogen levels peak at mid-cycle, when girls experience the highest desire for intimacy, socializing and verbal communication. Higher levels of estrogen also stimulate an increase in production of oxytocin and serotonin, and these chemicals cause girls to want to connect, be intimate, have greater empathy, feel more relaxed and joyful, and to feel good about themselves. All of these hormones activate a girl's brain centers for talking, flirting and socializing.

Connecting through talking also activates the pleasure centers, especially if what she's talking about involves secrets or romance. So they get an oxytocin and dopamine rush, which causes girls to want to connect more, and when they do they release more oxytocin…and a feel-good cycle ensues.

The third week of the cycle sees estrogen starting to decrease, which causes gradual withdrawal symptoms. Girls might become a little irritable and need more time and space to be alone. At mid-cycle, girls also ovulate, which coincides with a temporary increase in the male hormone testosterone. This rise in testosterone raises sex drives at the same time a girl is ripe for becoming pregnant. Ovulation causes a temporary rise in estrogen for several days, but then estrogen starts to drop again. Luckily the hormone progesterone comes to the rescue, at least partially. Progesterone causes the brain to be somewhat sedated, trying to mitigate the withdrawal symptoms from the decreasing estrogen. Progesterone, in combination with serotonin, acts as a kind of mood stabilizer that third week, but it also causes girls to be a little less focused and mentally sharp.

Week four is when the Titanic hits the iceberg and all hell breaks loose. Progesterone and estrogen levels rapidly decrease, and girls lose whatever calming effects progesterone had brought. They experience estrogen and progesterone withdrawal, and when their brains don't get the reassuring calming effects from these hormones, nor from oxytocin and serotonin, they become more irritable, stressed, moody, emotionally labile and reactive. They also show signs of being hypersensitive to approval/disapproval or to the comments of others. Some girls feel sad or can seem depressed. They appear to have lost their mojo and their self-esteem, and they want to be left alone. And they will fight for this alone space. Studies have shown that the girls with the lowest estrogen and progesterone levels end up having the most severe problems with mood instability and emotional upsets.

Too many girls have gotten the message that these signs and symptoms are 'all in their heads,' or they are 'just being dramatic'. That might be true for a minority of girls, but the reality here is that these behavioral changes are due to biology and physiology. It's imperative that girls understand the biologic basis for these emotional shifts; it helps them to face their cycles every month with more awareness and understanding. Remember, too, that once girls get to about age 20, the myelination of their nervous system will allow for faster connections between their emotional centers and their pre-frontal cortex. This enables them to handle their emotions and stress better, to be less impulsive and reactive, and not to get so overwhelmed with their emotions. The normal behavioral changes girls experience during adolescence due to the changes in their brains and hormones often come out as mood changes, becoming overwhelmed at times with their emotions, acting out of sorts and irritable, pulling away from people at times, having more anger and anxiety, worrying about how they look and what others think, comparing themselves to others, sudden bursts of energy at times, fluctuating levels of focus, and developing more negative self-talk.

All girls are different and don't exhibit all of these behaviors, nor with the same intensity. But these symptoms are common and universal. And unfortunately, I believe this is why parents, teachers and professionals working with adolescent girls often mislabel them as having poor self-esteem, anxiety disorder or depression. I can see why they might, but often I don't agree with their diagnosis. Another way to look at the behavioral changes girls undergo at puberty and during their cycles is to go back to our transformation metaphor.

In the big picture, girls are undergoing a major touchpoint, a transformation that involves some 'sleep' or going inward. This transformation requires girls to go into the forest or cave, do their work on their inner resumes, and then emerge at a higher level of awareness, energized and ready for what's next in their lives. We could look at their monthly cycles in a similar way, as another internal transformation, but a physical one. And it too requires some time to withdraw, to replenish the womb, and then come out the other side refreshed and renewed. This cycle of release and renewal continues until menopause, another big touchpoint for women. No woman enjoys having periods every month. But I've had many women who became conscious of the physiologic value of their cycles tell me they appreciate that every month their body metaphorically lets go of old, unneeded cells and rebuilds itself with new ones. There is something magical for them about the letting go of the old and embracing the new. It's a rebirth process every month for them.

There are many connections between the behaviors I describe throughout this book and the ways girls' brains are wired and hormonally influenced. These are the biologic, internal factors that shape girl behavior, thoughts and emotions. I want all middle and high school girls to understand their brain's unique wiring and the ways their hormones and their monthly cycles affect their emotions and behaviors. If they can understand that the ups and downs of their emotions and self-esteem are related to the changes in their brain chemistry and brain anatomy, they will feel more normal and hopeful versus crazy, stressed, depressed and hopeless. They will also feel more in control of what these processes are bringing to them each month and throughout puberty.

It's another important way for girls to know and understand themselves. And it's another opportunity for parents, teachers and other adults to offer girls education, guidance and support.

CHAPTER 5

FEELING MACHINES

Seventeen-year-old Becca's parents found out via Facebook that she had had sex with her boyfriend, Dan. They had dated for about two months after being friends since sixth grade. Becca's parents had tried to discourage her relationship with Dan because he came from a 'broken home' and had a reputation as a troublemaker. Now, they took away her phone and her computer, grounded her for a month, and told Becca she was not allowed to see or contact Dan. I asked Becca how she felt about not being able to talk to Dan, and her response was: "*I don't know. I feel like it's not fair that my parents are judging him based on some rumors they heard from other parents who don't even know Dan...*" Becca went on a rift from there, but couldn't describe what her feelings were.

Audrey, 12, told me that her biological dad left her and her mom when she was a baby, and then she and her mom were together for about 7 years before her mom's boyfriend moved in. At first she was happy because she thought she was finally going to have a 'normal' family like her friends, but then he started drinking more and more and becoming angrier. He yelled at her and her mom, and she saw him push her mom into walls several times. I asked her how she felt about that, and Audrey started going on and on about how she wished he would just go away and leave them so that they could go back to the way it was. But she had a really hard time labeling any of her feelings.

And that is the dilemma in these two stories, plus thousands of others I've heard over the past five to 10 years: girls experience some tough, challenging life events, and yet are unaware of their feelings about those experiences. I find so many girls today totally disconnected from their feelings.

I speak to classes of 12th graders at an all-girls high school my daughter attended years ago, usually talking to four to five classes each semester. And I've always asked the girls how many of them take regular time to be alone and quiet. In the past, I'd get six to eight raised hands out of a class of 20. That started changing about five to 10 years ago. I asked that same question of five classes recently, and guess how many hands were raised in the affirmative? One! A second girl raised her hand up and down, and I asked her if she took quiet time. *"Does it count if I'm on the computer?"* Nope, not a chance. Quiet time means being quiet, focused on you. And it can mean checking in and asking yourself questions like: *How am I feeling today? How do I feel about my family issues? Or my friends? Or my boyfriend? Or about the stress of final exams? Or about going to college next year?*

I think the main culprit behind girls being disconnected from their emotions is they neglect to check in with themselves, or to allow themselves to feel things. They are too busy, too distracted and running too fast. The most common answer to the question, "Why don't you have any quiet alone time?" is, "There's no time!"

As a culture, we've done a fabulous job teaching our girls to be busy, competitive, distracted and plugged into electronics. We've done a terrible job teaching them to be alone and quiet, and to know what they are feeling. Due to all the stresses and pressures I discussed in Chapter 3, girls feel a whole boatload of different emotions: sad, confused, stressed, disconnected, angry, frustrated, disappointed, pressured, and afraid--to name a few. They are not expressing their feelings in healthy ways because:

1. They aren't aware of what they are feeling.
2. They have learned to stay busy and distracted as a way not to feel, because they fear if they started to express things it would overwhelm them, like drinking water from a fire hose.
3. They lack the skills to express feelings in healthy ways; they just don't know how.

So the feelings get pushed underground, and girls get numb. But as the emotions build up, they show up in unhealthy ways:

1. They leak anger out on people who don't deserve it, i.e. parents, siblings, and friends. A small comment from a parent can result in a hurricane-sized reaction.
2. They experience somatic complaints. Our bodies are a great barometer for our emotional status. We all have a sensitive place where our feelings go when they have built up. That's why girls end up with recurring headaches or stomachaches. People get stiff necks, low back pain, bladder infections or other illnesses due to a lowered immune system. But it's the stored-up emotions that can be the cause of these physical problems.
3. They have trouble sleeping. I meet many girls in middle school and especially high school who have a hard time falling asleep. If I ask a group of 20 high schoolers at one of my retreats, "How many of you have a hard time falling asleep?" I typically get 17 to 20 hands raised. They have been experiencing life all day long, with its ups and downs. But they have been too busy and distracted with schoolwork, activities and electronics to pay attention to their emotions and thoughts. A lot of the busyness is put in place specifically to avoid feeling things and getting overwhelmed. So bedtime is

the first time all day they've been alone and quiet. And in this state all the thoughts and feelings they have been suppressing all day long come bubbling up, and it's really hard to shut off that flow. So it might take them an hour or two to fall asleep, causing them to become tired and sleep-deprived. Which then causes them to be more moody and crabby and more likely to ruminate and overreact emotionally to things. A vicious cycle ensues.

4. They exhibit 'Mean Girl' behaviors. I have found that some, probably a lot, of the relationship aggressions happening between girls is due to this overwhelmed state. All the suppressed emotions can leak out as sarcasm, critical comments, negative body language and aggression. They take out their pent-up feelings on each other. As we will discuss later on, it's more complicated than that, but I believe unexpressed emotions play a big part in all the dramas in girls' friendships.

5. They cause self-harm. My experience with girls who cut themselves indicates the main cause is feeling overwhelmed with emotions. The following are reasons girls have given me for why they cut, in their own words:

   a. Lila: *"When I can't understand or figure out my feelings, I cut because I can then focus on that; I can understand the physical pain."*

   b. Anna: *"It's much easier to deal with the physical pain of cutting compared to all the complicated emotional pains I feel."*

   c. Meg: *"I always feel so out of control. But cutting is something I can control; how deep and how long the cut is, and the amount of pain."*

   d. Dani: *"It gives me something to think about besides my problems. It's a great distraction. I get so tired and overwhelmed with my negative thoughts."*

e. Liz: *"It makes sense! You cut; you feel the pain, period! Everything else seems so complicated."*

f. Abby: *"It's a release. It feels like you're breathing. So much tension builds up inside me; the cutting releases it, and I feel more in control of it."*

g. Stephanie: *"All the overwhelming feelings I have turn into anger at myself, and the cutting is like releasing the anger onto myself."*

h. Maria: *"I get so mad at my parents, but I'm afraid to explode on them. So I take that anger out on myself by cutting."*

i. Tyler: *"I can't tell my parents and my friends how angry I get with them, so I cut myself to show them how much I am hurting."*

j. Lindsey: *"I cut because I know I can stand the physical pain; I can't handle the emotional pain."*

k. Avery: *"Cutting allows me to feel alive; I feel so numb and dead most of the time."*

l. Jenna: *"Cutting hurts less than all the crap going on around me in my family. I get tired of hearing my parents fighting."*

m. Sara: *"When I cut, my heart speeds up when I see the blood--because I know I'm doing something I shouldn't be doing, yet I got away with it. Then you go into a trance with the release."*

n. Laura: *"I want to stop, it feels so out of control and I know it's hurting me. But whenever you try, it just consumes you again."*

o. Carla: *"I have to wear layers of clothes to hide the evidence of my weakness. It becomes like a dirty little secret that adds to the anger I have at myself for not being who I really wish I could be."*

p. Kelly: *"It's weird, but I feel like it's a way to be mean to my parents when I'm mad at them. It's like I'm having them bleed, them feel the pain I'm feeling."*

6. They experience eating disorders. From articles and books I've read, and from listening to girls, this is also an avenue for unexpressed feelings. Here is how some teen girls describe their feelings about their bulimia:

    a. Fifteen-year-old Amy: *"I want to control one part of myself that feels so uncontrollable, so the rest of me can fall in line."*

    b. Fourteen-year-old Rachel: *"I can do this one thing right even if I feel worse afterward."*

    c. Fourteen-year-old Rana: *"I feel bad afterward, but there is a physical reason I can point to."*

    d. Sixteen-year-old Lexi: *"It doesn't feel like I have a disorder because when I do it, it feels like everything falls into place."*

    e. Seventeen-year-old Brianna: *"When you do it, hating yourself makes perfect sense. It's about self-hatred."*

7. Anxiety. For many girls, the result of being overwhelmed with emotions is anxiety. It's not the primary emotion, rather the result of not expressing or dealing with all their other emotions, pressures and stresses. As described in chapter 4 about the female brain, girls channel their feelings through their prefrontal cortex and verbal circuits, which sets them up to ruminate. And this chewing of thoughts over and over again tends to make mountains out of molehills. According to Louann Brizendine M.D., the female brain also activates more in anticipation of fear, pain and danger, making it harder for girls to suppress their fears. Not surprisingly, anxiety is four times more common in girls than boys, and it is more prone to escalate in the last week of their menstrual cycles, when they

lose the calming effects of progesterone, estrogen and oxytocin due to falling levels of each. Now, a mature prefrontal cortex allows girls to handle emotions and stress better; it allows them to be less impulsive and reactive. But girls' brains aren't fully formed until around age 18 to 20 years. The prefrontal cortex is building many more new cells, but the connections between the brain's emotional centers (the amygdale) and the prefrontal cortex are thin and unmyelinated. Therefore, girls get overwhelmed with their emotions, and quickly. After puberty, myelin will coat their connections, enabling faster conduction. This will allow them to stay calmer and handle stress more effectively.

8. Depression and self-hatred. Preteen and teenage girls also have higher levels of depression than boys. Instead of repressed emotions blasting outward as anger, for some girls these are directed inward as depression and self-hatred. Some girls numb themselves with alcohol or drugs; others use video games, TV or other electronics. Yet others use boys and sex to distract themselves from feeling. These activities tend to suck their energy, making them feel apathetic and blah. The lack of sleep mentioned earlier also contributes to their lower levels of energy and motivation. The part of themselves that knows better feels bad about the drug usage or being used by boys, so girls tend to further disparage and discourage themselves. And another negative cycle ensues.

Negative self-talk for many girls becomes a major contributor to their lowered feelings of well-being. Ask a middle school girl what she dislikes about herself, and be ready for a barrage of judgments. Girls judge their looks big-time, and there is no body part that escapes their oversight. Not even earlobes and toenails! The triple-bind pressures described in Chapter 3 give girls even more places and permission to be hard on themselves. The pressure and drive to be perfect has no bounds today. Perfectionism is the order of the day for appearance, bodies, academics, sports, activities, boyfriends, social networking sites--you name it. Girls feel they must be the best at whatever they are involved in. It's a 24/7 race with no end in sight.

One of my patients, Annie, described the pressures from her dad: *"I feel the pressure to be amazing!"* And anything less than perfect feels like a failure. Any glitch becomes a reason to further judge and dislike yourself. Any mistake becomes more evidence about why you are a loser, unattractive or not good enough. If you happen to have an intense, perfectionist, low-frustration tolerance temperament, you are really in trouble. The intensity of negative self-judgments gets really ratcheted up in these girls, as their own negative feelings mix with their perceived pressures from parents, teachers, friends, colleges, boys and the culture.

9. Thrill-hangover cycle. I first learned about this cycle in Anthony de Mello's book *Awareness*, and I have seen it play out in the lives of both adults and teenagers.

Gabby is a 15-year-old high school freshman who, according to her parents, has been 'boy crazy' for the past two years. She was adopted from a Russian orphanage at about 3 years of age, and had some attachment issues for the first several years with her new family. She had started asking more questions about her birth parents and the orphanage in middle school, but didn't seem satisfied with her parents' answers that they had no records about them. She grew more sullen, angry and distant at home, and her social life became everything to her. Gabby got her first boyfriend in seventh grade, and on their second 'date' she gave him oral sex because *"he told me I was pretty, and it felt good to be wanted by a boy."* After that night, he stopped talking to her, and she felt devastated and used. More important, it reaffirmed her belief that she wasn't 'lovable or wanted.' This belief started with her inner decision that the reason her birth parents didn't keep her was because there was something wrong with her, that she wasn't important or lovable. It was too painful to go to that place of feeling unwanted and unloved, so she distracted herself with friends and electronics. There were times when she'd feel depressed about her relationship with her family, and she turned to boys to fill herself up. She had hookups several times with older guys, and at least for that night, she felt wanted and attractive. But of course those feelings didn't last.

That's how the thrill-hangover cycle works. You feel unhappy, empty or depressed, and you unconsciously look for something to pull yourself out of your funk, i.e. a thrill. Examples include getting drunk or high, gambling, or stealing. While you are doing these things you don't think about your problems, and you are numbed to your feelings. But once the high wears off, or the luster and smell of a new car fades, you are right back where you started. Only now you feel a little emptier and more discouraged. That's the emotional hangover. And so over time it takes bigger thrills to make you feel good, causing deeper hangovers--and thus the unhealthy cycle.

Girls who I see stuck in this cycle use thrills like shopping, cheating on their boyfriends, sexuality, taking risks, sexting, hooking up with guys for one night stands, viewing pornography, sneaking out to meet boys at night, drugs and alcohol, going out with much older guys, going to parties in unsafe neighborhoods, experimenting with bisexuality, and skipping school. The initial high or rise they get from these behaviors works to distract them from their feelings and problems, but of course it wears off more and more quickly, as their depression and hangover feelings deepen. These girls are really stuck and hurting. To get out of this cycle, girls need to allow themselves to express their feelings in healthy ways, and to find healthy things to fill themselves up with. There will be more on that in Chapter 11.

10. Getting lost in electronics. There are so many ways today that girls use electronics to get numb. Even just constant texting can be a way to not be with yourself, to not focus on you. Spending hours on social networking sites can create the same kind of disconnection with yourself. Girls spend inordinate amounts of time creating avatars, or facades. It's a way to try to be someone they are not: someone flirtatious, attractive, popular and happy. It's a way to escape their real life for a while. Involving themselves in everyone else's business also allows them to not focus on their business, their feelings, their pain. Girls can leak out some of the anger I described in (1) and (4) above online, as well. It's easier to vent on someone who's not sitting across from you. And it's easier to say disrespectful, critical, 'mean' things online. Some girls spend hours in chat rooms talking to strangers whom they have 'befriended.' I have met many girls who like commiserating in chat rooms with others who also are depressed, cutting, or have experienced suicidal thoughts or gestures. But what they really are doing is wallowing in negativity and not addressing their own feelings or issues. In a sense, talking or gossiping about it in chat rooms becomes a way to avoid it.

Plain and simple, these electronics become major distractions and energy-drains. They keep girls busy and distracted from reality, and from dealing with issues and emotions they are experiencing. Conflicts don't get resolved, emotions aren't expressed, deep conversations are avoided, and real connection never materializes. And girls aren't learning to enjoy quiet, alone time by chatting online. They are not learning how to get quiet and check in with themselves, to know themselves.

Their activities merely deflect time away from the work of transformation.

CHAPTER 6

BEST FRIENDS, WORST ENEMIES

"Interestingly, I think that there is one thing that has killed more dreams than death itself; that is a person who is concerned with what others think." Unknown Author

Alice and Mandy were playing together in the sandbox at recess, fully engrossed in a make-believe game. Fellow kindergartener Chloe walked up and asked if she could play, and Alice and Mandy both said, *"No!"* they were in the middle of a game. Chloe teared up, and walked away crestfallen. Alice and Mandy looked at each other with a quizzical look on their faces like, *"What just happened?"*

What just happened is that Alice and Mandy got a taste of their social powers. They got a strong reaction from Chloe just by saying no. Their intention was not mean-spirited, but they learned a lesson about the power of their words and actions on other people. Some people describe these kinds of situations as 'playground politics,' meaning children are continually discovering the ins and outs of friendships. They must figure out how to include themselves, have a voice, set boundaries, resolve conflicts, not take things personally, handle gossip and drama, and a host of other skills.

In this chapter I will use a lot of stories from my Strong Girls Strong World program in schools, and from my retreats and camps, to bring out the kinds of friendship issues girls are dealing with today.

And I'll also show you ways I address these issues with both individuals and groups of girls, guiding them to healthy skill building.

Fifth-grader Catherine asked to do a conflict resolution with Hanna, and she agreed. So the two girls scooted into the center of the circle, and began. This scenario occurred while I was working with a class of fifth-grade girls. *"I felt really sad and left out last week when I went up to you and your friends at recess and they immediately told you they wanted you to go with them to the monkey bars. And you went with them, and I felt really alone."* Hanna mirrored all that back to Catherine and asked her if there was more she wanted to share. Catherine did. *"I've been feeling left out a lot lately, and I felt the worst when you did that. You were the first girl to befriend me when I was the 'new girl' in fourth grade and your friendship means a lot to me."* Hanna mirrored this back to Catherine and then it was her turn to share how she felt about this incident. *"When you asked me to play with you, I felt really torn because my other friends had asked me to do something and I didn't want to hurt anyone's feelings. So I went with them, but I checked back with you a minute later to make sure you were OK, and I saw you were playing with Alison, so I figured you were OK."* Catherine mirrored Hanna back, and then Hanna made a new commitment to Catherine, along with a request. *"You can count on me to include you more with my group of friends, but I also want it to be OK that sometimes I play with different people in case I don't want to do what you're doing."* Catherine agreed to this, and committed to work on finding new friends to play with, and to include herself more with groups instead of trying to pull Hanna away to have her all to herself.

When I work with classrooms of girls, I always spend time teaching them skills to handle their conflicts and upset feelings directly. What most girls do is get their feelings hurt, and then tell other girls about what a jerk their friend B is, and then those girls become mad at B too and ignore her and harass her. B tells other girls her plight, and they take her side and get mad at friend A and her group, and the drama unfolds and escalates. This is probably the main cause of drama and fractured classrooms of girls, and it is totally preventable. So why don't girls handle their conflicts directly with other girls? In my experience, I have seen several reasons.

For one, they don't know how; they don't have the words or framework to do it effectively. At home, most parents get too involved in their children's sibling rivalry, so kids don't learn how to handle conflicts themselves. They've grown up thinking it's the adult's job to do it. Thus, tattling becomes endemic, and kids fail to take responsibility. Schools also have dropped the ball. In recent years, the intense pressures of testing and No Child Left Behind have meant there is little or no time left for social-emotional learning. Teachers, principals and schools aren't willing to give up class time to allow kids to be trained in and practice skills like these. So conflicts and feelings get shoved below the surface, and more 'mean girl' and relationship aggression (RA) behaviors emerge as a result.

By the way, I will be using the term relationship or relational aggression at different points in this book, so let me explain what I mean by it. Rachel Simmons in her book *Odd Girl Out* discussed research done at the University of Minnesota that defined relational aggression to include acts that harm others through damage (or the threat of damage) to relationships or feelings of acceptance, friendship, or group inclusion. In these acts, the aggressor uses her relationship with the target as a weapon. These acts can be direct or indirect and hidden. It is the negative body language, the exclusion of people, the criticism and judgments, the sabotaging of friendships with other girls or boys, or the catty comments that are meant to hurt.

Back to the reasons why girls don't handle their conflicts directly with other girls. The good girl conditioning also contributes here. Girls are reluctant to stand up for themselves or to confront friends because they are afraid of hurting people's feelings or being labeled a bitch or losing them as a friend. They want to please other people and be liked by everyone, so they bite their tongues and act like everything's just fine. Girls' brains are wired to bond and connect, so avoiding conflict and confrontations seems the best way to maintain social harmony. The old cliché is that when boys have a conflict, they slug it out and move on. There's a lot of truth in that. And there's also a lot of truth in the cliché that girls hold grudges and create dramas out of small potatoes.

When I get girls sitting together on the floor, and they handle conflicts one-on-one in front of the group like Catherine and Hanna did, they often work on issues that occurred months and years ago that were never really resolved. Feelings fester and come out as sarcasm, criticism or other RA behaviors. Girls may have avoided each other for years, and almost always over a misunderstanding. A few more real examples illustrate my points.

Lilly and Rachel were fifth-graders who had been tight friends starting in kindergarten. At the start of fifth grade, Lilly noticed Rachel hanging out with Ashley a lot, and felt jealous. By the time they faced each other in our circle, they'd grown distant. *"I've been feeling sad and left out since the school year started because it seems like you're always with Ashley. I don't know what I did to make you mad at me, but I'd like to start over,"* Lilly said. Rachel repeated what she heard back, and when it was her turn to share some interesting thoughts came forward. *"It's just that I've become good friends with Ashley. We were on the same softball team this summer, and we got to go to some out-of-town tournaments together, and we went with our families on a vacation to Florida right before school started. When school started, you acted like you were mad at me, and I didn't know why. So I guess I figured you didn't want to hang out with me anymore. I still would like to be friends and do stuff, but I want it to be okay that I'm friends with Ashley too."* Both girls made commitments to each other; they hugged, and sat back in the circle feeling happier, like a weight had been lifted from their shoulders.

I hear about misunderstandings like this all the time, and they cause friendship problems and drama. Here's another example involving two sixth graders, Rainey and Brianna. *"I've been upset about you since school started. You've been really crabby and disrespectful to me, and it seems like you only have time for your two new friends. You're always with them. We've been best friends since first grade so this really hurts,"* Rainey said. Brianna mirrored her back until Rainey felt heard, and then shared her feelings. *"Sometimes I feel annoyed when I'm with you because you tell me things I already know. Like the other day you told me I dropped my pencil. I feel like sometimes you say things just to get attention even if it doesn't fit. It's like you're trying too hard, and it gets annoying."* Rainey reflected all of this back, and then started crying. Through her tears she explained that her mom has been threatening to move her brother to another school because he has no friends and is always complaining he's being bullied. Rainey has been worried her mom might pull her out of school too if she doesn't make more friends, so when Brianna started pulling away, it intensified her fears and caused her needy behaviors. Brianna committed to hanging out with Rainey more and including her with her new friends. Rainey committed to checking in with Brianna if she feels Brianna is mad at her instead of avoiding her or being needy and annoying to get her attention. Both girls felt relieved.

Every time girls handle a disagreement like this, they and the whole group learn something about the participants. One of the most important things they find out is the ways each girl is sensitive and why. Danielle and Karlena, two fifth graders are a good example of this. *"I felt upset and hurt when you wanted to get in line yesterday and you just said, "Move!"* Danielle told Karlena. Karlena mirrored this, and asked if there was more. *"Yeah,"* Danielle responded, *"I felt disrespected and pushed aside…"* At this point Danielle started crying and we held up the process for a moment. When she could, Danielle continued, *"I have a temper sometimes, and I've gone off on people in the past. I was bullied a lot in my school last year and I put up with it for a long time. One day I'd had enough and I lost it. I got punished by my teachers, and the rest of the year was horrible. That's why I changed schools this year. I don't want to have to go through all of that again."* Karlena reflected back all of Danielle's feelings, and then she teared up. She thought she was in trouble, so we reassured her she wasn't; we were just giving Danielle a chance to clear something up. Karlena didn't even remember saying *"move it"* and we told her this process was about becoming aware of how sensitive Danielle was to being bullied because of last year. Karlena could see why Danielle might interpret her actions that first week of school as, *"Here we go again."* Karlena and the whole class committed to being aware of Danielle's sensitivity. And Danielle committed to working on being less sensitive and to not bringing last year's issues into her new school. Both girls scooted back into the circle happier.

I can't tell you how valuable it is for all the girls to recognize why Danielle acted the way she did. Understanding why people behave as they do allows us to not judge them or react as much to them. The whole class now appreciated why Danielle was so sensitive to being teased and left out. And my experience in working with groups of girls like this is that they don't use this new awareness to tease that person. This is especially true when you keep working with the group over time, allowing many girls to share their stories. It brings them closer together; they care about each other more deeply. And this level of consideration becomes the most important determinant in them not teasing or excluding people.

By the way, if you're wondering how these girls know how to manage their one-on-one conflict resolutions so well, it's because we had worked with them in previous sessions. We taught them a method to work through conflicts peacefully and effectively. The following explains that process.

Steps for Conflict Resolution

1. ASK PERMISSION:
   "There is something really important that I need to talk about with you, and I just want you to listen. Is this a good time?"
2. AFFIRM THE RELATIONSHIP:
   "Our friendship means a lot to me, and....."
3. I STATEMENTS:
   "I felt ___ "(only use ROOT BEER FEELINGS)
   "when you___"(be specific: what, when, where)
   "and what I want is___"(be specific)
4. MIRROR:
   "What I heard you say is___, did I get that right? Tell me more."
   Repeat until the sender feels heard
5. UNDERSTANDING:
   Sender: "Why do you think it bothered you so much?"
6. LISTENER MIRROR ALL OF THIS
7. REVERSE ROLES AND REDO ABOVE STEPS
8. WIN-WIN SOLUTION:
   Brainstorm solutions together- pick one or more
   "What you can count on me for is___" (often relates to your contribution)
9. FOLLOW-UP AND ACCOUNTABILITY:
   "How are we doing with each other and what we committed to?"

I've used this format in working with students as young as second grade, and in my camps with 8 to 10 year olds. We go through the steps, explain why each step is important, and then ask for volunteers to try one, using a real situation, not a made-up one. And I've never had a group where someone didn't find the courage to start us off. Once the first pair completes the process, the group learns several things. For one, no one gets in trouble. That is one of the reasons girls normally don't want to call someone out. The group also sees a happy resolution to the conflict, letting them know that as scary as it might appear to be, the process works. Teachers tend to be fearful about having girls resolve conflicts in a group setting like this. They are afraid girls will use what they see and hear as more ammunition to hurt each other later on. And I can see why they worry. Here is how I answer these concerns.

1. Relationship aggressions are group issues that usually affect more people than just the original two girls. Many girls often get pulled into the conflict, feel pushed to take sides, add to the drama, and all feel the effects of it on the mood and spirit of the classroom. Seeing it as a collective matter leads me to want to deal with it as a class, and the solutions become applicable to the whole group.

2. Seeing the procedure in practice helps girls learn the steps better. Sometimes it's easier to see your own mischief if it's played out indirectly by other people. You can recognize your conduct in others, and also see how those behaviors affect them. I always ask the group what they learned by watching two girls work through a conflict resolution, and I always get lots of raised hands. They learn a ton about themselves, other people, and relationships.

3. Seeing positive results shows girls that the process is safe and it works. They see that people are lighter and happier and closer at the end. It gives them the courage to come forward and handle their concerns. In my experience, after the first pair finishes their conflict resolution, the other girls line up eagerly to share theirs. We usually run out of time and have to put some off until our next visit.

4. The group is much more likely to play a positive role in holding each other accountable as well. The class knows what's going on, they've heard commitments made, and they've shared what they learned. It feels like a collective solution and agreement. And we've done many exercises and discussions that have already empowered the members to take responsibility for the tone and spirit of the class. And accepting your part in conflicts in front of everyone makes it much less likely that you will repeat the same mischief.

I love how much the girls learn about each other through this practice. Let me illustrate with a few of examples.

Kara was an eighth grader who volunteered to do a conflict resolution. She wanted to address some concerns with two girls, but we had her work with just one, Ava. We've found that the process works best if it's one-on-one. *"We were all best friends since fourth grade,"* Kara said to Ava. *"But it seemed like when we came back this fall you two kind of ditched me. I'm not sure if it has to do with me playing on the freshman volleyball team or not, but you seem like you don't invite me over or want to hang out with me at school anymore."* Kara was talking through her tears by the last line. Ava mirrored her back several times until Kara felt heard, and then Ava shared. *"When we came back to school you seemed really distant to us, like you were too good for us now that you were playing up in volleyball. I felt really hurt and betrayed; it was like you were too cool for us because you were hanging out with high school kids all the time. So Mary and I figured we'd move on too."* Ava, too, was in tears as she spoke. Kara mirrored Ava until she felt heard, and then Kara spoke again. *"One of the things I didn't tell you guys was that my dad moved out this summer, and my parents are getting a divorce. My summer sucked! I was too embarrassed to tell anyone. Going back and forth between houses has been really stressful, especially since school started. So yeah, I was pretty quiet and crabby, but it wasn't about you guys, at least at first. Once you acted like you didn't want to hang out, I was mad and hurt too."* Ava then responded. *"We notice you being more withdrawn, and I guess I thought you were just avoiding us because it might look 'lame' for you to be talking to us. I'm so sorry about your parents, I wish you would have called me and told me."* At this point, Ava and Mary scooted over and hugged Kara, and all three cried on each other's shoulders for a moment. You could've heard a pin drop in the room, as everyone was so focused and respectful. But the learning wasn't quite over. Ava and Mary shared how they both had an older sister who was the star of the family, getting straight A's and being a super athlete. Both had felt 'less-than' and not as good as their sibling, and had become sensitive to being compared. When they saw Kara moved up to freshman volleyball, it triggered their not-good-enough buttons, especially when they saw Kara talking to high school kids. It was kind of like, *"Here we go again, another place where I feel less-than."* The girls made commitments about spending more time together and also expressing their feelings and needs to each other.

In another interaction, sixth-grader Brooke asked Becca to join her in the middle. *"I felt really hurt and left out the other day when I came up to you and asked if I could do something with you,"* Brooke said. *"And you kind of rolled your eyes and turned away. Then you walked away with your group and started playing a game."* Becca mirrored her back, but Brooke had more to share. *"I really like you as a friend, and I really want to be part of your group."* Becca reflected what she had heard. And I asked Brooke to share why she thought Becca's actions hurt so much. *"My parents got divorced three years ago, and I hardly ever see my dad anymore. He never calls, and I haven't been over to his condo for four months. I'm adopted (Brooke started crying at this point) and I don't know who my birth dad is. And I feel really insecure and sensitive about people making fun of me because of it. I've always felt different because of being adopted, and even more so now that my dad isn't involved in my life. It really*

hurts to go to your house and see how close you are with your dad."
Becca looked stunned, but she did a great job mirroring her friend.
Then Becca spoke. *"I would never make fun of you about your dad or
being adopted. And I don't remember rolling my eyes the other day,
but I want you to know that I value you as a friend. You can count on
me to include you in my group, and if you ever feel like I'm not, I'm
open to you telling me."* Brooke committed to including herself more
instead of waiting to be asked, and to be more honest with Becca.

In the first story, the whole group learns how sensitive Ava and
Mary are about being compared and feeling 'not good enough.' They
see how tender Kara is because of her family situation. And they also
appreciate how a misunderstanding has created distance and bad
feelings because it wasn't addressed. In the second, Brooke's class
now knows how sensitive she is to being adopted and about not
having a relationship with her dad. And they comprehend how her
feeling left out of a group would bring up a lot of feelings because of
her family problems.

Sometimes I'll have the girls brainstorm how they can support
someone like Brooke who has just shared. The whole group can
become more inclusive and look out for her more. If they notice her
being quieter or withdrawn, they talked about checking in with her to
make sure she's okay. It is imperative for teachers to allow time for
these kinds of interactions. When disagreements and their resulting
feelings are not given a voice, it's hard for girls to feel safe or focused
on schoolwork. They become more sensitive and reactive, causing
more snippy behaviors and more meltdowns. Girls tell me they worry
about the drama all day at school, and they take it home with them as
well. They'll ruminate about it all evening, and they worry about
going to school the next day, causing sleep disturbances. They scour
the social network sites for any words against them, and often
overreact to and misinterpret messages they read. They'll text their

friend about it, who then text other friends, and the hive starts buzzing from the dispute.

Girls wake up worried about what this day will bring, and walk in to school expecting the worst. Great way to start the school day, right? Schools and teachers tell girls just to ignore negative comments and behaviors, as though it is easy just to wish feelings away. But the reality is what is unexpressed becomes unmanageable!

In my Strong Girls Strong World Program, I like to work with a class or group of girls every two weeks at first, creating the atmosphere of safety needed to get down to it. We usually teach them the conflict resolution model during the second visit and have several pairs work through their quarrel. On return visits, we open up the floor to anyone who has something they want to handle, and we usually get a few takers. Our hope is that teachers will allow a 30- to 60-minute class meeting every week for girls to work on community building. Resolving conflicts is just one area to be addressed. The meetings also are meant to teach the other social-emotional learning and leadership skills discussed throughout this book.

Girls need to know that this process is not a one-and-done phenomenon. Regular follow-ups keep them accountable to their agreements and intentions. It is incredibly valuable to check in with pairs who've previously worked through a problem and see how things are going. Without this follow-up, girls can regress and take out retribution on each other. A girl who's been bullied or excluded by a group needs to know that the teacher and the class is taking her issue seriously, and that they will not let RA behaviors continue. Additionally, these kinds of skills build over time. Because girls are traversing this touchpoint, adults must assume there will be ups and downs in their emotions and moods. They will make mistakes as they play with their social power and stretch themselves. Stuff happens! What's important is that girls know that there will be time and a practice to manage things that come up. They will be heard, and action will be taken.

"The opposite of courage in our society is not cowardice...it's conformity." Rollo May

Before I move on, I'd like to spend a moment talking about the whole notion of 'fitting in.' There is way too much emphasis placed on fitting in and having a sense of belonging.

"I didn't belong as a kid, and that always bothered me. If I'd only known that one day my differentness would be an asset, my earlier life would have been much easier." Bette Midler

Kids internalize fitting in as 'being like everyone else' in dress, language and behaviors. Parents, teachers and the culture have conditioned them to strive to be accepted and popular and to belong. I say, *"Why would you want to belong to anybody?"*

"Why are you trying so hard to fit in, when you are meant to stand out?" Unknown

Despite the fact that the female brain has wired girls to want to connect, I dislike the herd mentality; girls become way too dependent on externals for their sense of themselves, like puppets on a string.

"When you judge another, you do not define them, you define yourself." Wayne Dyer

If a girlfriend says she likes another girl's new outfit, the second girl feels great about herself, and that comment can carry her through the day. But if you give others that power to make you feel good, you have set yourself up to feeling bad when you are criticized. If that same friend says, *"What's with that outfit?"* the second girl is in a bad mood and suffers from insecurity the rest of the day. So her feelings, mood and sense of herself go up and down depending upon what others say or don't say, do or don't do. She has given her power away, plain and simple. This necessity to belong and fit in drives kids to give up who they are. Girls tell me all the time they believe they need to filter everything they say and do, and it's exhausting!

Seventeen-year-old Lizzy is a vivacious, spunky theater kid who came to see me because she had gotten overwhelmed with emotions and asked her parents to take her to a counselor. Lizzy first started feeling down in 4th grade when her best friend Andi started to hang out with the popular group and left her behind. She drifted from group to group for the next 2 years, but never really found a home. And that's when she started to doubt herself. She wondered if she was too 'out there' and needed to tone it down a bit. She had a flair for the dramatic and wore her emotions on her sleeve. I asked her what she gave up to appear more 'normal' in hopes of fitting in. *"Well, Andi and I always liked to wear clothes with wild colors and different accessories. The hardest things for me to give up were my purple tennis shoes; I loved those shoes! They were so me!"* As she spoke these last lines, she looked up at me with a sheepish look on her face. It was like she was embarrassed at her excitement and passion about her interests and her unique look.

That's what I mean by girls filtering their thoughts and feelings. She was worried I'd judge her as being crazy or silly, so she was tempering her remarks and enthusiasm. That's the 'good girl' part of her: not too different, not too loud, not too out there. This kind of filtering goes on a lot with their peers, and sometimes for good reason. In many groups, you can be kicked out in the blink of an eye if you are wearing the wrong brand of clothes, hanging out with the wrong people such as some dorky, unpopular girl, or not having the latest technology. Girls experience this as pressure, an ever-present tension.

For Lizzy, it was important to take back those parts of herself that she had hidden or lost due to the pressures of fitting in. I knew she was on track when she showed up for a visit wearing some really wild purple tennis shoes. The grin on her face said it all: *"I'm back!"*

I'll talk more about how girls can break free of this compulsion to fit in, but I hope you now better appreciate what girls experience in their friendships, and also what they require.

CHAPTER 7

YOU ARE IN CHARGE OF YOUR STORY

"Ultimately it is not the stories that determine our choices, but the stories that we continue to choose to believe." Unknown Author

Fifteen-year-old Tia has an older brother Ryan who was the 'star' of the family. He got good grades without much effort, but more important, he was a stud basketball and football player. Colleges were calling him for football scholarships, and Tia's parents were absorbed in that whole process with Ryan. During Ryan's senior year, Tia started acting out some. She snuck out several times to meet up with boys, her grades slipped, and she got caught stealing earrings at the mall. Her parents grounded her and raised a short-lived fuss, but quickly became distracted again with Ryan's football season. I saw Tia because her parents found out she was cutting. When I asked her how she felt because of all the attention lavished on her brother, Tia at first lashed out with some angry statements about how she didn't care anymore, she just wanted to be with her friends. After mirroring her anger for a while, Tia suddenly started sobbing. And once she started, she couldn't stop. I remember her apologizing to me for *'losing it,'* then she'd start crying again. It had been a long time since she'd felt anything but anger. She eventually shared that she felt sad, hurt and lonely. I told her that in my experience, when kids bring up those kinds of intense emotions, they always ask themselves questions in their heads.

"Do you remember times when you felt really alone and hurt?" I asked. *"Yeah, all the time,"* Tia said, *"especially the past three years."* I followed up with a second question. *"Do you remember asking yourself questions like 'Why aren't they paying more attention to me?' or, 'Why don't I get much time with my parents?'"* *"Yeah, I did a lot, especially at night when I was crying myself to sleep,"* Tia responded. I then said, *"The important thing isn't the questions we ask ourselves; it's how we answer the questions in our heads. How did you answer those questions? What did you say to yourself?"* Tia answered, *"That I wasn't as important as Ryan, so I guess I figured that I wasn't important. Sometimes I wondered what was wrong with me; was I not good enough? Maybe if I was prettier or a better daughter they'd notice me more. At my lowest I'd feel unloved, like my parents really just didn't love me."*

That was the pay dirt. And it's what I look for when I work with girls because these thoughts are incredibly powerful; they drive girls' actions. A simple chart illustrates what I mean.

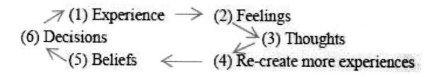

Let's use Tia's example to demonstrate this process. Tia's experience was having parents who became distracted with her brother's sports and college process. She felt hurt, left out and alone. Her private logic, those thoughts in her head she generated to answer questions about why, told her she was not important, not good enough or pretty enough, and unloved and unlovable. Because she felt this way about herself, she allowed girlfriends and guys to take advantage of her. She put up with a lot of abuse, and she acted in ways that caused people to exclude her. She re-experienced many of these same emotions, and her thoughts started turning into solid beliefs about herself and her relationships. Tia decided she was ugly, weird, not good enough, and that she didn't fit in. These judgments then were at the root of her poor boundaries and of her not taking good care of herself.

Let me share another example of a 14-year-old girl who made unhealthy decisions about herself. Angela's parents got divorced when she was 9 years old, and her dad moved 1,000 miles away within a year. According to Angela, it may as well have been a million miles away, based on her dad's actions. *"At first, he used to call a couple times a week and my younger brother Adam and I would fly to his city every month or two. We'd also spend three to four weeks with him in the summers. Then a year and a half ago, his girlfriend Whitney and her 4-year-old son moved in with him and everything changed. He hardly ever called, and when he did he sounded really distant. I started not liking visits because he spent most of the time with his girlfriend. For the past year, we only saw him every two to three months. When we were there last week, he sat us down and told us Whitney was six months pregnant and they would be using my bedroom for the baby, so I'd be sleeping on a mattress in the basement!"* Angela had been speaking fast and furious until she shared about her bedroom, at which time her eyes welled up with tears. And she slowed down considerably when I asked her how all of this made her feel. *"I feel like I'm not good enough for him, and that his girlfriend and their new baby are more important than me. I asked him once what I could do to be a better daughter, but he never answered me."* More tears followed this statement. I asked her what else she had been thinking in her head because she felt this way. *"Well, I feel unloved by my dad, and I feel alone, especially when I'm with him. I also feel really confused and lost. I used to know what a good relationship was, but now I'm not so sure. It's harder for me to trust people."* I asked her, *"Why is it harder for you to trust?"* Angela responded, *"My dad promised us that we would always be his priority and that we'd have a place in his home. Whitney has taken our place, so I feel like he lied. I decided I have to take care of my brother, and that I would have to be strong for him. And I hate seeing my mom cry about all this, so I usually don't talk about it at home either."*

A couple of entries in Angela's journal might shed more light on her feelings and decisions.

- *"I'm angry that I don't have the guts to tell my dad how I really feel. I acted happy when he told me Whitney was pregnant, and I was a little excited because I like little kids. But mostly I'm mad because he already is spending almost no time with us. I'm also mad because I let my dad's actions affect me and upset me in a way that makes me want to hurt myself in some way."*
- *"I'm confused about why he's caring more about the baby and his 'new family' than his two blood-related kids."*
- *"Although this may sound mean, I'm glad I live with my mom full time instead of with my dad!"*

Whew! There certainly was a lot of emotion bottled up inside Angela, and she looked relieved at the end of her venting and crying. She had started making a lot of unhealthy decisions about herself and life based on her experiences with her dad. She was thinking, *"I'm not good enough, I'm unlovable and not important, relationships are scary and I can't trust people, I have to put my feelings and needs aside to take care of others."* She had a lot of negative self-talk too, about being mad at herself for not expressing herself to her dad, for blaming herself for her dad's actions, and for thinking about hurting herself. Angela had been worrying that her friends were prettier and smarter than she, and that boys noticed them more too. So her dad's behaviors reinforced some already percolating thoughts.

These stories show us what is going on in girls' heads and hearts. When their emotional centers light up with feelings, much of that energy gets channeled to their prefrontal cortexes, causing girls to ruminate; they think about it and think about it, turning the experience over and over again in their minds and oftentimes escalating mole hills into mountains. This process also builds mere thoughts into beliefs, resulting in unhealthy and untrue conclusions about themselves, relationships and life.

Decisions like the ones Tia and Angela made hurt their self-confidence, self-esteem, and sense of what they deserve from life. This affects their body language when they walk into school or social situations. It makes it harder to stand up for themselves and to set firm boundaries. It influences whom they befriend and hang out with. And it shapes their ability to cope with future stresses and feelings. That's why it's critical for adults who care for and about girls to help them see what's really going on below the surface, beneath the facade that makes them say, *It's no big deal* or, *I don't care.*

In my programs with girls in high school, we engage them in a process that helps them figure out how they have interpreted past life experiences. It's a multi-step process of identifying feelings, thoughts, decisions, the cost of those decisions, and how to re-define what they have lived through.

"Never be bullied into silence. Never allow yourself to be made a victim. Accept no one's definition of your life, but define yourself."
Harvey Firestone

I want girls to know they are in charge of their stories. I helped Angela re-define some decisions she'd made about herself. She became clear that her dad's mischief was not about her; that she was not only good enough but also deserving of love. She reached out to some other dad figures in her life for love and support, and she started to release her feelings and thoughts onto her journal pages. The journaling was especially valuable and healing for Angela. Once she saw and read her emotions and views on paper, it was easier to make better sense of them and to process through them. Angela got her confidence back and felt more grounded and more herself. She has more work to do, but she's well on her way. Her dad, I'm not so sure about.

Stephanie asked Sean into the circle one day as my wife and I were working with their fourth grade class. *"I felt hurt, sad and mad when you didn't pass the ball to me at recess during our basketball game, even though I was open a lot,"* Stephanie said. Sean mirrored her, and asked if there was more. *"Yeah, I wondered if you don't think I'm very good, or if you don't like me or don't want me playing with you guys."* Sean again mirrored her, and I asked Stephanie to share why it hurt her feelings so much. *"I'm really sensitive to being left out of sports because I'm a girl, and I'm really competitive and I play on a traveling basketball team. That's why it bothers me so much when some of the guys don't pass to me when we're playing a game."* This led us to talk about the cost to us when we make assumptions about things instead of checking them out. (You can see more about girls and assumptions in Chapter 13.) Sean responded. *"I like it when you play with us. I think you're a great player; that's why I choose you for my team at after-school care."* As Stephanie mirrored Sean, she looked happier and lighter already. Sean continued. *"You can count on me to pass to you more at recess."* To which Stephanie responded, *"And you can count on me to tell you if I'm upset about it again and that I'll play harder."* This incident occurred right before our session. I was proud of Stephanie for dealing with it right away. And if you think I'm making up the way these kids talk during their conflict resolution, you're mistaken. We had taught the conflict-resolution model to this class, and their teachers gave them opportunities to handle things in-between our visits. So even fourth graders can use this kind of language. They're incredible if we only allow them to step it up.

Here's another case in point of a sensitive girl who got her feelings hurt. *"I felt hurt last week during four-square when you were in the king's square and I was in the queen's square,"* Ilana said. *"And you kept making a funny whiny noise. It felt like you were making fun of me."* Autumn mirrored her back, and asked if there was more. *"I'm really sensitive to people teasing me because I'm so small, and they think I'm not good at sports because I'm the smallest in the class."* She started crying a little, and Autumn and the rest of the group respectfully gave her a moment. I remembered that during our 'cross the line' exercise in the first session with them, Ilana was the girl whose contribution was, *"Cross the line if you ever feel like a speck of dust."* When it was Autumn's turn to share, it was clear that Ilana's words had touched her. *"I'm so sorry you felt hurt that day, I really wasn't making fun of you, but I can see why you might have thought that. You can count on me to be more sensitive to your feelings from now on."* To which Ilana responded, *"You can count on me to be less sensitive, and if I feel upset, to check it out with you right away."*

We worked with this class on not allowing words to hurt them, and not giving their power away. I'll discuss this in detail in Chapter 12. But you can see how a prior belief of Ilana's, that she's small and therefore less capable and unimportant, has made her overly sensitive to other people's comments and actions. And it also affects her confidence when it comes to including herself.

Here's another good recess story. *"I felt mad, hurt and embarrassed the other day when you were pitching in kickball,"* Jessie said, *"and I asked you if I could pitch some too and you said you would let me in a little while, but then you never did."* Katie mirrored her back, and asked if there was more about that. *"I told two of my friends because I was so upset, and when you tried to talk to me I was still too upset. I'm not very athletic; I'm actually terrible at sports. If there were 35 people being chosen for teams, I'd be like the 34th person picked. It makes me feel really embarrassed and less confident.*" Katie did a great job reflecting all of it, and you could see it really bothered her that Jessie was hurt. *"I'm really sorry I forgot to let you pitch,"* Katie responded. *"I'm super-competitive, and it upsets me when people don't take the games seriously and goof off. I think I was just thinking about that and forgot what I'd told you."* Jessie mirrored that, and asked Katie what she wanted. *"I just want to be your friend again!"* Katie's eyes teared up. She had noticed Jessie was upset after recess and had tried to find out why. She committed to being more mindful of Jessie's feelings of exclusion during recess games, and Katie committed to going directly to Katie to tell her how she feels versus telling other girls first. They hugged and sat together the rest of the session. Awesome!

So when you see girls who are angry, sad, withdrawn or just not themselves, you should wonder what life experience they are operating from. I'd be curious to know their beliefs are about themselves, friendship, trust and life. This is especially true if they'd experienced something in their lives that aroused strong emotions: things like being teased or left out, living through family issues like divorce, experiencing significant loss, being compared to siblings, or having parents who are distracted or unavailable for various reasons.

That pretty much includes almost every girl I have ever met in grade school, middle school and high school! It doesn't take a major trauma (in the eyes of adults) to cause this cycle of beliefs to start. Being harassed on the bus or losing your friend group in fourth grade can be enough to start an unhealthy progression rolling. This is why girls need sacred spaces to deal with their emotions and life experiences.

CHAPTER 8

YOU ARE MORE THAN YOUR SPORT

Lisa was a level 10 gymnast and a high school junior when I met her. She requested an office visit because she had been feeling more and more depressed since she injured her wrist at a meet two months prior. It was her fifth wrist fracture, and she had torn ligaments for the second time in a year. When I asked her what she had been feeling lately, she went on and on about missing the competition, falling behind in her training, and having a hard time focusing in school. In other words, lots of head talk, but no emotions. What finally got her to get more real was when I asked if she ever worried that her gymnastics career was over, along with her dreams of getting a college scholarship. That's when some tears came, although she fought hard to remain in control. *"Yeah, I've thought about that a lot. I would be ...devastated. I've been doing gymnastics since I was 4 years old, and hard-core since I was 7. I don't know what I would do."* *"It sounds like gymnastics has been everything to you,"* I said, *"and you'd feel lost without it."* Lisa nodded. *"I feel lost already. I'm not even sure my doctors are going to let me compete anymore. It's so hard to watch my friends at the meets. I'm still on the team, but it's not the same."* I responded, *"It sounds like the doctors and your body are telling you something. Would it be okay if you stopped gymnastics?"* Lisa paused, and then answered. *"My parents would be really upset. They have invested so much time and money in this, I'd be afraid of disappointing them. A lot of their friends are parents of my friends on the team, so they'd lose all that too. Plus I'd be letting down my coaches and my teammates. I don't know if I could just walk*

away from it." In response, I asked a couple of additional questions. *"What could you do with all that extra time? What are some things you have an interest in or a passion for?"* Lisa answered, *"That's the scary thing: I don't know. I don't know what I like or what I want. I'm so used to this regimented schedule. I feel really confused and lost right now. It's depressing not knowing what you want."*

I have worked with elite girl athletes like Lisa, especially in the past 10 years. They play at the highest level in sports like gymnastics, swimming, soccer and ice-skating. I saw them because injuries were severe enough to cut short their careers. And they all shared many of the same fears and sentiments Lisa did. *Who am I without my sport?* That question rattled around in all their heads. That male energy part of them I described in Chapter 2 had pushed them to high levels of ambition and competition. But they were out-of-balance with it. They had no life outside their sport. Even their social lives were impacted. Most of these girls had been so preoccupied with practices, games, meets, tournaments and out-of-town competitions that they had little free time to spend on friends or sleepovers. They perceived their only identity as being a soccer star, and feared that without it people wouldn't know how to connect with them. It was like starting over as a new sixth-grader at a new middle school. That's how awkward and insecure they felt socially. Many of these girls had kept busy and distracted from their emotions, which of course had built up over time. For Lisa, it had turned inward to depression. For others, it was cutting. Several of them had been sexually active in middle school, and many had become angry, with their anger misdirected at their moms or friends.

As more and more girls become heavily invested in club sports teams starting as young as first grade, I worry about their psychological and emotional health. Overuse injuries in females have risen dramatically in the past 10 years, and that takes a psychological toll on these girls too.

And girls in sports struggle not just because of career-ending injuries. I've seen young girls devastated by not making the cut for select teams. Their lives, and their family's lives, revolve around these activities. Even their parents' social lives are wrapped up in which teams their kids make. Many girls lose their friend groups if they don't make the cut, because their friends on the team are busy most weekends with tournaments, games, practices and out-of-town competitions. And everyone at school knows who's on which team. It creates a hierarchy that's tough to break into. Similar problems arise if a girl doesn't make her high school team, or doesn't get that college scholarship her family has been hyper-focused on since kindergarten. Girls can allow it to mean they have failed, or worse yet, that they are failures. These athletes believe they have let their parents and coaches down, and they take it very personally. Worse, they don't have the tools to put it in perspective or to express their concerns. So they suffer, needlessly.

The good news is that career-ending injuries or not making teams also can be viewed as new beginnings: a fresh start, a chance to redefine yourself. It can be a time to experiment with new interests, to be open to discover, *What do I like? What are my passions?*

I encourage these girls to think back over their lives and remember any activity they either tried and liked or wished they'd had time for. What strikes them as being fun or interesting? What do they seem drawn to? What kind of biographies do they enjoy reading? Who do they admire? If they knew they couldn't fail, what would they try for? It's trial and error, the same as we all experience throughout our lives. They just got a little behind, that's all. They have the rest of their lives to create new experiences and stories about who they are and what their purpose is. But the first step is to slow down and go inward in order to figure out what they are feeling, and then to express those emotions in healthy ways. They need to take time to grieve, because this really is a significant loss for them. Failing to do so will result in an unhealthy manifestation of their emotions.

Allow yourself to go through your feelings. Make good sense of your experience. Honor the lessons and gifts you received from the sport and the injuries. Let go of any negativity. Move forward with anticipation and joy and excitement for the next leg of your journey.

CHAPTER 9

SLOW DOWN, YOU'RE MOVIN' TOO FAST

"It is good to be solitary, for solitary is difficult; that something is difficult must be a reason the more for us to do it."
Rainer Maria Rilke

I was working with a class of sixth-graders at an all-girls school a few years ago and heard once again evidence of how busy girls are today. I had them close their eyes and did a visualization in which I asked them to think about how they felt 'different.' By different I meant in a bad way, for example the things about themselves they judged negatively and wished would change. We went around the circle and had every girl share. It was Molly's disclosure that struck me most.

"I feel different because I'm so busy every day. I have gymnastics six days a week and do out-of-town tournaments twice a month," Molly said. *"And I hear about my friends talking to each other every night and doing stuff after school and on the weekends. By the time I get home from practice at eight, I have to eat dinner and do homework, and there's no time for being with my friends. So I feel different because everybody else seems like they have so much time just to have fun."* As Molly shared, her voice became more soft and distressed. The look on her face when she finished talking was one of sadness and resignation. What was fascinating was that before we had finished getting around the circle, five other girls shared similar

stories of busyness and no time for friends. I was glad Molly didn't seem so alone in her experience, but how sad for all of them!

As Rilke so eloquently pointed out in his quote, it's not always easy to be alone and silent. That has become especially true for this generation of kids, who seem to have come out of the womb with headphones on. Girls have been inundated with electronics of all sorts since they were in grade school, and the toddlers of today are ahead of that curve. All the noise and distraction and momentary thrills from texting, social networking sites, Skype, YouTube and the like make tranquil times seem so foreign. Plus many girls' schedules are packed so tightly, that there seems to be no time for solitude even if they wanted some. And yet, our girls all need 'Sleeping Beauty' time.

"There is more to life than increasing its speed." Gandhi

"The necessary thing is after all but this: solitude, great inner solitude. Going into oneself for hours meeting no one – this one must be able to attain." Rilke

Randi is the 55-year old mother of two college-age children. I asked her when she felt like she had made the transformation from a girl to a woman. She had to think a while; the answer at first was all over the place. But in the end it came down to quiet alone time. *"I didn't date much in high school,"* Randi said. *"I was into sports, and I was never one of those girls who always had to have a boyfriend. My second year in college I started dating a guy, and it was one of those love-at-first-sight kind of romances. We got engaged my third year and started to argue with each other more and more. Right before I was supposed to send the wedding announcements out, I broke it off. I was so afraid of how angry my mom was going to be; the wedding was only six weeks away. After the breakup, I was single for a year, and I think in that time I kind of grew into myself. I just felt more confident and sure of myself. It's hard to pinpoint exactly why."*

I asked her, *"Why do you think you broke up with him? How did you know what was right for you?"* *"You know, I'm not sure,"* she responded. *"But now that I think about it, I tend to figure things out by processing them in my head. Even today, if I get into a fight with my husband, he'll come to me wanting to talk about it. And I push him away because I need time to think it through. It might take me a couple of hours or even a couple of days, but then I'm ready to talk. And I guess that's what I did in high school and college. I'd go for a walk or a run, or even just walk across my campus to have quiet time to think. There was no TV in my room or dorm, no phones or computers, so I had a lot of time with myself to think about things. I wish I had more of that time today."*

That solitude is one of the missing pieces in our Sleeping Beauty puzzle. As I have mentioned before, the times when girls are alone with their thoughts and feelings, they tend to get overwhelmed. So many emotions build up with so many views rattling around in their brains. It's easier just to avoid it with busyness and distractions.

"Embrace your solitude and love it. Endure the pain it causes, and try to sing out with it. For those near to you are distant." Rilke

When girls have had a chance to release their pent-up emotions, and have been guided to process through their judgments and worries, they become lighter and calmer. They learn to love having time to themselves, and they miss it when they slip back into their hectic pace. They discover how to be alone without being lonely.

"You will never feel alone if you like who you are with."
Wayne Dyer

A large part of the adolescent touchpoint is to figure out who they are and what is right for them. Self-awareness, self-discovery and self-acceptance are key components of a girl's transformation.

Sleeping Beauties, Awakened Women

Cinderella worked in solitude for years, suffering as she waited for the day when she was ready to meet the world. She realized she could live without her parents, and she learned to love herself without the acceptance of her peers. She relied on her inner strengths and self-reliance, not her good looks. This strong sense of self, this vibrant life force that coursed through her being, is what attracted the attention of everyone at the Prince's ball. From her profound inner work, Cinderella had discovered and acknowledged the princess within herself. She didn't feel alone because she loved and accepted herself as she was.

"You are not too old and it is not too late to dive into your increasing depths, where life calmly gives out its own secret."

Rilke

A more modern fairytale that illustrates this process is the movie *Runaway Bride*, with Julia Roberts as the princess-in-waiting. Roberts' character was stuck, and she wasn't even aware of it until Richard Gere's character came along to prod her awake. She had on three occasions been to the altar to get married to three different fiancés, and every time she got cold feet and fled. We can see in several ways how lost Roberts is and how little self-awareness she has. When they show her being asked, at breakfast with each of her fiancés, what kind of eggs she wants to order, she unflinchingly answers, *"Whatever he has."* Her mom is dead, as is common in most of our princess tales, and she has had to take care not only of her alcoholic father but his hardware store as well.

She puts on a fake tattoo for one fiancé, and gives up on her dream of making designer lamps. As she walks up the aisle to wed Gere, a camera flash wakens her out of a lustful reverie, and once again she runs. Actually, she jumps onto a Federal Express truck and drives away from a frantic Gere. The next part of the movie is the more meaningful part. For what seems like the next year, she finally gives up rebounding and remains single. There are scenes of her exercising, and one where she has about eight plates of different kinds of eggs in front of her. She's about to figure out *"What kind of eggs do I like?"* A subsequent incident shows Gere walking down a street in a big city one day where he sees one of her designer lamps in the display window. She's living her dream! In the final scene, Roberts breaks into his apartment, sits him down, hands Gere her running shoes, and delivers a speech that basically says the following: *"I realized I couldn't marry you because I needed some time to find myself. How could you be in love with me when I didn't even know who me was? I like poached eggs, and I love my new lamp business. I'm ready to marry you now, on my terms. I don't need a man to complete my anymore, because I have connected with myself at the deepest levels."*

This was her Sleeping Beauty time, her time to get quiet and go within to find herself and expand, and to actively discover her wants, needs, desires, and passions. The secret Rilke is talking about in his quote is the innate sense of who each girl is, at her deepest and most real level.

"But your solitude will be a support and a home for you, even in the midst of very unfamiliar circumstances, and from it you will find all your paths." Rilke

This is one of the most crucial missing pieces for girls today. The paths Rilke touches on are not the paths of straight A's leading to an Ivy League school or playing club sports 24/7 from first grade on in hopes of attaining a college scholarship. Those routes have been laid out by parents and the educational system and the culture.

"I'm glad I paid so little attention to good advice; had I abided by it I might have been saved from some of my most valuable mistakes." Gene Fowler, journalist

Sleeping Beauties, Awakened Women

I'm talking about an authentic, personal course here, where girls find their own journeys, where girls create their own stories and destinies. These paths are found during the inward journey, undeterred and uninterrupted by the media, peers and other externals.

"...keep growing quietly and seriously throughout your whole development; you cannot disturb it more rudely than by looking outward and expecting from outside replies to questions that only your inmost feeling in your most hushed hour can perhaps answer." Rilke

Our educational system and parenting are driven a lot by externals. We are still stuck on the old carrot and stick approach to motivate children. We've been riding the self-esteem wave started in the 1990's that overvalued praise and rewards. This kind of conditioning has created the prototypical child of today who, when asked to study for a test or do their chores, answers, "What will I get for it?" We have sucked kids dry of their love of learning, playing for plays sake, doing the right thing because it's the right thing to do, and being self-motivated. When you ask a kid or teen today to assess their artwork or schoolwork, they become paralyzed.

Todd, a 12th-grade art teacher at a public high school, told me an interesting story about a conversation with one of his students. Hannah turned in her drawing, and Todd decided to handle it differently this time. Instead of praising her work and telling her what a great artist she was, he instead turned the tables on Hannah with a very simple question. *"So what do you think about your drawing?"* Hannah paused. *"Uhh, I don't know, what do you think?"* To which Todd responded, *"I want to hear first how you think you did?"* Hannah stood there uncomfortably. Amazingly, *"Well, I...uhh..."* was as much information as Todd could get out of Hanna. And he realized in that moment that after 12 years of schooling, no one had ever asked Hanna what she thought of her work.

The cost? We are conditioning girls to look outside of themselves for their sense of themselves. They become way too dependent on what other people say or don't say, do or don't do. The last thing we want for our girls is to look to movie stars, models, rock stars, reality TV stars, or peers to assess if they are good enough, pretty enough and thin enough. But that's exactly what all this emphasis on externals is doing.

"All of mans miseries derive from not being able to sit quietly in a room alone." Blaise Pascal, French scientist and philosopher

The best answers to these kinds of questions come from within. It involves listening to your inner voice, trusting your intuition, becoming aware of your 'knowingness,' shutting out all the distractions and voices of the world, and listening to your inner wisdom and heart. And it involves moments of silence where you are undisturbed. *Should I stay with my current friend group or find a healthier group? What should my boundaries be with others? What do I want to do after high school? Should I sign up for the club volleyball team or just stick with my high school team? Is it okay to try some weed or not? Am I getting too fat or is it just the normal body changes of puberty?* Girls are constantly asking themselves questions like these, and unfortunately, they are looking for the answers on Facebook and Instagram, in the look on their friends' faces, in whether or not a boy asks them out, and by checking out women in magazines and TV shows.

"One of the greatest necessities in America is to discover creative solitude." Carl Sandburg

"What lies behind us and what lies before us are tiny matters compared to what lies within us." Ralph Waldo Emerson

Sleeping Beauties, Awakened Women

We need to teach girls how to settle their bodies, impulses and minds so they can turn inward for their answers. The following are ways girls can accomplish this.

First, journaling. This is a terrific technique for girls to take all the ideas they are ruminating about and release them onto their journal pages. It's often best when unedited and free-flowing, in other words, just let 'er rip. I tell girls I'm not talking about a travelogue of what they did all day. It's about getting thoughts out of their busy brains, about taking a load off their shoulders.

Fourteen-year-old Sara, writing in her journal about her dad, who had just moved in with his new girlfriend and her 2 young children *"When you told me you were moving in with Mary and her two kids, I acted like I was okay with it, but I'm not! I'm upset because I think you love her more than me, and you promised after the divorce that you would always be there for me no matter what. You lied to me, and I feel really hurt and left out. I want my old dad back!"* In this entry, Sara had written four pages. She had been scared to be honest with her dad, so it felt safe just to lay it all out in her journal. She told me journal writing meant healing to her.

I also tell girls that journaling is no different than math or soccer; it takes practice to get better at it. You don't miss soccer practice for a year and then show up at the national championship game expecting to play brilliantly. The same goes for journaling. Writing most days or every day allows girls to get better and better at getting their deepest concerns up and out onto the paper. Even if nothing huge is happening that day, it's still good to discipline themselves to write. This practice allows them to be more effective at it when there are heavier things going on. It helps if they make it part of their evening routine, just like brushing teeth. Journaling quiets down busy brains, and it helps girls to decelerate and decompress. They can reread previous passages, and then respond with how they feel about that issue today. It becomes a way to think through issues, and to get clear about what you want or need or feel.

At my retreats and summer camps I like to get middle and high school girls outdoors to write. They seem to settle into the practice more quickly in nature. There are a number of good books to prompt and guide girls in becoming skilled at journaling. I've listed several in my bibliography, but don't get too caught up in finding the perfect, fancy diary or one with too many directives. Keep it simple and straightforward. Stream-of-consciousness writing is one technique I've used at camps and schools to get girls started. I have them put their pen tip onto the page, and then tell them to just start writing out whatever thoughts pop into their heads--just don't take their pen off the page or stop writing until I say stop, usually after five to 10 minutes. If all that comes up is, "This is stupid," then they should write that. After just a few minutes, almost everyone ends up writing about more important matters. It's an excellent jump-starter for anyone with journal-block. I will talk more about channeling emotions in Chapter11.

Second, arts and crafts. For many girls, arts and crafts are calming activities that can help them become more still and present. They get engaged in their art, and all the worries and cares fade away. Whether it is sketching, painting or sculpting, it serves the purpose of shifting into a more reflective space. I've also met quite a few girls in middle school and high school who knit or crochet as a way to put the brakes on. And you don't have to be Picasso or Georgia O'Keefe to get the calming benefits of artwork. It's about the process, not the result.

Third, time in nature. There is something relaxing and grounding about spending time in nature. I encourage girls to find themselves a spot outdoors to call their own. It could be by a creek, pond, lake, river or ocean. For some it's a walk in the woods, climbing a tree, sitting in a tree house, swinging on a swing, or lying in a hammock under some trees. At our summer camps, one of our favorite before-bed rituals is to lie out on some tarps in the middle of a field and star gaze. We make sure it's a low-energy area. It's okay to talk and hang out, but we ask the rowdier kids go inside the mess hall if they want a louder time. Most kids have never just sat outside and stared at the sky, waiting expectantly for shooting stars. It's incredibly relaxing, and our repeat campers tell us they can't wait to do it. They have so little downtime in their lives that stargazing is a real treat.

For more information about the positive effects of being in nature, read the book *Last Child in the Woods* by Richard Louv. He cites good studies showing the calming effects of time in green space on kids with attention deficit disorder and on kids in general who spend time outdoors.

Fourth, bringing yourself to the present moment. Most times when girls are worried, fearful or anxious, it is about something that might happen in the future. They become apprehensive because of an upcoming test, whether they will be asked to homecoming dance, how girls will treat them tomorrow when they get to school, or whether they will be accepted into the college of their choice. The truth, for most people, is that what we are so anxious might happen rarely does, or if it does it's rarely as bad as we thought. Yet we've wasted a ton of time and energy worrying needlessly. So I encourage girls to stay in the moment, to bring themselves into the here-and-now. Because in this instant, it's all good. Right now, they are fine. I teach girls several techniques to bring themselves to the present.

1. Breath Work – Focusing on your breathing is a simple way to be in the moment. I have girls just become aware of their respirations. Is it shallow? Deep? Are they breathing mostly from their diaphragm or chest? Can they feel the air going through their nostrils? Is it cool? Warm? I also have girls count in their heads as they breathe in and out. I'll have them inhale over five seconds,

hold the breath for two counts, then slowly exhale while counting backward from five. When they do this with their eyes closed for a minute or two, their bodies calm down, and so do their brains. It's very relaxing.

And when your total focus is on your respirations, your negative or worried thoughts go away. You are drawn into your body, and into the present.

2. Focus - Focusing on one sense allows the girls to focus in on what's at hand. Here are some examples of how I do this in my camps and classroom work with girls:

    a) Visual. I pair girls off and have one blindfolded. Their partner guides them, usually outside, and brings their face up to something interesting. This could be a flower, bark pattern on a tree, or an insect. When they lift the blindfold off, the sight they are looking at comes vividly into focus, especially since they've been in the dark for several minutes. Or we'll lie down under some trees and just watch the leaves and branches swaying in the wind. Or they will hold a pretty flower up to their face and stare at it for a few moments. They are amazed at what they have been missing because they rush around so distracted. I also have girls sit quietly and stare at a candle flame in the fireplace or campfire. Or we'll lie on the ground and soak in the stars on a clear night.

    b) Auditory. It's amazing how many different sounds you can hear when you just sit in silence out in nature. The girls hear different birds calling each other, insects, and the wind rustling through trees. I have them do it for at least five minutes, because sometimes it takes them awhile to get settled and focused. It helps, too, for them to close their eyes so they can use one sense at a time. I also play many different kinds of music for them: melodic soundtracks, New Age, Native American flute music, different kinds of chanting (including just the 'ohm' sound), or Tibetan singing bowls. I also play nature sounds like ocean waves, mountain streams, babbling brooks, gentle rain showers, or rainforest sounds. The key is to have them experience all kinds of quieting methods, because one girl's ceiling is another girl's floor; they need to find which sounds work for them. Finally, I'll have them experience some of these sounds live. We'll go sit by a waterfall for some meditative time, or under a pavilion and listen to a rainstorm, or by the creek to listen to its sounds.

c) Smell. Sometimes I will bring several different varieties of roses from my garden, all with their own unique fragrance. I'll have the girls close their eyes and just smell the roses, literally. I have read that roses vibrate at the highest frequency of any flower, and that smelling their fragrance is medicinal. What I know from experience is that this activity does bring girls into the moment.

d) Touch. If you are used to being around girls, you know how freely they use touch to connect. Whether it is braiding or brushing each other's hair or sitting in tight clumps, this kind of touch is grounding for girls. They love giving each other back or shoulder massages too. One exercise I do with girls on retreats or at camps, after a day or so of getting to know each other and feeling safe, is 'Jessie's eye exercise.' We all stand up with a partner, hold hands, and then stare into one another's eyes for about 30 seconds. At first there are giggles and comments as they work through their discomfort, but we remind them to stay quiet and stay with it. We keep changing partners until everyone has done this with about 10 people. And we also tell them before we start not to force things; just look into your partner's eyes and notice what you experience. When we're done, we'll sit and process it. Almost everyone ends up liking it a lot, once they get past the initial discomfort. We hear comments like, "I felt like I could tell what she was feeling or thinking" or "I had never noticed how pretty her eyes were," or "I feel a lot closer to everyone now." Someone will comment about the eyes being the "window into someone's soul" and how it kind of felt that way during the exercise. Everyone at the end feels calmer, more peaceful, and closer. In their everyday lives they have never slowed down enough before to really look into people's eyes. It's very soulful.

e) Kinesthetic. We also use exercises like yoga to slow girls down. We'll do some fun postures, having them focus on their breathing as they do them. We also have girls do a progressive muscle relaxation exercise, where they tighten specific muscles for 10 to 20 seconds and then slowly release them. We'll start at their feet and work our way up to thighs, buttocks, stomach, chest, hands, arms, shoulders, and even their faces. We play some quiet music and have them lying down as they do this. And it really makes them feel relaxed. Focusing their full attention on a sense like this is calming, and it does bring them into the present moment.

3. Mindfulness – I am a huge proponent of doing one thing at a time, despite tremendous cultural pressures to multitask. There is good research showing that performance quality goes down when we multitask. And girls today are the queens of doing many things at once. Research also shows that the body rewards them with a shot of dopamine to the brain's pleasure center, giving them a kind of multitasking high. The neurochemical reward is what creates the seeking drive, the need for more technology. All the while, everything they do is degraded in quality.

It's nothing for girls to be doing their homework, snacking, texting, Face- booking, listening to music, and all with the TV on at the same time. And even though girls are continuously connected to people through technology, they rarely get anyone's full attention. Everyone is there but not there. And this instant, 24/7 connectivity becomes a craving for girls, and they grow to need it. One of the consequences of all this is that there is no time to be alone with yourself, to reflect and gather yourself. "Loneliness is failed solitude" makes a wonderful and fitting quote for this phenomenon.

At retreats and camps, I have girls experience the benefits of doing one thing at a time. We'll have them do a variety of everyday tasks, like brushing their teeth, vacuuming the carpet, eating a meal, walking to the lake, or listening to the sounds of nature with their eyes closed. We encourage them to be 100 percent focused on that act, trying to block out distractions. Having this single-pointed attention allows girls to fully experience whatever they are doing, and it has a calming effect on them.

Another concept that fits here is the idea of flow. Flow is what happens when you are fully engaged in something you have an interest in or passion for. You get so into the activity that you lose time. You might be working on a song on the guitar, and you look up and two hours have gone by, even though it felt like 15 minutes. I'll talk more about this in Chapter 14. There are some powerful words we seem to have lost sight of in our hectic, noisy culture. Words like solitude, reflection, daydreaming, soul searching, deliberateness and mindfulness. Erik Erikson said, *"Teens need places of stillness where you can gather yourself."* For girls to effectively grow through their transformative touchpoint, they need this still time as well. Stillness and solitude allows girls to think their own thoughts, process through their concerns and feelings, and to really know themselves inside and out.

"By far the greatest number of new ideas occur during a state of reverie, intermediate between waking and sleeping. The creator needs to be able to be passive, to let things happen within the mind." Anthony Starr, in his book Solitude: A Return to Self.

"Art is emotion recollected in tranquility." Wordsworth.

Girls need time alone and disconnected, where they are undisturbed, uninterrupted, and unreachable. Creativity springs forth during these times, as do new perceptions and perspectives. Girls will be more free and effective in exploring their emerging identity if they have enough still, quiet moments. That's why the metaphor of sleep is used in so many fairy tales and myths.

Let me leave you with one of my favorite poems I read to girls on this topic.

> *There Is A Voice Inside Of You*
> *That Whispers All Day Long,*
> *"I Feel That This Is Right For Me,*
> *I Know That This Is Wrong."*
> *No Teacher, Preacher, Parent, Friend*
> *Or Wise Man Can Decide*
> *What's Right For You, Just Listen To*
> *The Voice That Speaks Inside.*
>
> Shel Silverstein

CHAPTER 10

SACRED SPACES

Sixteen-year-old Keegan was having a hard time setting healthy boundaries with boys. We were sitting on the carpet in front of a crackling fire one winter morning at a high school weekend retreat. Keegan seemed to have it all together: honor student, varsity athlete, and lots of friends. We decided to do an exercise with her to figure out why she was letting guys push her sexual boundaries.

We had her stand up on the carpet and sent one of the teen guys to the far end of the room. We told him to slowly walk toward her, and as soon as she felt any discomfort, she was to tell him, *"Stop."* So Zach started walking toward Keegan, and when he was about 20 feet away, we noticed a shift in her body language, but she said nothing. Zach kept walking until he was, literally, right in her face before Keegan let out a soft, giggly, *"Stop."* We asked her if that was when she'd first felt uncomfortable, and she said yes. When we asked the 19 other teens present, they reported she looked uncomfortable 20 feet earlier. Had Keegan noticed that? *"Well, yeah, but...,"* she answered and then she burst into tears and started relating how bad she felt after letting guys go further sexually than she wanted. *"It's just that...I like the attention. I like it when guys want me, or find me attractive, or pick me instead of my friends. I know it's bad, but..."*

As Keegan processed through her feelings, she shared a story about her dad. Her parents divorced when she was 5 years old, and her dad saw her fairly regularly for several years. Then he got a girlfriend, and they quickly got married and had a baby together. And as time went on, Keegan's dad saw her less and less. What started out as every other weekend became once a month, then every six to eight weeks, then almost never. He'd go months without seeing her, and he rarely called. When she was 10 years old, she remembers him calling out of the blue one day and inviting her to spend the weekend with him. Keegan got really excited and remembered sitting on the steps outside her house, with her pink suitcase by her side, waiting for her daddy to pick her up at 5 o'clock. Five o'clock came and went, then 5:30, 6, and at 6:30 she trudged back into the house, crushed. She could recall asking herself, *Why doesn't my dad see me? Why didn't he show up? He promised!* Her private logic told her: *Maybe his new family is more important than me, and therefore I'm not important, or I'm not good enough, or maybe if I was prettier.* Those thoughts eventually became solid beliefs about herself.

Because of those beliefs, her sense of what she deserved was low. If you think you're not important or lovable, then you don't feel deserving enough to set good boundaries and take care of yourself. You can push yourself to get straight A's and become the captain of your varsity lacrosse team, but inside you still feel not good enough or unworthy. Thus, Keegan was needy for boys' attention, and their words of *"You're so beautiful"* or, *"You're so hot"* or, *"Do you want to go out"* made her, for a while, feel attractive and wanted. That's why she was willing to loosen her boundaries for guys.

From the stories in this book, I hope you realize just how much girls have going on in their lives today. The pressures, stresses and life experiences they go through create a swell of feelings and the need to work things through. I like the concept of 'sacred space.' To me it means having a place to get away from it all, to let your hair down, and not to have to worry about impressing people. It's situations where you can be honest, real and not be judged. It's spaces where you can be accepted and loved for exactly who you are, and where you feel safe to express your deepest thoughts and feelings and desires. That's why I started my retreats and camps back in 1991. I wanted to create a nurturing, safe, home-away-from-home for kids and teens to come to relax, de-stress, and learn more about themselves and other people. There is a strong need for kids and teens to have better social-emotional learning like this, because most schools don't have the time or expertise for it, and what parents can do in the home is not enough. Some lessons, especially social ones, can be learned only in a community of peers.

Because of the way they are wired, girls, especially, need this kind of safe space. They love to talk about their lives and their stories. It's one of the most important ways that they connect and figure things out. Out of all the many things I do in my career and life, my most fulfilling and fun times are sitting on the carpet at a camp, retreat or classroom with a group of girls sharing. They just come alive! They share, they cry, they laugh, they get silly, they get serious. They are so genuine and in-the-moment. That's one of the main reasons I believe girls need these sacred spaces. For some girls this means having their most trusted friend over and acting silly. They play dress-up, play board games, put on music and dance crazy. There are no boys to impress, and no catty girls to judge them. Every girl deserves a friend they can be like this with. Some girls find this safety in a youth group at church, or on service trips. The reason to be together in these groups is not to look good or be popular or hook up. It's a much higher purpose: getting out of yourself and filling your spiritual cup.

I read a book years ago called, *Smart Girls Gifted Women*, by Barbara Kerr that we'll discuss in detail in Chapter 14, but for now I want to mention her take on this concept. My favorite part of the book was her nine biographies of famous women like Marie Curie, Gertrude Stein, Eleanor Roosevelt, Margaret Mead, Georgia O'Keeffe, Maya Angelou, Katharine Hepburn, Beverly Sills and

Rigoberta Mencer. These eminent women had many things in common, including sacred space. All these women were voracious readers growing up, not very popular with their peers, and spent time alone. But they used this time to develop their talents, be it singing, writing or painting. So when they finished high school, they had already developed their passions and interests. They found their tribe of friends and supports in later high school and after. But having time in solitude during their adolescence to fully engage in their passions helped these girls define themselves and their life's purpose.

I worry today that our over-scheduled, hyper-busy and distracted girls don't have any time for such endeavors. Everything is so supervised and pre-scripted. There is little time or energy left to explore their passions, initiate, create or daydream. No time for sacred spaces. Having places to gather to share their stories and to hear other girls' stories is a critical piece of social-emotional learning and for their leadership development. The following stories from my retreats and camps will give you get an idea of what girls like to share when they feel safe and accepted.

Ten-year-old Jennifer was the only child of older parents. Her dad had two adult children in their thirties from his first marriage, and her mom was 39 when she had her. Jennifer shared in our circle that her dad left the house before she woke up, and didn't get home most days until 9 to 10 p.m. He rarely tucked her in, and even his weekends were spent working either at the office or at home. She experienced a lot of sadness about wanting him around more, and felt hurt when his behavior didn't change after she shared these feelings with him.

Nina was an eighth-grader at one of our all-girl middle school retreats. The theme of this particular weekend ended up being stress and pressures, and Nina was the poster child for the group. She played select soccer year-round, and shared through tears how her dad was critical of her play. Whenever she'd look over at him during games, he'd have an intense look on his face as he yelled some directive at her. On the car rides home, he often went on and on about the girls on her team who scored or made great plays. And so Nina felt not only compared, but that her dad liked her teammates better. She worked her butt off for her straight A's, yet he never commented on that. She pushed herself to be perfect at everything, and when she wasn't, she could be really hard on herself.

Fifteen-year-old Meg's dad had recently gone to a treatment program for alcohol abuse, and it had really shaken up the family. We did some journaling one day at camp, and reading her entry will give you an idea of what she was going through. *"I am feeling very angry with the way you have been acting lately, you are better than that. Coming home late, falling down the steps, cussing at a 15-year-old teenage girl, driving after many rounds of beer, that's got to stop... Don't blame Mom or your kids. Blame yourself... I am beyond proud to call you my dad, but when we are out with friends and you drink five or more beers or you blow up at us for the smallest mistake because you are trying to sleep off a hangover, I admit I am embarrassed. Why do you think I turn away from your hugs and never want to snuggle with you? Or ignore you when I get home from school? I've seen how close my friends are with their dads, and I wish my dad understood how hard being perfect is and how hard it is to be me... I am mad at you; how am I supposed to know how to handle my anger and my frustrations? It's easier to ignore you because I'm scared of how you are going to react if I tell you how I feel. Although it sounds like we are all mad at you, that's just us releasing these feelings that have been kept inside for so long... We love you; we believe in you, work hard and stay focused."*

That letter still brings tears to my eyes. And it was so therapeutic for her to write it and share it with us.

Sleeping Beauties, Awakened Women

Sixteen-year-old Gail shared at a high school retreat that she always felt like an outsider, like she never fit in. We asked her when she first started feeling that way, and she recalled that in fourth grade her best friend moved to another state and the cliques in her class started excluding her. One girl in particular, of the Queen Bee variety, led the popular group of girls in harassing Gail at every turn. In sixth grade, she found two friends who at first included her, but when seventh grade started, they ditched her. Gail released a lot of hurt and pain in her story, with the most emotion coming from sharing how lonely she felt. Once Gail shared her story, it led to most of the girls telling their stories of being teased or excluded and how they could relate to what she felt. What a gift that was for Gail, knowing she wasn't the only one who felt that way or who had experienced 'mean girl' stuff.

Fifteen-year-old Eva seemed pretty anxious when she arrived at her first weekend retreat with us. After Gail and a number of other girls shared Saturday morning about their friendship issues, Eva felt safe enough to share her story. She talked about having a lot of social anxiety, especially with new groups like this one. *"I walked in here last night wondering: How will they see me? What will they think of me? How will they treat me?"* And the answers in her head were, as usual, negative. She shared that, like Gail, her troubles started in fourth grade, where she was harassed every day by a group of girls. She finally made a good friend in seventh grade, who turned on her for no apparent reason. I asked Eva what she decided about herself because of these experiences. *"I'm weird, awkward, too shy, my interests are too different. I feel like when I speak it comes out wrong and I trip over my words a lot,"* she said. *"I also worry I'm not pretty enough or cool enough. So I usually just keep quiet in groups and observe."* Eva had a lot of work ahead of her to switch all of that negative self-talk and those decisions about herself. Just being heard and not judged at the retreat was a huge confidence booster for her. She also realized she wasn't alone with what she was facing.

That is one of the most valuable gifts girls experience by sharing in a sacred space like this, the realization that they are not alone in their struggles, feelings and challenges. The groups quickly come together, judgments are dropped, and girls allow their real selves to come out to play. I love seeing girls like Gail and Nina and Meg and Eva, who had been weighed down with feelings and thoughts and pressures, come alive at a retreat or camp. It's magical. If you were to meet any of these girls, you'd fall in love with them immediately: for their openness, their spunk and their vulnerability. And you'd never guess they had all this stuff going on below the surface. After all these years running retreats and camps, it still amazes me to see what complicated lives so many kids live today.

I started these retreats, camps and my *Strong Girls Strong World* classroom program some years ago because girls relax more and share quicker when their sacred space doesn't include boys. I've run co-ed camps for 22 years, and girls and boys learn a ton of personal growth during them. But I've come to believe that, especially for girls in grade and middle school, girls need a space without boys for this kind of process. It's true of high school girls too, but as the girls mature, boys become less of a distraction.

Do I think boys need more help with their social learning? You bet! But boys learn differently than girls, especially at the younger ages. And the methods we use in our programs are geared more to the way girls learn. After a week of our camp, most girls say the 'courseroom' learning times were their favorite part of the week; few boys say that. They are more likely to complain about being bored with the sharing parts. Sometimes people ask why I don't create a curriculum and camps for boys. Pure and simple, my interest and passion is in working with girls on these unique and critical developmental issues. I've devoted the past 22 years to creating programs for girls; I'll leave it to someone else to create them for boys.

CHAPTER 11

EXPRESSING FEELINGS

"I feel like my parents can't let me grow up. They are constantly on me and telling me what to do," seventeen-year-old Tessa told me. *"So how do you feel when they do that?"* I asked. *"I feel like they're treating me like a baby,"* she responded. *"They've been talking about me being an engineer for years because I'm good at math. And I think I might want to be one, but I really want to go into aeronautical engineering because I love airplanes; I have since I was a kid. But my parents keep harping on me going into mechanical engineering because there are more jobs in that field."* *"What's the feeling when you think about your parents still directing so much of your life, and even your career?"* I asked. At this point, her eyes teared up, and she started crying. *"I feel sad because it feels like my parents don't trust me or believe in me. And I feel disrespected and angry because it's supposed to be my major and my career and my life."*

Finally, we get to the feelings. Tessa had been withdrawing from her parents for the past year, sharing less and less with them. She also had a few episodes where she exploded with anger at seemingly small incidents, and had become increasingly disrespectful when speaking with her parents. All of this was the result of not expressing her emotions and troubles in beneficial ways. In chapter 5, I shared 10 ways suppressed emotions can show up in unhealthy ways. But there are other harmful ways that girls try to deal with their emotions.

1. They collect evidence. When some girls feel sad or upset, and they have a head full of stinking thinking and negative decisions about themselves, one way they attempt to deal with it is by 'collecting evidence.' Refer to the Decisions Chart in Chapter 7. Once girls have started acquiring negative beliefs about themselves, for example, *No one likes me, I'm weird* and *I don't fit in,* or other similar thoughts, they sometimes end up recreating negative experiences to validate those beliefs. But they don't do it consciously. Using Tia's story from Chapter 7, the reactions she had about her parents giving her brother more time and attention led her to believe that she was unimportant and not good enough. So, if at school one day she flirts with a boy she likes, and he doesn't pay any attention, in her mind Tia is likely to go right to, *Here we go again! I'm not very pretty or desirable, I'm not as cute as the other girls, and once again I feel unimportant and unlovable.* This type of negative self-affirmation keeps girls stuck in an endless negativity loop, and leaves them feeling hopeless. The other tactic Tia chose was to avoid her parents because she was mad at them. Her parents interpreted this behavior as Tia saying that she needed more space from them, and so they backed off, which of course made Tia feel more left out...you get the picture. She ended up creating more of what she didn't want.

2. They blame others and make themselves the victim. Some girls deal with their emotions by blaming other people for their woes. If they feel left out because a friend has excluded them, instead of allowing themselves to acknowledge their feelings and handle these directly with that friend, it's easier sometimes just to blame the other person for what's going on between them. Blaming other people and not being willing to take responsibility for their part keeps girls stuck in a victim role and mentality. And this victimization makes it harder for them to have the courage to confront people and deal with their

issues. So these girls' feelings keep building up, and their stinking thinking becomes stronger, and they find it harder and harder to bust out of this cycle of discouragement.

3. They withdraw. Instead of expressing their emotions, some girls choose to withdraw; to isolate themselves as protection from more hurts. It seems safer to shut down and numb out, because the hurts that have built up over time appear overwhelming. *"I'm afraid if I start to cry I won't be able to stop!"* Emily said. Shauna added, *"There were a few times when I started to feel, and a rush of emotions swept over me and I felt like I was drowning. I just felt so overwhelmed, like it was too much."* Of course, this pattern is just a short-term stop-gap, because the feelings don't go away. They just keep building up; the piper has to be paid at some point.

4. They descend into denial and apathy. When 10-year-old Jennifer from Chapter 10 first started sharing at one of our retreats about her dad being absent a lot, she came off as being pretty indifferent. *"I don't really care that he's never around; I have my mom and it's not like he was ever really there for me anyway,"* she said. *"How about the times when you and your mom are fighting?"* I asked. *"Do you wish he was there for you then?"* Jennifer thought for a second. *"Well, yeah, sometimes I wish he was there to take my side. My mom is always on me, and I wish he was there to back me up."* At this point, Jennifer started to cry. Through her tears, she shared more of her hurts. *"Sometimes when I'm at my friend Carly's house I get sad because her dad is so nice to her and me, and he makes us breakfast and plays board games with us. That's when I think about how my dad is not there for me."* Underneath her indifference, that attitude of *I don't care*, are many significant feelings she is suppressing. Jennifer feels sad, hurt, angry, lonely, unimportant, neglected and unloved. But

it's easier to hide behind a mask of apathy than to be vulnerable and allow herself to feel all of that. This is especially true for those who have been avoiding or stuffing these emotions for months.

5. They numb out. There are many things girls can use to avoid their emotions, most commonly alcohol, drugs and sex. Some girls I've met are on several medications that have a sedative effect on them. They may not be depressed or anxious anymore, but now they feel like zombies. *"I had gotten so tired of feeling depressed, so I was willing to try an antidepressant,"* eighteen-year-old Sophie told me. *"And I guess it does take care of the deep downs I used to sink into. But now I also don't feel any of the old highs. I can't seem to feel excited about things I used to get excited about. I just feel kind of blah."* Fifteen-year-old Isabel expressed similar feelings. *"I was put on some medicine for my attention deficit hyperactivity disorder, and also something for anxiety because I had a hard time not getting all worked up about tests. I do get more homework done now and faster, but I feel like a zombie. It's like I'm there but not there. It's hard to explain. But I don't feel like myself anymore."* As described in Chapter 5, I've also met more and more girls who numb out via electronics. They become addicted to being constantly connected into everybody's business, through texting, Facebook, Instagram and phone calls. A small number of girls also lose themselves by hanging out in chat rooms. Being constantly plugged into TV shows, chat rooms, and social networking sites results in a mind-numbing experience. It's a way to avoid what's going on in the real world.

6. They use distractions. Keeping busy and distracted is yet another way not to think about problems or avoid emotions. And unfortunately, our culture provides more than enough

avenues to do this. Some girls distract themselves with drama. If you are flitting around like a bee from flower to flower, or in this case, from drama to drama, you don't have to feel what's going on inside. Girls get caught up in everyone else's business, and it diverts them from thinking about and having to deal with their own. Boys can be a huge distraction as well: thinking about, talking about and gossiping about boys. Girls will focus on who likes them or who doesn't, text and Instagram friends for the latest updates, and drift from one boyfriend to the next. For some, it's just excessive busyness with anything and everything that can keep them from feeling. Seven hours of school, two to three hours of sports or other extracurricular activities, two to four hours of homework, while at the same time being plugged into numerous technologies, as the girls shared in Chapter 9; there's just no time to go inward and connect with their emotions. Busy and distracted seems to be the new normal state of existence for kids and teens today. Unfortunately, the main casualty of this phenomenon is that girls are unable to recognize and work through their emotions .

So let's move on to some beneficial ways for girls to express their feelings.

First let me explain the concept of Root Beer Feelings (RBFs). At retreats, I will bring in a mug sitting on a saucer and start pouring a can of root beer into it. At first, there is some root beer on the bottom of the mug and a little foam on top. Then I'll ask the girls what will happen when I continue to pour the root beer; they describe how the foam will build up, then overflow the mug and make a mess. And they all agree that the root beer itself is more important than the foam. I'll then equate the root beer and foam to our feelings, as a metaphor. The foam is our anger family of feelings: angry, mad, frustrated, annoyed, pissed off. I'm quick to remind girls that these are not bad feelings; they are just feelings. But if you express or vent anger at people, that's when they can make a mess of your relationships. But underneath the foam, underneath the anger, lie much more significant feelings, our root beer feelings, or RBFs. These are actually felt first, but instead of articulating them, we tend to blow off foam feelings. So if Mary is walking down the school hallway with an armload of books, and an immature boy runs by and purposely bumps into her and her books go flying every which way, the first emotion Mary might feel is embarrassed. But instead of communicating that, she'll just get angry.

Most girls have experienced being really mad at someone or something, and started yelling and venting. And before you know it, they are crying. That's the RBF under the foam. I want girls to release their anger in healthy ways, but it's not enough. If they don't figure out the RBFs underneath the anger, and express those, they will remain and build up and cause the mischief I described in Chapter 5. But what I have found in working with kids and teens and adults is that if you can figure out what your RBF's are and just articulate those, the anger disappears. It's not about the anger, it's about channeling those more important and primary root beer feelings.

Girls ask me if physical exercise channels these RBFs and I answer no. Going out for a run or hitting a punching bag blows off steam and releases your 'foam feelings.' And that might allow you to get to your RBFs. But exercise alone isn't the answer. When I work with girls, and also in presentations with parents or teachers, I'll do an exercise where I ask everyone to remember the last time they were really angry at someone. And then, usually in pairs, they try to come up with what their RBFs were at that moment. It can take some practice, because in our culture, we tend to be more comfortable foaming than expressing RBFs.

Remember Becca from Chapter 5? She was mad at her parents because they wouldn't let her see her boyfriend. I pushed her until we could get below her foam to what was really going on. *"I feel disrespected and controlled,"* she said. *"And I also feel like it's unfair for them to judge Dan because they don't even know him and they're judging him on rumors they heard from some other parents."* I then asked a question. *"How else does it feel when they are controlling you?" "I feel sad and hurt,"* Becca responded. *"They don't trust me or my judgment at all. It's like they don't really see me or know me anymore."* So what's most essential here is Becca feels hurt, sad, not heard, mistrusted, disconnected, disrespected and controlled. If she could start a conversation with her parents by conveying her RBFs like sadness, hurt and not being heard, she would have a much better chance of getting them to listen to her. When she starts out by foaming, for example yelling and accusing her parents of being controlling, what she gets back is more foam. And Becca and her parents end up foaming on each other, with no resolution in sight and more hurt feelings.

So let's get onto healthy ways for girls to express their emotions.

1. Allow your feelings to come up. That sounds so easy, but just letting yourself feel whatever RBFs are inside is beneficial for anyone. I use a cloud-gazing metaphor to illustrate how this might look. Imagine yourself lying down on a hillside, looking up at the sky. You see some large puffy white clouds slowly passing across your line of vision, from left to right. You don't try to stop these clouds from going by; you just allow them to pass through until they are out of sight. The same goes for your feelings. Just like with the clouds, you can become aware of your feelings, and then allow yourself to be with them for a while. If you don't fight them or avoid them, they will slowly just pass through you. And you will be left feeling lighter, like a weight has been lifted from your shoulders. Most girls can connect with past experiences where they felt relief and like a wet noodle after a good, hard cry. Girls also describe becoming

more clear, like they can figure things out better. They are more aware and subsequently can trust their intuition because of this clarity. Despite girls' fears that if they start they may never stop, what they will experience is control over how, when and how long they feel. They do not have to get overwhelmed with these emotions. It's not a bottomless, endless pit.

I've suggested to many girls that they even make an appointment to feel. It may not be appropriate to do it at school, but at night, after their homework is done, they might decide to have some quiet, alone time where they will let concerns come up. They might emote for a half hour or so, and then move on, just like with those clouds. Feelings arise, they feel them, and they pass through.

One other thought about crying. Help girls become aware of the negative judgments people have about crying. It's described as 'losing it' and having a 'meltdown,' and being a 'basket-case,' or 'she's a mess!' I want girls to understand it's normal, healthy and crucial to let feelings go.

2. Keep a journal. I described this tool in Chapter 9 on Slowing Down, but I want to explain in more detail how journaling can be used to express emotions. For one thing, girls need to know that their journal entries will be private--for their eyes only. I want them to pour their hearts and souls out onto the pages, and to feel safe and free to write down any and every thought and feeling. They will hold back if they think their parents or siblings are going to sneak a peek. Many girls start out trying to express their emotions in journals and get stuck. When they ask themselves the question, *What am I feeling?*, oftentimes their knee-jerk reaction is, *I don't know*, and then they quit! So I encourage them to get more still, and quiet themselves even

more (see Chapter 9). If their brains are on hyper-functioning mode, it may take a little while to slow down enough to allow themselves to connect with their inner world. I recommend turning off all electronics, except perhaps music that is relaxing and soothing. Some girls need to exercise physically first to blow off some tension and foam. I also coach girls to ask themselves some questions. I'll have them fill in the blank on sentence stems like, *If I were feeling sad about anything, what might it be?* or *If I were feeling worried about anything, what might it be?* And they can plug in other feelings like hurt, disrespected, misunderstood, scared, etcetera. I also have them put in emotions like happy, excited or proud to focus on the positive.

In my counseling practice, I'll do a 'verbal journal' where I have girls share out loud the answers to those questions. It helps them feel more comfortable with the process before they go home to write. Or I'll have them journal right there in my office. And I also have girls do a lot of writing at my camps and retreats. The more they practice, the more comfortable they become, and the more effective they are at getting their feelings out onto the pages. The following are some journal entries girls have given me permission to share in this book.

"Why are you comparing me? You are always trying to make me what I'm not," Claire wrote. When Claire showed me this journal entry, I encouraged her to write more, to dig deeper. How does it feel to have a dad who doesn't accept you for the way you are? How does it feel when he compares you to siblings and other girls?

Angela, whose father is always on her about her grades wrote, *"Why are you doing this to me? Other dads aren't doing it! It makes it so hard for me to not be hard on myself."* I encouraged Angela to keep writing more about this issue. How does it feel when you see friends' dads treat their daughters differently? Write more about how you feel when you get down on yourself. What do you say to yourself? How do these negative thoughts affect you?

Fourteen-year-old Callie wrote, *"Mom, I hate it when you are always on the computer or phone working! When I try to tell you things that are important to me you are like in la-la land. I know you aren't listening even though you act like you are. It pisses me off! I hate your f---ing job!!!"* Wow! There was so much more-pent up inside Callie, so I encouraged her to get it all out. I told her not to worry about her words being politically correct or sounding bitter. She was concerned about being a 'good girl' and not sounding mean to her mom. But holding onto it was causing Callie to have more and more anxiety.

So, you get the idea. I encourage girls to write in their journals most evenings. Before bed seems to be a good time for most girls: they are operating a little slower, it's easier to turn off electronics and distractions, and it helps them to fall asleep better once they've unloaded their troubles.

One other thing about journaling. It can be extremely valuable for girls to write down what they are experiencing one night, then put it away and come back to it in a few days. They can reread their entries, and write about whether they still feel that way. They get some distance from what was bothering them, and they have time to think about it or bounce ideas off other people. In this way, they are processing their issues internally, figuring things out, making better sense of their feelings and experiences. This is an extremely beneficial process for all girls to learn.

3. Write letters. Some girls express themselves better by writing than by talking. So writing a letter to someone they are upset with can be very therapeutic. They can pour it all out onto the pages; just vent and not worry about what they say or how the other person will react to it. Once they are done writing, they can go back and read what they wrote and then decide if they want to actually send the letter or just rip it up. Most of the time it's better just to shred it, because they don't want to foam at the other person. What's most important is getting things off their chest.

But I have had many, many girls write and send letters to estranged parents. Girls feel safer about being honest in their letters than they would saying those things in person, when a mom or dad or friend is standing in front of them. Many girls are more worried about not hurting the other person's feelings than they are about sharing their truth. In person, they also are more worried the person will get angry or not listen, so they shut down. Another advantage is that the letter recipient can read and reread the letter, and oftentimes they'll hear the message better because they are less defensive by not being put on-the-spot. They also might process what the writer is saying better because they can take some time to reflect on what they've read and because there is less emotion involved.

4. Write stories. Creative girls who have good imaginations and who like to write stories can use this as a channel for their emotions. I have girls write a story about this other girl, a fictitious girl, who is facing the same challenge and feeling similar emotions as they are. By writing about how this girl works through her issues, girls are really processing their own situation. I have read biographies of writers over the years, and many of them got their start doing this kind of writing. For

most girls, it's just another way to get inside and express themselves fully.

5. Write poetry: Some girls do a good job of releasing their feelings through writing poetry. If they have read much poetry, they will recognize it as a valuable art form through which to channel their concerns.

6. Write songs. Writing song lyrics is similar to poetry. I remind girls to think about the lyrics of their favorite songs, and in them they will recognize many emotions. Most songs are written because someone is sad about a breakup, happy because they are in love, angry at society, or confused by a situation. For musically inclined girls, this can be a great tool.

7. Play music: Playing an instrument can be a way to channel emotions. Whether you are riffing on an electric guitar, beating the drums, or wailing on a saxophone, it's a way for emotions to come pouring out. Think about musicians you've watched who get into that flow zone, and when they are done they are exhausted. They have literally let it all hang out. Singing is also a good emotional outlet for some girls. I always think of watching Whitney Houston sing *I'll Always Love You.* You can feel her emotions and her soul as she belts it out. I know of girls who sing out the blues in the shower or while driving alone in their cars.

8. Create art: There are many ways artistic girls can use their favorite mediums to express what's going on inside them. Some girls will just draw what they are feeling; it can look like anything, and it's often very abstract. Or they can draw a picture of their experience that also reveals their emotions. Other girls will take the opposite tack and draw what they want, what they wish would happen. Some girls will use clay

to sculpt their emotions, and again this could take any number of creative forms. In my retreats, I've had girls pick different-colored pipe cleaners to illustrate their emotions or represent their body image. I've also met many girls who use knitting and needlepoint as a way to slow down, and get focused. Sometimes they will use this kind of activity to get themselves into the space where they can know what they are feeling, just as some athletic girls use exercise or sports to blow off foam to get to their RBFs.

9. Just dance. And then there are our dancers, who use the movement of their bodies to express emotions. Interpretive dancing and ballet come to mind as ways for girls to tell a story or paint a picture about their world or feelings. When you've seen someone fully engrossed in dancing, fully in the moment, you've caught a glimpse of their souls.

10. Share things. Last, but not least, talking about your feelings is another way to get things out. It's so valuable for girls to have a parent or parents they can trust with their innermost concerns. Parents who have been good, non-judgmental listeners over time have provided a track record that says they are safe and trustworthy. Girls also want to know that if they share something in confidence with a parent it stays with the parent. I've met too many moms who break this trust and tell their daughter's secrets to their friends or their own mothers or sisters. These moms feel worried, confused or overwhelmed with their daughter's issues, and like their daughters, they want to talk about it! But in doing so, they break their daughter's trust and then wonder why they won't talk to them anymore.

When a girl's family is going through a separation or divorce, sometimes she needs a counselor to talk to, someone who is not Mom or Dad. These girls worry that if they talk to one parent, it will be viewed as taking sides. And they don't want the other parent to be upset with them. They also don't want to end up in the middle of their parents' problems. I have met hundreds of younger girls who talk about their problems and hurts with a trusted stuffed animal. Their tried-and-true fluffy friend is always there for them, never interrupts, never judges, and always listens. Many girls also talk to live pets. Dogs and cats have absorbed many a sad story, and they too can be trusted always to be there, listen and love them unconditionally. And of course, girls talk with their friends who have proven themselves to be trustworthy. So many girls have felt burned by others they thought were their best friends only to find out they betrayed their trust by telling their secrets to a third party. It's one of the deepest hurts girls experience, because their close friendships are so important to them, and so are their personal feelings and stories.

Too many girls today make the mistake of talking about their secrets and problems online or in texts, which of course sets them up for a lot of people knowing their private business. When secrets go viral, girls can become devastated. It can throw them into depression, anxiety and even suicidal impulses. It feels like their whole life is over, and it makes it hard for them to trust anyone with their feelings again, so they struggle on alone. I heard of a good metaphor for learning how to trust your friends more from Rachel Simmons, author of *Odd Girl Out*. I have adjusted the metaphor for the work I do with girls.

I have girls imagine they have a big winter overcoat on, and it is buttoned up to the top. When the coat is fully buttoned, it is a metaphor for protecting yourself by not revealing anything personal to friends; you don't trust people at all. If they want to start trusting a friend more in order to become closer, then they can share a little about themselves and then see what the other girl does with it. That's the equivalent of unbuttoning a few buttons. If the friend keeps her trust and doesn't spread the info to other girls, then you can feel confident to share a little more and be a little more vulnerable; thus unbuttoning a few more buttons. You get the idea.

The truth is that many of us have some friends we trust implicitly and can take the overcoat completely off. We can be honest and transparent with these friends. There are other people in our lives with whom we keep our coats buttoned up to the top, because they have shown with past behaviors that they can't be trusted with our secrets. I tell girls they can still be friends with girls like that; just don't share meaningful things with them. This concept allows girls to feel in control of how much they share of themselves, how vulnerable they get, how open they are with friends. Girls can look at their friends and tell you who they can trust and who they can't. And if they worry that they are being too sensitive about trusting people because of past betrayals, they can just hit the restart button and unlayer themselves one button at a time; on their timeline.

I love it when girls have adults other than their parents whom they trust enough to share their problems with. Grandparents, aunts and uncles, teachers and coaches can fill this role. Because girls get real and vulnerable and tell their stories at my retreats and camps, our staff often becomes important confidants for them. Girls need adults who their parents trust to listen to them and to guide them. We all needed people like that growing up. I remember as a teenager going down to our neighbors, Herb and Jackie Gittleman's house. They were a young, hip couple with two preschool-aged daughters. And on summer evenings, all the teenagers in our neighborhood would hang out in their front yard. We loved going there because, unlike our 'idiotic' parents, the Gittlemans listened to us; they didn't judge us; they understood us in a way that it seemed our parents couldn't. Provide trusting adults like that for your daughters. It's invaluable for them to have people like that to share their problems and concerns.

The point is, it's important for every girl to figure out which of these tools of expression works best for her. And it's great to have several such tools in her toolbox. The more girls practice these skills, the more effective they become. And once they get into something like journaling or drawing in this way, they'll miss it if they take time off from it.

Learning to slow yourself down, get quiet, go inward and know what you are feeling and what you need: these are essential skills all girls need as they undergo their transformation from girl to woman. The time our fairy tale heroines spent metaphorically sleeping (Sleeping Beauty and Snow White), or wandering in the desert (Rapunzel), or working and suffering on their own (Cinderella), or taste-testing different kinds of eggs (*Runaway Bride*)—those are the times girls work on their inner resumes. Those are their times of self-discovery.

And becoming aware of, understanding, and adopting healthy ways to express all of their emotions is an important piece of this transformation.

CHAPTER 12

NAVIGATING THE SOCIAL SCENE

"Each friend represents a world within us, a world possibly not born until they arrive, and it is only by this meeting that a new world is born." Anais Nin

In this chapter, I want to give parents and those who work with girls some ideas about teaching them how to deal with teasing, harassment, gossip and drama. Most teachers would verify an upswing today not only in the frequency and intensity of relationship aggression (RA) in girls, but also in its prevalence among younger and younger girls. I have been called to schools in recent years to work with 'tough' classes of first-grade girls, which is a whole lot earlier than the middle and high school dramas of their moms.

First off, I want girls to understand why their classmates behave this way. When I've asked groups from grade school on up to high school to list reasons for relationship aggression, here are some of their most common answers:

- Girls want to be noticed, get attention or be popular.
- They are angry at someone or something else and take it out on people who don't deserve it.
- It's a way to feel powerful or in control.
- They are afraid if they don't tease people they won't be included in a group where others act that way.
- They may have been overpowered, yelled at, or hit at home so they bring their anger to school or online.

- They are stressed out and can't control themselves or their feelings.
- It's a way to try to make yourself look better or to feel better about yourself.
- They are doing it to get revenge on girls who have hurt them.
- Some girls don't know better ways to connect.
- If they don't gossip or join in on teasing people, they feel out of the loop/excluded/ not in-the-know.

I would add a few more reasons to this list, based on conversations I've had with girls over the years:

- They don't express their emotions in healthy ways, so their feelings build up and it doesn't take much to cause them to explode.
- Girls don't handle the normal conflicts and disagreements that occur in their friendships and groups, so negative feelings fester over time and leak out as relationship aggressions.
- Girls have been given permission and opportunities to be competitive, assertive, aggressive and ambitious with a winner-take-all and I'm-willing-to-step-on-anyone-to-the-top attitude. This leaks into their relationships, causing mischief.
- Girls don't do a good job of handling sarcasm and verbal insults. More-so than boys, they tend to take teasing much too personally, make false and negative assumptions (see Chapter 13), and ruminate about every word and gesture they experience from other girls all day long at school. They make mountains out of molehills, carry grudges, and have a hard time letting things go.

All this results in girls being more reactive, sensitive and prone to drama. And this causes more hurt feelings, vengeful reactions, and seemingly endless cycles of relationship aggression.

Hormonal changes that occur during their monthly menstrual cycles have a profound effect on a girl's mood and ability to control their emotions and reactions. When girls go through their estrogen/progesterone withdrawal during the fourth week of their cycle, they tend to be more irritable, want to be left alone, have a dramatic increase in their stress level and emotional reactivity, and get overwhelmed. I've met numerous girls whose friendship crises occur only at the end of their cycles, but no one has made that connection for them. So they are left feeling guilty and out of control.

Also, girls don't have the skills to handle their conflicts and hurts directly and effectively. For more on this, re-read Chapter 6. And most schools and classroom teachers have not taken the reins in providing girls the skills to create more caring classroom communities. Teachers are reluctant to carve out time for this social-emotional learning, in large part because of pressures to teach-for-the-test and also because they've never learned those skills themselves. It's also interesting to note that the vast majority of teachers in grade and middle school are women. And when I do workshops with teachers, most admit that even now in their adult lives they have a hard time handling their conflicts in a direct way with spouses and friends. They never learned these skills themselves growing up, never got training on this during their education classes, and so feel ill-prepared and lack the confidence to teach this to their students. It's a vicious cycle.

Last, but not least, our entire culture seems to have become more disrespectful. Just notice how college and professional athletes and politicians conduct themselves. Characters in TV shows are incredibly sarcastic and disrespectful, and that includes shows for kids and families. Just compare *Father Knows Best* and *Leave it to Beaver* with *Family Guy, South Park*, or any sitcom that involves families. There's a huge difference in the tone of their conversations and connections. So why would we expect our kids to be any different? They emulate what's modeled for them. By the time girls are 18 years old, close to 40 percent of them have been through a family divorce. So they have also seen their parents be disrespectful to each other, and oftentimes, for years.

The next topic I want to cover is "who gets teased or harassed?" I guess the simplest answer is every girl.

When I do a 'cross the line' exercise with girls, it's easy to see just how many are affected. We have all of them stand on one side of a rope, then we throw out statements that begin with, *"Cross the line if you..."* The sentence endings include phrases like: *have been teased or made fun of, been excluded, been bullied, had your trust betrayed by a friend, have been the subject of gossip or rumors* and *felt like you had to choose between two friends who are fighting.* Ninety-five to 100 percent of the girls cross over the line by the time all those statements have been made, and that figure is constant whether it's girls in grade school or high school. When we ask: *"Cross the line if...you have ever teased someone, excluded someone, talked about someone behind their back or gossiped",* again 95 to 100 percent of the girls cross over.

Interestingly, when I do this same exercise with adult women, i.e. mothers and teachers, asking about what they experienced in grade, middle or high school, I get pretty much the same numbers crossing over. So it's not a new phenomenon, although women agree it started for them later, usually in middle school, and seemed less aggressive and physical. So again, for the question of 'who' gets teased or harassed, I'm confident in saying nearly every girl I've worked with has experienced these relationship aggression behaviors at some level and at some point in time. But I also find that some girls seem to be targeted for teasing and bullying more often than others.

Here is a list of the kinds of girls I see targeted for bullying.

1. Girls with poor social skills. They might have some auditory processing problems that cause them to be a step behind when groups of girls are bantering back and forth. They do better one on one, but in groups they seem lost, and they feel socially awkward. They tell me they don't know how to include themselves or join conversations gracefully. Girls on the autism spectrum, i.e. with Aspergers syndrome, fit this bill too. They don't pick up on social cues, so they have a hard time connecting with peers.

2. Quiet, shy girls. These often have good social skills, but are just quiet by nature and slow to warm up in social situations, especially new or large ones. They tend to hang out on the outskirts, sometimes alone or with their one good friend (who is often shy too). Sometimes their shyness is misinterpreted as being snotty or 'too good for us' or not interested in playing or connecting. Some of these girls also are less inclined to stand up to the louder girls, preferring instead to hide out or stay out of the spotlight. They feel it is safer to fade into the background or be invisible, because that allows them to avoid being teased. But, of course, it also causes them to be alone.

3. Sweet, innocent girls. In their own ways, I actually think all girls have this side. But some girls are so sweet and empathetic that they seem to fly above the hostilities/gossip/drama radar. They sometimes don't even realize they are being teased because they see the best in people and are sort of oblivious to the mischief. Many of these girls look younger in some ways, but in other ways they are very mature. They are not the racier girls who have sharp tongues and are into boys at an early age. They aren't the girls who push limits and want to grow up fast. On the contrary, these girls like staying young and innocent. They play with dolls longer than other girls, love imaginative

play, and tend to be homebodies who are just as happy hanging out at home with their family as they are at a sleepover. I love how they stay little girls longer and retain that sense of innocence. Adults love these kinds of girls, but peers may pick on them as easy targets to antagonize.

4. Girls who start puberty early. I really feel for these girls. These are the fifth- graders who tower over every boy in their class. And worse yet, they are the first ones to sprout breasts and need bras. They also break out with acne, and the final blow is starting their periods as young as 9 or 10 years of age. Boys and girls alike tease these girls for all of the above reasons. It's impossible to hide your newfound height, curves and pimples. These girls often become extremely self-conscious about their looks.

Elise (16) had a hard time standing up for herself when girls harassed her. As we explored why she had problems setting boundaries, the answer ended up having its origin in fifth grade. *"I was the first girl to go through puberty, and I was by far the tallest in my class,"* she told me. *"And people started calling me names like giraffe and Cyclops. Boys in my class made comments about my looks, and older guys in my neighborhood started hitting on me. I was overwhelmed and I felt so different, so not-like all my friends. I felt lonely all the time, and I felt no one could possibly understand what I was going through."* *"When all this was going on, were you asking yourself questions in your head like: Why is this happening to me? Why are they making fun of only me?"* I asked. *"Yeah, all the time,"* she responded. *"The important thing is how you answered those questions,"* I said in response. *"What did you say to yourself?"* Her response was direct. *"That I'm ugly and there's something wrong with me. I'm different; I don't fit in anywhere; no one understands me."* Because of these, Elise didn't think she was worthy of taking good care of herself, and thus had a hard time sticking up for herself. In her mind, she wasn't worth much.

This is an all too common story for girls who start puberty early or are the first one in their class. And it often provokes teasing and harassment from classmates.

5. Pretty girls. I've met so many girls, especially in middle school and beyond, who ended up hanging out more with guys than girls because of all the crap they received from girls. Girls who get a lot of attention from boys, even if they don't want it or ask for it by flirting, are often recipients of relationship aggression from their classmates. Girls become jealous because boys are always hitting on these girls, wanting to go out with them, or just hanging out with them. I've also found that girls assume 'pretty' girls are popular and thus snobs or catty, and often they either avoid them or lump them in with the 'mean' girls. This is like the book that gets judged by its cover. Additionally, many girls feel intimidated by these good-looking girls. When I do exercises to mix up girls in a group, a good approach is to ask them to share why they may have avoided each other or not become friends. One of the common reasons given is this sense of feeling intimidated by pretty girls. Girls are surprised with how 'normal' and nice these girls are, and they feel bad about judging them so harshly.

6. Girls who are different. Differences come in many styles, but just the fact that she is different sometimes makes a girl the target of ridicule. The color of her skin, having red hair and freckles, being short or tall, thin or heavy, really smart or a student with learning disabilities, being a tom boy or a girly girl, having immigrant parents with different customs and foods, or having a unique interest in something like whales,

Anime, or playing the accordion can set a girl apart causing her to become a target.

7. Needy girls. Girls who try too hard to fit into a group often end up the brunt of teasing and exclusion behaviors. These are girls who don't feel included in any group, or lack good friends. So they are willing to do anything to get into the group they've picked out. And their needy behaviors just push people away more, and the cycle ensues. I've seen many girls who are late bloomers or who aren't too spiffy with their social skills trying hard to get into the most popular group in their class. And they just aren't there yet with the ability to banter and joke around or to keep up with the conversations. They really need to find some girls who are more at their level socially, but oftentimes they aren't aware of the mismatch that seems so obvious to people on the outside. So they get a lot of teasing and abuse from the racy, popular group. It's really sad to watch.

Let's delve now into what girls need to learn in order to better navigate the current social landscape.

"I will permit no man to narrow and degrade my soul by making me hate him." Booker T. Washington

Don't give your power away! This is a central concept I want all girls to understand and embrace. The way I teach it is through a fun exercise. I face off with a volunteer who stands a foot away, and we both raise our arms chest high, with our palms facing out. The goal of this Push Game is to see who can win the most points, with points being scored when you can knock the other person off balance by gently pushing on their palms. I usually provoke my opponent by telling them I have never been beaten, ever! And I'll tease them by calling them a weak girl, etc. And then the game begins.

There are two ways to make the other person lose her balance. One occurs because they are so determined to beat me that they shove hard, and I totally let go of tension in my hands and arms: they stumble forward and I win a point. The other way is when I push on their hands and they resist, which causes them to fall backward and again, I get a point. After I win two to three points (did I mention I have never lost?), I stop and ask the girl and the group what they have observed. I point out the two ways my opponent has lost. Now that I have their attention, the teaching begins.

Pressing on each other's hands is a metaphor for teasing someone, calling people names or pushing their buttons. Losing their balance, metaphorically speaking, is losing their emotional equilibrium, for example. getting angry and hurt and then reacting in some inappropriate way.

"The most common way people give up their power is by thinking they don't have any." Alice Walker, author of *The Color Purple*

When girls argue that I won because I'm bigger or stronger then my opponent, I prove that isn't true. I teach my partner how to totally let go of any resistance in her hands and arms when I push them. I've never studied judo, but I think it's that same principle of absorbing the other person's energy and letting it go. Once the girl has learned this trick, I start shoving her hands, harder and harder, until I am pushing with all my might, and I cannot knock her backward. The girls are astonished, especially when I do this with a third-grade wispy girl who probably weighs all of 50 pounds.

How do I tie this in with teasing? I remind the girls of a famous quote by Eleanor Roosevelt that goes something like, *No one has the power to make you feel anything unless you give them permission.* I want girls to really embrace this concept that they are always responsible for their feelings and their reaction to things, including being made fun of.

"No one can harm you except yourself." Gandhi

I tell them that no matter what other people say or do to them, they never have to allow themselves to get angry or upset. If they do, or if they react by saying something back, they have 'lost their balance' and they are now engaged and part of the problem. If they walk into school in a good mood, and then someone criticizes their attire and it upsets them, they have given their power away in that moment. They were feeling good, and with one provocation, they are hurt and can't stop thinking about it all day long. In essence, they have said to that person, *You are in charge of my mood and my happiness.*

Let me give you some more ideas about the concept of girls giving away their authority. I'll give you some ideas about how girls do it, how they feel when they do it, the costs to them, some detrimental ways they react because of these feelings, and finally ways to stay strong and in control.

Ways Girls Give Their Power Away:
- Worry about what others think of you
- Compare yourself to others
- Controlled by other's judgments
- Doubt yourself / engage in negative self-talk
- Deny your feelings
- Do whatever peers say to fit in
- Put up with abuse
- Worry about others feelings more than your own
- Not listening to your intuition, heart, gut, inner voice
- Lose control or have meltdowns with your parents
- Avoid conflict & not stand up for yourself or friends
- Not stay true to you

- Not ask for what you want
- Act like you don't care when you do
- Let your buttons be pushed
- Spend a lot of time and energy trying to make everyone happy
- Pleaser - make choices so others will like you or not be mad at you
- Allow yourself to be seen/treated like an object
- Apologize when you did nothing wrong in order to save a friendship

Emotions girls feel when they give their power away:

discouraged • angry • resentful • frustrated • confused • sad • ashamed • anxious • defeated • guilty • powerless • out of integrity • unhappy • pulled/conflicted • weak • out of control • trapped/stuck • lost • sense of loss • overpowered • disappointed in yourself • self-doubt • worthless • stupid • overwhelmed • helpless

Harmful reactions to these feelings and other costs to girls:

- Apologize for no reason
- Take anger out on people who don't deserve it
- Become controlling in other areas of your life
- Overpower others
- Distract yourself/numb out
- Not feel worthy/deserving → poor boundaries
- Feelings fester → unhealthy expressions
- Easier to give in and give up authentic self
- Lose yourself, your voice, your emotions
- Disconnected from yourself and others
- Negative self-talk
- Disappointed in yourself

How to keep and reclaim your power:

- Visualize self as powerful/taking care of self in relationships
- Find best picture of yourself when younger & powerful → remind yourself that she is still in you
- Switch negative self-talk/coach yourself
- Become aware of costs to you when you give power away
- Express all feelings in healthy ways (especially Root Beer Feelings)
- Nurture yourself/take time for yourself
- Watch your words: avoid statements like "she made me feel ____" or "I need _____ to be happy."
- Create clear, firm boundaries before you get into situations/not let yourself be used
- Focus on making yourself happy vs. just make others happy
- Ask for what you want – start small and build
- Have an opinion and state it with respect, authority, conviction
- Decide on your sexual boundaries ahead of time before you get caught up in the heat of the moment
- Create BFF voice in your head to encourage/coach you
- Surround yourself with nurturing/trustworthy friends who build you up
- Listen to people who want what's good for you vs. media/boys/advertisers etc.
- Be a good friend to others
- Do things you love to do and bring you fulfillment
- Find groups/activities with a higher purpose
- Catch yourself when giving power away → pause → coach self → do it different
- Work on increasing your self-confidence and self-acceptance

Dr. Tim Jordan, M.D.

By not allowing words or comments to hurt you, you are saying to people, *I am in charge of how I feel about myself, not you. I am not giving up my power to anyone!*

I usually have all the girls in a class or retreat pair off and practice letting go of their partner's energy. Some of them have a tough time not pushing back; they are in the habit of fighting back or responding to other people. I encourage them to see themselves, in their minds, letting taunts go whenever they are confronted with a 'mean girl.' It's a great metaphor, and a great image to remind them of staying strong.

After the push game, I usually introduce the concept of 'tomato words.' I'll pick out a girl in the group and ask her how she would feel and reply if I called her a tomato. I'll usually say, *"Eww, you're a tomato!"* a few times for effect. And her response is giggling and laughter. When I ask her why she is smiling instead of feeling hurt, she tells me it's because what I said is silly and stupid. *"I know I'm not a tomato; I'm not a fruit!"* she'll say. And I say, *"That's right! The reason you don't react to that word is that you know you aren't a tomato, or some other funny words I use ('You're toothpaste' or, 'You're a Volkswagen'). There is no energy around that word because you are clear that it's not true, thus you have no attachment to it."*

The challenge I then give girls is this: turn every word, every name you are called, into a 'tomato word.' Just as in the push game, they have the ability never again to let any words get to them. Here is what I suggest they say in their heads if someone is calling them names or trying to provoke them. *"Just relax, Sally; I'm not a tomato; it's just a word; I know I'm not a ____; I'm not a tomato; I'm not willing to give my power away; it's just a word; I'm not a tomato; they're just trying to get a rise out of me..."* In essence, they are coaching themselves to stay calm and true to themselves, and 'to not go there.' I then suggest they smile at the other person, and walk away. But I want girls to understand that this approach is a lot different than letting words hurt them, trying to act like they didn't hurt, and ignoring the other person. That's what parents and teachers tell girls: *"Just ignore her!"* In order to do that, they need the vision and framing of the push game and skills like tomato words. *"I actually didn't think it would work,"* Fifth-grader Tess told me when we were talking about the Tomato Game. *"But I tried it with this one girl who has been harassing me since last year. And after a couple of days, she stopped bugging me! I feel so powerful! Like I can really not let people get to me anymore."*

That is exactly the response I hear from girls who put these concepts into play. They feel proud of themselves, and much more in control. From then on they walk into school and social situations with a lot more confidence. At this point, I tell girls, *"From this day forward, there are no mean words, only words. If someone calls you a name, you can let it hurt your feelings, and thus make it a 'mean word,' or you can make it a tomato word, keep your power, and stay true to yourself."* Even if someone addresses you with the nastiest, cuss word-laden comments, you have the power to let it slide off so that nothing sticks. Sometimes I'll have girls imagine they have sprayed themselves with emotional Scotch Guard, so that negativity doesn't stick.

> *"The person who upsets you the most is your greatest teacher, because they bring you face to face with who you are."* Lynn Andrews

What makes it easier to not take teasing on is if you truly believe you are not that word they are throwing at you. The words that bother us are the ones we judge in ourselves as true and bad. For example, if you are short, but are totally okay with your height, and someone calls you shorty, it has no effect. But if you are sensitive to being short, then those taunts could hurt. It's not because the words are mean; it's because you believe it and have judgments about that characteristic yourself. The same goes for any reason you are being made fun of: wearing glasses, your height or weight, your academic standing, your athleticism, any birthmarks, your race or religion. If you accept all parts of yourself, then you no longer will give power to anyone's words.

The mantra I wish for all girls to adopt is, *There are no mean words. I am in charge!*

A good book I read years ago was *Sticks and Stones: Seven Ways Your Child Can Deal With Teasing, Conflict and Other Hard Times* by Scott Cooper. It is geared for kids in early grade school. One of the skills he suggests is the Mighty Might for when someone says something provocative. So if someone says: *"You're an idiot,"* you respond with a smile and say, *"You might be right."* If they keep pushing: *"You're such a nerd,"* you keep calm and just respond, *"You might be right."* After a few times, I encourage kids to smile and walk away. And they walk away having retained all of their power. They've taught the teaser that she can't provoke you into a negative reaction. I tell girls that, through their actions and words, they are always teaching people how to treat them. If they keep their authority by not allowing any harassment to get to them, they've taught people they are not a good target.

This holds true for when girls hear they are the subject of negative gossip or rumors. A common response is to get upset, talk about it with people who are not the originators of it, and then get others to gossip about the person who started it. Drama, drama, and more drama! Instead of playing this game and becoming part of the problem, girls can choose to rise above it. If Mary tells Gina that Sammi has been talking about her, Gina could go directly to Sammi and check it out. Here is how the encounter played out.

"Sammi, I heard a rumor that you were making fun of me behind my back. Is it true?" Gina said. *"No, I never said that,"* Sammi responded. *"I think people are just trying to stir something up."* Gina answered, *"Well, I'm glad you didn't do it. I'm not willing to be friends with people who gossip about me, or about anybody for that matter. And you can count on me never to talk about you behind your back either."*

That short confrontation taught Sammi a lot about Gina: she's powerful, a loyal friend who can be trusted, and someone who will have your back. Gina has also given Sammi valuable information about how she needs to treat her if she wants to be her friend.

This kind of conversation feels foreign to girls. They are so afraid to confront their buddies because they fear it will result in losing that friend and possibly others as well. They haven't been given the language to take care of themselves like this. And they also will have to fight through and break the 'good girl' code that has been telling them this kind of action is mean. Girls tend to confuse being assertive and setting healthy boundaries with being aggressive and a bitch. Please educate them on the benefits of taking care of themselves like Gina did.

"Great minds discuss ideas; average minds discuss events; small minds discuss people." Eleanor Roosevelt

Another way of handling rumors and gossip is to make sure it stops with you. Don't pass it on. Just say, *"Thanks for telling me,"* and then drop it. The gossip stops with you. Or you could decide to become a 'By Player' instead of a 'Bystander'.

This is a critical concept for girls to incorporate into their thinking. So many of them stand by quietly and watch their friends get bullied, harassed and excluded. They feel paralyzed and impotent; part of them wants to speak up, but their fears hold them back.

"The ultimate tragedy is not the oppression and cruelty by the bad people, but the silence over that by the good people."
Martin Luther King Jr.

I have girls perform role-plays of someone being teased by a 'mean girl,' or someone who is being excluded by the girls at the popular lunch table. I'll ask them why each of the girls in the skit--the excluded girl, the alpha female who leads the exclusion, and the silent bystanders--might act that way.

The reasons girls give for remaining silent when others are being teased and left out are numerous:

- I'm afraid if I say something I'll be the next target.
- The alpha girl is so powerful.
- I worry that if I stand up for someone, no one will have my back and stand up for me.
- I don't know what to say. I've tried to say something but it either comes out wrong or I get ignored.
- It took me forever to get into the group, and I don't want to get kicked out.
- I'm afraid I'll lose my friends in the group and be alone again.

"You are not only responsible for what you say, but also for what you do not say." Martin Luther King Jr.

We then discuss the costs to them individually and as a group/classroom community if people remain bystanders to bullying. Girls become aware that they feel guilty and out of integrity; they feel discouraged and are mad at themselves because they lacked the courage to do the right thing. And their silence and lack of action actually gives the aggressor permission to keep on going.

"When you are silent, someone is speaking for you."
                                                    Elizabeth Eckford

They also need to be awakened to what all this means about the quality of their friendships. Are these really the kind of girls they want to hang with? There is always an underlying tension when they are in the group: *Am I dressed OK? Saying the right things? Am I in or out? What if they find out who the real me is? What if they see through my facade and discover how uncool, ordinary, and insecure I am?* Review the friendship tensions list I presented in Chapter 6.

"The ultimate measure of a man is not where he stands in moments of comfort and convenience, but where he stands at times of challenge and controversy." Martin Luther King Jr.

I would apply this quote also to the measure of a woman and a community. A community of bystanders doesn't have the safety and closeness all girls want and need. Girls don't feel comfortable being real or speaking their truth. Thus, the group misses out on so many good ideas, diversity of personalities and opinions, and spontaneity. Everyone feels constricted, careful, or wary. Girls also often don't feel supported by their teachers or the school. Even though character education and anti-bullying policies may be in place, these don't really get to the grass-root, everyday needs of girls. Girls tell me all the time that even though they believe their teachers care about what's going on, they don't really know what's going on. This kind of relationship aggression doesn't happen in front of adults, of course. And the anti-bullying programs tend to be too superficial and top-down. Meaning, there is too much responsibility given to teachers for stopping it, versus empowering, educating and coaching girls to take responsibility for these issues.

I finish up the bystanders role-play by having a handful of girls volunteer to show us different examples of how they could stand up to the alpha female in the lunch table skit. And I coach them on how they can be assertive and powerful without being aggressive. They need to understand that if they become disrespectful or snippy with the alpha female, they are adding to the drama and will probably provoke a disrespectful or aggressive response. Some girls in the skit take action by creating an empty chair next to them for the targeted girl to sit in, ignoring the alpha girl. If the alpha girl keeps trying to argue her point, some girls stand up and tell the new girl to follow them and they go sit at another table together. It's fun to see how creative they can be with each other. I encourage the new by-players not to argue with the alpha girl; that usually just fuels an instigator and those girls tend to be good at words and arguing. Take some action without generating any drama or response.

After the skits are over, I ask the class or group of girls if they'd like to commit to becoming by-players, both individually and as a group. It's a lot easier to have the courage to stand up for a friend if you know others will support you. The class commitment to doing it differently takes the control away from the perpetrators and places it in the hands of the group. Research has shown that the most effective anti-bullying programs are the ones that focus on the bystanders, not just the bully and victim. And it also has been shown again and again that the best programs are the ones that are school-wide, with participation from parents, teachers, principals and the district. It tells everyone that this issue will be taken seriously, we are all in this together, and we are going to be held accountable to agreements.

Another suggestion I have for girls regarding friendship issues is to be careful about the language you use. For instance, I've stopped using labels like 'bully' and 'victim'. The bully label is extremely negative, and doesn't take into account why girls act that way. I don't like labels of any kind because they are so limiting and carry too many judgments.

As I explained at the start of this chapter, there are reasons why girls engage in these behaviors. They are not really mean people; they just do disrespectful things sometimes. I find that many of these girls are really powerful creatures who like to be in charge, like to be in control, like to be the leader, and like to have things their way. I prefer to describe them in the most positive light: as incredibly influential leaders who still have a lot of rough edges to work out. Quiet, passive kids need to learn how to be more vocal and assertive; alpha females need to learn how to be strong leaders without being overly controlling or aggressive. They need our support and understanding as much as the 'victims' and bystanders. After hearing and reading so many stories about powerful women feeling constricted in their leadership attempts, so often being judged negatively as 'bitches', I don't want strong girls to lose their spirit. They need understanding and guidance, not labels and punishment.

I also don't want kids to become 'victims.' Most times, they don't initiate teasing or bullying behaviors. But how they respond affects whether it continues and worsens or goes away. I teach girls skills like the mighty might, tomato words, and not giving their power away. I help them switch negative beliefs about themselves that could have resulted from past experiences, since these can cause them to remain or become targets. And, again, I work with the whole class of girls, putting everything out on the table. The girls are encouraged to engage in conflict resolutions with others they feel hurt by and to clear things up. The group makes commitments and intentions about how they want to treat each other, and also about stepping up as by-players. In total, it makes a world of difference in the classroom community.

I also caution parents to be careful about how they handle daughters who are experiencing problems with friends. When a girl comes home with a story about being teased, I tell parents to listen, mirror back what they've heard, and be sure, first and foremost, that their daughter feels understood. At this point, you could ask a few questions to get them thinking for themselves about why the hostilities occurred. Then assist them in problem-solving what they could try to make things different. I equate this to coaching a basketball team. If things aren't going well for a player, you take them out of the game and coach them a little on the bench. Once they've calmed down and have a new plan, you send them back out there and see what happens.

If your child tries several tactics and the teasing persists, then I would call the teacher and make them aware of what's going on. Oftentimes, they don't know it's happening. You can suggest the teacher bring the involved girls together and guide them to work it out. Then the teacher can check in with them every few days to make sure they are honoring their agreements with each other.

Christy was a quiet, sweet sixth grader who started being harassed by two girls in her class. One day when Christy put her lunch down at a table and went to get a drink, they threw it into the trash. They called her names, and made fun of her in front of their guy friends. Christy did a good job of trying to set boundaries and take care of herself. But the girls wouldn't stop. When I saw her for an office visit, I encouraged her to ask the school counselor to bring the three girls together and work it out. Christy made sure the counselor agreed not to get the girls in trouble, and the meeting occurred. The two girls weren't happy about it, but the counselor guided them all to make agreements about ending the harassment. When I saw Christy two weeks later, she was really relieved because there had been no more incidents. The three girls never became friends, but the teasing stopped.

I like it when girls take responsibility for taking action, like Christy did. She learned some invaluable lessons about taking care of herself.

I also warn parents, especially those who tend to over-protect their children, not to 'Mine for Pain'. In other words, when their daughter comes home from school, they should avoid asking leading questions that infer something probably went wrong. I've met some kids with enmeshed mothers who felt like if they didn't have a sad story every day to report, Mom would be unhappy. So they'd often make up tales or exaggerate to appease their moms. If you expect and look for problems, you'll either find them or create them unnecessarily, which can keep daughters stuck in a 'target' role.

I would also avoid calling other parents if you think your daughter is being teased or bullied. Instead, work with her using the tools I described earlier, and if there is still no resolution, contact the teacher. I have seen far too many instances when such a phone call created much more drama than the girls did. And also, don't play 'Hot Potato' with your daughter's emotions. If she comes home upset and vents to you, listen and validate, but don't take it on. Oftentimes, the next day at school the girls make up or forget about it, but parents are left feeling angry and upset. Sometimes they don't let go of negative judgments about the other girl for a long time, or never, even when the girls are best friends.

Julia was an eighth grader at an all-girl weekend retreat who had seemed depressed for about two months. Her problems arose because of the actions of her friend group. *"I've been friends with a group of about eight girls since I was in first grade,"* she told me. *"I guess everyone considers them the popular girls. This school year they started doing things I didn't like. They all got boy crazy, and that's all they want to talk about. And in the past couple of months they have been sneaking alcohol from their parents and drinking it at parties." "How do you feel about what they're doing?"* I asked. *"I feel really uncomfortable,"* Julia said. *"I drank a little alcohol one night, and I didn't like it." "Have you tried letting them know how you feel?"* I asked. *"No, I don't think they'd listen or care,"* Julia responded. *"They are so into the partying now. I just don't know what to do. They've been my best friends for so long, and I don't want to lose the group."* She liked hearing other girls share similar stories all weekend, and knowing she wasn't alone. We encouraged Julia to have some quiet time to journal and think about what felt right to her. I wanted her to learn that she really did know what to do; that the answer was inside her. She came to my office for a visit about two weeks later and seemed so much happier and relaxed. *"So what happened with your friends?"* I asked. *"I decided to stop hanging out with them on the weekends,"* Julia answered. *"And they noticed and got mad at me and won't talk to me now." "Why did you decide to stop hanging with them?"* I asked. *"I didn't like the way I felt when I was with them,"* Julia said. *"And I didn't like what I was becoming."*

Wow! That took a ton of courage and wisdom for Julia to make that decision. She still felt a little sad sometimes because she hadn't found a new group yet. But making a bunch of new buddies at the weekend retreat had given her the confidence that she was okay, and deserved to have good friends. At a follow-up visit a month later, Julia shared with me that she now had a healthier new friend group at school. She had continued her journaling, because she liked how calm it made her feel, and she had discovered that she could make better decisions in that quieter space.

I want every girl to develop the self-awareness and courage that Julia showed. And I think it's crucial to note that during a challenging time like that, she needed some guidance from caring adults and peers.

One final suggestion about supporting girls with their friendship issues. I often encourage girls to make a list of the qualities of a good friend, a best friend forever if you will, and to be sure to include how this friend would treat them and other people. I saw 11-year-old Eleanor recently, and this was her list: Respectful * Kind to everyone * Includes everyone * Doesn't gossip or talk about people behind their backs * Likes sports * Would call me to do stuff as often as I call her.

Once they've made their list, I have them do the following with it.

First, become the list! I tell girls that if they want to attract friends who match their list, it's important that they live those qualities too. If you want a friend who doesn't gossip, then don't gossip. Because if you are spreading rumors, there's a good chance you'll attract others who do it too. If you want a friend who won't exclude you, be really inclusive of everyone.

Secondly, I have them think about the friends they hang out with the most, and check out how these girls live out those attributes. Some girls are shocked at how few of these traits their friends display. It really makes them think about whether or not their current friend group is healthy for them. And coming to this realization on their own is much more powerful than adults telling them to find new friends.

"You can tell more about a person by what he says about others than you can by what others say about him." Leo Aikman

Lastly, I have the girls think about all the girls, or boys, in their class, even the kids in the grade above or below them. By their observations and past experiences, I encourage them to notice who fits their list of characteristics. Sometimes girls will take a week or two and really observe how people treat them and other kids. I tell them to look for people who are kind to everyone, include everyone, and stand up for their friends. Sometimes these girls are not the loud, aggressive, popular girls who get all the attention. They might be quieter, or hang out on the fringes. These are the people they can befriend. In this way, girls find kindred souls like Julia did. They also grow in relationship areas where they might need to grow. And their new friendships are more nourishing and fulfilling.

Let me close this chapter with a summary list of skills girls can use to deal with and prevent relationship aggression behaviors.

1) Understand why girls become aggressors, targets, and by-players
2) Make friends of different ages and in diverse groups and schools
3) Don't gossip- drama stops with you!
4) Accept/love yourself, be true to yourself, speak up for yourself
5) Assess your own behavior and your part in conflicts
6) Be a leader- stand up for yourself and others
7) Spread kindness and compassion- include quiet, alone, new kids
8) Ask friends to stop gossiping- hold others accountable to the mind trust
9) Make a contract to stand up to aggressors- create allies; you're not alone
10) Let your friends know how much your care about and appreciate them
11) Remember you are not alone! - share fears and desire to do it differently
12) Express all your feelings in healthy ways
13) Don't take your anger from RA out on others
14) Have a sense of humor
15) Do not give your power away!
16) Girls interact better with each other if they know each other more deeply

17) Focus on team intentions, making all successful vs. competition, achievement

18) Encourage activities that requires cooperation, service, higher purpose

19) Handle conflicts in group setting- deepen understanding, sensitivity to others

20) Safe space to talk about feelings, RA, needs, solutions

21) Use older girls for role models and confidants

CHAPTER 13

STINKING THINKING

"It is hard to fight an enemy who has outposts in your head."
Sally Kempton

Mara is a freshman in high school who came to see me because she thought she was depressed. The oldest of three children, Mara had undergone some major life changes in the past six months. At the beginning of the summer, her parents separated. It was a shock to all three kids because their parents hadn't been arguing or fighting. Dad moved out, but because he hadn't been very involved with the kids, it didn't have much effect on Mara. His new apartment had only one bedroom, so he either came to the house for dinner or took all three kids out once a week. The big shocker came a month ago, when Mara's dad told her the reason for the divorce was that he was gay. Her initial reaction was that it wasn't a big deal; she had a few friends who were gay and she had no judgments about it. But as time went on, her thoughts about it became more conflicted.

"I mean I don't really care that he's gay," Mara told me. *"Two of my friends are gay and it's no big deal to me. But then I started wondering how I'd tell my boyfriend someday that my dad is gay. I mean, I don't even have a boyfriend, but I'm worried a guy might think it's weird, you know? And then I keep having this nagging thought: Am I gay? I mean, I know I'm straight; I like guys a lot. I'm attracted to guys. I've never been attracted to girls or anything. But I can't get that thought out of my head."*

She went on from there into some other riffs about her dad walking her up the aisle at her wedding and how people at school might react if he showed up at one of her plays with a partner. There were many tears shed off and on during her venting, and it was a continuous flow of concerns and feelings that had been building up for a month.

Mara was displaying something extremely common in girls: ruminating. To ruminate means 'to chew,' and in the case of Mara and many other girls, it means to chew on thoughts. Girls will take a thought or worry, oftentimes something fairly small, and think about it and think about it, and turn it over and over in their minds. They often end up making mountains out of molehills. For information of the neurological reasons why girls ruminate, see the chapter 4 on the female brain.

Girls who exaggerate like this become stressed and anxious. They are internally distracted, and their schoolwork and performance in activities suffer. The constant barrage of thoughts makes it hard both to fall asleep and to sleep peacefully. They toss and turn, wake up, and then can't fall back asleep. Girls who cogitate also put themselves into confusion a lot. They doubt themselves, can't make decisions, and over-think problems. And they often lose sight of reality, as they make a lot of assumptions and also make up stories in their heads. They don't know what's what any longer.

I have come across many girls who have been medicated for diagnoses like attention deficit disorder, OCD, depression or anxiety disorder, yet no one has addressed their rumination, which is the likely the source of their symptoms. That's disturbing and sad. Mulling ideas over and over is one reason that our sleeping beauties develop negative self-talk during this touchpoint. And many of the middle and high school girls I work with have a lot of unconstructive thoughts.

"I can't stand it when people at my school make comments about my makeup," thirteen-year-old Liz said. *"This bitch the other day came up to me and asked why my neck looked a different color than my face, and I yelled at her that I'm terrible at putting on my makeup, OK? I wear it to cover up my zits, and I never have just one; it's like my whole face is covered. As if I'm not insecure enough, I don't need people pointing out that I have acne. I know I'm not very pretty, and the zits just make it worse."*

Wow! Can you imagine walking around each day with all of that going on in your head nonstop? During a girl's transformation, with all of its associated changes, it's easy to see why she succumbs to being hard on herselfAs described in Chapter 3, girls have been fed a steady diet of images and conditioning that allows no room for 'average,' errors or imperfections. The triple-bind messages have forced girls to strive for an unrealistic standard of being perfect at everything and being everything to everyone all the time: perfect student, perfect athlete, perfect daughter, perfect sibling, perfect friend, perfect teenager, perfect wife, perfect mother, perfect bread winner, all with the perfect body, and so on. It's no wonder young women in their twenties and thirties feel lost and empty. Young girls look at magazines, TV, movies, musical stars, billboards, ads and models and say to themselves: *That's how I am supposed to look; that is the expectation. Otherwise I am ugly and a failure; I don't measure up; I'm not as pretty or good as everyone else.* This is where so much of their dissatisfaction with their bodies comes from. Girls compare themselves to models, movie stars, and especially to their peers, and find something in the comparison to feel bad about.

On my retreats, we do an exercise where we'll go around the circle and have every person share what they judge negatively about their body, and everyone has things they don't like. And it's not just the biggies like height and weight. Girls might judge their fingers, their toenails, ear lobes, eyebrows and eyelashes, nose, lips, hair color and texture, feet, hands, knees, legs, booties, breasts, shoulders. I have heard every conceivable body part mentioned as a negative. Girls with straight hair wish theirs was curly or wavy. Girls with wavy hair iron their hair flat every morning before school. Their breasts are too big or too small; same with their booties. It just goes on and on. Every time they look into a mirror, the harmful judgments about their bodies and appearance arise. These also appear when they see their skinny, twiggy, blonde friends. And it comes up big time whenever a boy rejects them or doesn't show interest in them. Girls go straight to, *I'm ugly, fat and unattractive.* They also lack information about the universal body changes they undergo during puberty. There are normal, biologic and evolutionary reasons why girls get curves and put on weight in different places than boys.

When I talk to a group of high school girls about the female brain, hormonal changes during puberty, and their monthly cycles--and how all this affects their bodies and emotions--they are spellbound. No one has even told them this information, which they need to make sense of all the changes they have been experiencing. It's the first time they really get it, and this understanding allows them to relax and judge themselves less.

Girls also compare themselves when it comes to academics, sports and activities like dance, singing and debate. They have been conditioned to look outside themselves to assess whether or not they measure up and are okay. This, of course, is a trap, because you can always find someone who is smarter, faster or more talented. It sets girls up to feel inferior, and to develop more destructive self-talk. And then there is the whole issue of boys. At some point, girls become super-sensitive to how attractive they are to boys. The large rise of estrogen in girls and testosterone in boys primes them for the important task of reproduction and propagating the species. It's been built into our DNA and brain wiring. The sexual-pursuit circuits in the hypothalamus of pubertal boys grow twice as large as those in pubertal girls. And the mate-detection circuits in boys are primarily visual.

Louann Brizendine, M.D., in *The Male Brain*, uses research to show that males alive today have been biologically selected over millions of years to seek out fertile females and to zoom in on certain features that indicate reproductive health. And this is true across all cultures. Men for millions of years have been attracted to the proverbial hourglass figure: large breasts, small waist with a flat stomach, and full hips. They also prefer women with clear skin, bright eyes, full lips and shiny hair, all of which are strong visual markers of fertility and good health. And so from an evolutionary standpoint, I can understand why girls are worried about how they look to boys.

The combined effects of perfectionism, lookism, the triple-bind pressures and expectations, and the early and sustained oversexualization and objectification of girls cause them to feel self-conscious, insecure and substandard. Combine that with trying to come to terms with their physical changes during puberty, and you can see why the wrong glance from a boy or being teased or ignored by a boy they are attracted to could throw a girl off course. And it doesn't help that girls hear comments all day and all night long about boys, who's attracted to whom, and who said what about them. These comments are reported directly and overheard in classrooms, hallways and cafeterias, as well as on social networking sites. It's a 24/7 news cycle, and it creates constant tension for girls about their position with friends and guys. *Am I in or out?* Stay tuned. There will be an update every few minutes.

You can see why girls become preoccupied with their appearance and with their attractiveness. And ruminating about it can create damaging self-talk, assumptions, and decisions about themselves. I see so many girls who have so much garbage in their heads; so many un-truths and misunderstandings. They have accumulated negative decisions about themselves. So how can we help girls not fall into these traps and become so discouraged?

"We cannot control the parade of negative thoughts marching through our minds. But we can choose which ones we will give attention to. Picture your thoughts as people passing by the front of your home. Just because they're walking by doesn't mean you have to invite them in." Gladys Edmunds

First and foremost, they need to become aware of what they are saying to themselves and what they have decided about themselves. For most girls these thoughts have become unconscious and automatic. I do an exercise where I have them fill out a self-talk sheet showing a girl at the bottom of the page with five large thought bubbles coming from her head. These are labeled family, friends, self, body and future. The girls write all the negative thoughts and beliefs they have about each of those areas of their lives. Here are some examples girls have shared in each area:

- Family: I'm different than my family, I don't fit in, My parents love my siblings more than me, No one understands me, I'm not important, No one cares, I'm invisible, I'm unlovable.
- Friends: I'm different, I don't fit in, no one likes me, I'm weird or a freak, I'm nerdy, I'm awkward or too shy, I'm too bossy, I'm invisible, I'm alone, No one cares, No one notices when I'm absent, I'm left out and alone, I'm not as good as others, I never know what to say, I say weird things, No one understands me, I'm the only one who feels this way.
- Self: There's something wrong with me, I'm not good enough, I'm hopeless, I'm lazy or stupid, I'm weird, I'm way behind my peers, I'm not lovable or important, I don't measure up.
- Body: I'm ugly or unattractive, I'm fat, I'm not athletic, No boy will be attracted to me, I'm too ____, I hate my____.

- Future: I'll never be good enough, I won't get into the college I want to go to, I won't get a college scholarship, I won't make the team, play, or cheerleading squad, I'll never get the grades my parents and teachers want me to get, I won't get asked to the dance or prom, I'll never be happy, I'll never be satisfied with my body and appearance, I'll never attract a cool or hot guy or get a boyfriend., This will never change or get better.

"The soul becomes dyed with the color of its thoughts."
Marcus Aurelius, Roman emperor

After the girls share their negative thoughts, we have them figure out the costs to them if they hold onto them. They come up with costs like*: I feel discouraged, down, depressed, anxious, unhappy and discontented; it cuts my motivation; I'm less confident and give up easier; I don't raise my hand, take risks, or put myself out there; I'm reluctant to try to include myself; I feel insecure and worry about what other people think all the time; I give my power away and don't have good boundaries with friends and boys; I'm less optimistic and hopeful; I don't trust myself or my intuition; I constantly doubt myself and my decisions.* Whew--that's a depressing list, isn't it? But talk to girls or to adult women, and I promise you they will connect to that list of beliefs and emotions.

"Worry doesn't empty today of it's trouble; it empties tomorrow of it's strength." Saint Francis

Becoming cognizant of the price of hanging onto their negativity can become the greatest motivation to change it. Most girls are unaware of them, or they haven't made the connection between the feelings and symptoms and the thought/beliefs.

"Good thoughts bear good fruit, bad thoughts bear bad fruit-and man is his own gardener." James Allen

I also challenge girls to focus on their inner dialogue all day long, and just notice how often destructive chatter pops into their heads. I tell them, "Don't judge it, don't criticize or get mad at yourself when you catch yourself drifting into this stinking thinking; just notice it." I want them to be gentle with themselves. They've probably been bad-mouthing themselves for months or years, so I encourage them to be patient as they work to change that. And how do you change it once you've become aware you are doing it? Here are a few suggestions I give to girls:

1. Reality Check. I'll have them challenge every negative thought that arises, whether on their self-talk worksheet or just in their heads. *Do you really have no friends? Are you really stupid, or do you just have a hard time with math? Are you really fat, or do you just have a muscular build because you play sports?* You get the idea.

   I have them fill out another thought bubble sheet titled, 'the truth about me.' They write what's real and true about every harmful thought in their bubbles. Then they share what the positive effects on them would be if they really believed these positive truths about themselves. Girls share benefits like: I'd feel more confident and happy; I'd be more motivated and persistent; I'd put myself out there more and not be afraid to speak up or include myself; I'd trust myself and my intuition more; I'd raise my hand more in class; I'd join more clubs or teams; I'd worry less about what others think and do things because they feel right for me; I'd take better care of myself and set good boundaries because I would believe I deserved better. That sounds a lot better.

2. Mantras. A mantra is a word or phrase you say over and over to yourself to change your thinking. The best example of one that

most kids have heard before is in the story The Little Engine That Could. I have altered the story over the years so that it relates better with the message girls need. This train engine was stuck going up a steep hill on a hot, sunny day. And she started out saying to herself, *"This hill is too steep, I'll never make it to the top; it's too hot; I can't do it."* So she couldn't. In my version of the story, a farmer has watched this drama unfold, and he walks over and tells the little engine: *"Your problem isn't the steep hill or the hot sun. Your problem is your stinking thinking! You need to change what you are saying to yourself."* So the little engine starts to say aloud: *"I think I can, I think I can,"* which is a positive mantra. And lo and behold, she starts to move. She keeps repeating her mantra and gets more and more excited, and builds up more and more speed and momentum. And before you know it, she crests the hill and speeds happily all the way home!

So I have girls select a mantra they can say to themselves that would switch some negative thought pattern. And this mantra has to be all positive, no negative words or thoughts. So if a girl is worried about an upcoming test, she would not say: *"I'm not going to flunk, I'm not going to flunk"* because then what is she actually thinking about? Flunking! Instead, she could say: *"Relax Mya, you're going to do fine. You always do fine, relax Mya, you're going to do fine."* If she gets fearful in a situation, she would not say, *"I'm not going to be scared"* because again, she'd be thinking about being scared. Instead, she'd say something like *"I feel safe and loved."* If she's thinking about giving up because she's getting frustrated, she could say over and over to herself: *"You can do it!"* Or *"I know I can do it!"*

You get the idea. Mantras are extremely powerful, and can be used any time, any place and no one knows you are doing it. You can repeat it to yourself over and over until you switch out of your stinking thinking.

3. Another way to switch negative self-talk is to spend some time releasing it. You can get these thoughts out of your head by verbalizing or writing them. Girls can journal these thoughts, write them out in a letter and then rip it up, or write a story about a girl with these negative thoughts who ends up switching her thinking. Negative thoughts and feelings can be expressed through art, music or dance, as well. So instead of ruminating and allowing your thoughts free will, channel them out of your head.

"A grateful heart a garden is." Unknown

4. Gratitude. One of the best avenues to change out of stinking thinking is to express appreciation. You can not be in a state of gratitude and any negative thoughts/feelings like anger, frustration, fear, stress, or worry. It's impossible! The following are ways to express gratitude.

1) Express gratitude in person
2) Gratitude Journal- be specific- write about others or yourself
3) Mentally count your blessings regularly
4) Write gratitude letters to people who made a difference in your life or the lives of others
5) Remember "bad times", contrast that with where you are now, and focus on how far you have come
6) Forgiveness- focus on the gifts and lessons that the person/experience gave you
7) Learn prayers of gratitude
8) Use positive, appreciative language: encouragement, gifts, giving, blessings, blessed, fortunate, abundance, appreciation, content, thankful, grateful
9) Look for things to be grateful for; think/speak positive thoughts

10) "George Bailey Effect"- imagine what life would be like without a major blessing like a spouse, children, a positive life event, a good friend, even yourself!
11) Give credit to other people
12) Focus on your senses and appreciate the miracle of our bodies and being alive
13) Gratitude through prayer and meditation
14) Gratitude clubs, assemblies, writing assignments at school
15) Express through poems, pictures, songs, stories, notes
16) Gratitude begets gratitude!!!

There has been good research that demonstrates the positive benefits of expressing gratitude, especially by Robert Emmons. Kids, teens, and adults who practice gratitude: are less materialistic, are more optimistic and happier, have higher life satisfaction and joy, act more generous and compassionate, and experience less of the negative things like depression, greed, illness, and social isolation. The benefits for kids and teens in particular who focus on gratitude: better grades, set higher goals, feel more satisfied with friends and family and school, and become more resilient during times of stress. Sounds like a no-brainer, right? The benefit that pertains here is that it is also a terrific way for girls to switch out of a negative self talk pattern.

"If you're not enjoying the journey, you probably won't enjoy the destination." Joe Tye

5. Come to the present moment. Refer back to chapter nine on how to slow down and come into the present. Most of a girl's anxious thoughts have to do with the future, about what might happen tomorrow at school, or next week or month. Staying in the here and now takes away worries and fears, because in this present moment, it's all good.

6. Belief systems. Finally, I like to help girls go back over negative experiences that may have caused some of their destructive thoughts and beliefs. Girls may come to think they are weird or don't fit in because their best friend betrayed them two years ago. They may think they are ugly because their parents compare them to their 'perfect' older sister. They might have decided they are unimportant or unlovable because after their parents' divorce, their dad rarely calls to see them. Girls can be guided to work through what they've come to believe as a result of what they have lived through. When they re-decide healthier, more accurate versions of these events, they won't develop this stinking thinking. They can understand and decide that their dad not calling them has nothing to do with them; it's his issue and his loss. It's crucial to learn not to take on unconstructive beliefs when friends do hurtful things, and not to take such behaviors so personally. Processing through past experiences is an extremely helpful way to redirect unproductive thinking and decisions.

Now let's spend a few minutes talking about assumptions, another behavior girls engage in all too frequently.

When girls make assumptions, they are making judgments about what something means without knowing the actual facts. Let me share some real examples from girls I have worked with.

"When I walked into class after recess, I saw two of my friends talking in the corner," fifth-grader Reed said. *"When I walked over to them, they stopped talking."* Reed's assumption was, *they were talking about me!*

"My three best friends were huddled together at recess, and they were all laughing really loudly," fourth-grader Ava told me. *"I came over to see what they were talking about, and they stopped laughing immediately. I asked them what they were talking about, and they*

said 'nothing.' I felt hurt, so I walked away, and as soon as I turned my back on them they started laughing again."* Ava's assumption was, *they're making fun of me!*

"I got on Facebook Saturday night, and I saw that my three best friends were having a sleepover and hadn't invited me," Anna confided. Anna's assumption was, *they don't like me anymore, I'm being left out, something must have happened...* and the suppositions begin.

Anything can set off assumption alarms. It might be someone's body language: eye rolling, turning away, a frown, a certain glance. It could be things that peers say or don't say when you expected a different response. Reading entries online can be misconstrued as negative. Girls have told me they got upset because their friend didn't end an online conversation with 'lol' or didn't use an exclamation mark when they usually do. Online, you can't read facial expressions, tones of voice, or body language, so there is immense opportunity for conjecture to go wild. Girls who are the most insecure, or who feel left out and alone are probably the most vulnerable.

All girls need to identify the costs to them when they stew on these false hypotheses. They must walk through scenarios like Reed, Ava and Anna's. My groups are then guided to list all the possible negative assumptions they could make because of someone's actions, which usually include five to 10 possibilities. Then we make a list of all the emotions a girl might feel because of making these guesses. Common feelings they come up with are sad, hurt, left out, betrayed, confused, worried, angry, embarrassed, or alone. Next we have them describe how they might act or react with these emotions driving them. Common responses are crying, saying something mean or vengeful, gossiping with other girls about the people who angered them, avoiding those friends, withdrawing or isolating themselves, tattling to a teacher, trying to go home early from school, or avoiding going to school the next day. Unfortunately, this solves nothing. And they usually make the person feel worse, as well as often compounding the situation. I've seen so many girls hold onto grudges and hurts for months and years because of an assumption. When we give the girls space to talk through what occurred, it almost always turns out to be a misunderstanding; the girl misinterpreted the behavior and has been upset for no reason.

After fleshing out several of these kinds of scenarios as a group, we switch it up. We have the girls come up with a list of positive possibilities for what the behaviors might represent.

Reed's example could have represented one of her friends needing to share something personal and just wanting to talk to one person about it. Another possibility Reed's class came up with was that maybe they were planning a surprise birthday party for her. And, unbelievably, this is exactly what happened that Friday night!

For Anna's situation, there's a good chance that the mother at the sleepover house would only allow her daughter to have two friends stay over. Or maybe they were all on the same basketball team and after their evening game just decided on the spur of the moment to go to someone's house. You get the idea.

Rachel Simmons, author of *Curse of the Good Girl*, suggests girls use the phrase *"I wonder if..."* to come up with positive possibilities about what's going on, versus the pessimistic theories. That would prevent girls from going right into their Stinking Thinking mode. Once the girls have a list of 'I wonder if's...', we go on to list how they'd feel with these positive notions in their head, and then how they might act if they had *that* thinking in mind. Of course they'd feel happier, more confident and included, and what proceeded would flow from being in that mindset. Perhaps most important of all, we discuss what they could do if they see or hear something that bothers or confuses them. If you're not sure what a friend's facial expression means, or don't know how to interpret what someone says, the best way to know the truth is to check it out! And check it out directly with that person.

Far too often, a girl's response is to go to other people and ask them what's going on with their friend. When more people become involved, there is a higher likelihood of gossip and drama. Ava could have gone to some other girls and told them how mean those three girls were. She might get them on her side and get some affirmation about how horrible those girls are. Her new posse will add their horror stories of previous encounters with the mean girls, and they would have connected through their negativity. Of course, a member of the new posse might leak information to the 'mean girls' that Ava has been talking smack about them, and then a full-scale drama unfolds, and all because Ava didn't go directly to her friends to clear things up.

I described in Chapter 6 on friends about teaching girls how to directly, peacefully and effectively handle issues like these. Misunderstandings would be redirected right away; no fuss and no mess. It takes courage for girls to confront their friends and peers because they are so afraid it will cause others to be mad at them, resulting in the loss of that relationship. The more girls go through the conflict resolution model and see the constructive results, the more likely they are to trust the process. The outcome is more closeness, not less. They end up feeling more confident and empowered. They have kept their power and their integrity; they've done the right thing. And that feels far superior to the previous way.

Assumptions are a critical issue to make girls aware of. Guidance and skills in this area prevent a lot of unnecessary stinking thinking and drama.

Sleeping Beauties, Awakened Women

One final issue that falls under this section is questions that girls ask themselves as they progress through the adolescent years. Here is a partial list of uncertainties they have shared with me:

1) Am I okay? Am I good enough?
2) Am I pretty enough to deserve friends or a boy friend?
3) Will I be left out and alone? Bullied, teased or rejected?
4) Who will I sit with at lunch or play with at recess?
5) Who will talk to me when I walk into school, in the hallways between classes, and in class?
6) Middle school and high school are harder; will I make it? Do good enough?
7) Will I disappoint my parents if I don't get perfect grades or not do the activities they want me to do or befriend who they want?
8) Why don't people call me to do stuff on the weekends? Why do I always have to call them first?
9) What would happen if I let everyone in on my secret ...who I really am?
10) Should I be someone I don't want to be (me) or someone nobody wants or likes?
11) Why don't boys notice me like they do the other girls?
12) Do other people think I'm as ugly as I think I am?
13) Will I ever have the courage to be true to myself?
14) Does anyone understand what I am going through?
15) Am I the only one???

As I have mentioned previously in this book, it's not so much the questions girls ask themselves, it's how they answer them. If girls go into rumination mode with queries like these, they will tend to end up thinking/deciding worst-case answers: *I'm ugly, no one likes me, I can't trust anyone.* You'll hear a lot of extremes, like no one..., everybody..., never..., always. And none of it is based on truth or reality.

So it's important to flush out what specific worries and judgments are rattling around in each girl's brain and guide them to more realistic and healthy answers. Girls need people in their lives whom they can trust with these sensitive thoughts and feelings. If they feel heard, they are much more apt to listen to that adult's wisdom, suggestions, and guidance. And, the answers to their internal questions won't end up becoming more stinking thinking.

There is also tremendous value in girls having safe places to discuss these kinds of issues, worries and concerns with other girls. I've been privileged to sit on the floor with circles of girls for 23 years, talking through these topics. It is vital for girls to know they are not alone, and they are not crazy for having these kinds of notions. They are actually quite normal.

And the more these concerns are brought out into the open, the more they lose their power over the girls. Remember, what is unexpressed becomes unmanageable. Bring these subjects out of the dark and into the light of awareness and understanding; it is a powerful protection against negative self-talk and harmful conclusions.

CHAPTER 14

PROTECTIVE FACTORS

"Embrace your solitude and love it. Endure the pain it causes, and try to sing out with it. For your solitude will be a support and a home for you, ever in the midst of very unfamiliar circumstances, and from it you will find all your paths." Ranier Maria Rilke

In her book, *Smart Girls Gifted Women*, Barbara Kerr studied the lives of 33 eminent women to determine the factors that helped them carry childhood talents into adulthood. She found several commonalities among the women, and she wrote biographies for nine of them in her book, including Marie Curie, Gertrude Stein, Eleanor Roosevelt, Margaret Mead, Georgia O'Keefe, Maya Angelou, Katharine Hepburn, Beverly Sills, and Rigoberta Marden.

For various reasons, all had spent time alone in girlhood, allowing them the freedom to pursue their passions without the many distractions that consume most preteen and teen girls. They used this time to read voraciously, study their crafts and learn to love working in solitude. Interestingly, these women experienced some social awkwardness as adolescents, and felt like they didn't fit in. Because of this, they were able to internalize the benefits of nonconformity, and this allowed them time to focus inward on their needs and dreams and passions. By the time they left high school, they had well-developed skills or passions, and this led to a lasting and intense interest in their subject. These girls had experienced being in 'flow', and it lit a fire in them. All had received individualized instruction as children, either from teachers, trainers or mentors. This allowed them to pursue their interests at their own accelerated pace. The mentors took an interest not only in their talents but also in them as people. Their strength of character helped them disregard socially or culturally accepted gender limitations. They felt a sense of equality with men, despite cultural messages to the contrary. Last, these successful women somehow balanced relationships, motherhood and full careers. They decided they could live their lives to the fullest, and were able to make it happen.

I have used this research, my other readings, my experiences counseling girls, and my work at mother-daughter and father-daughter retreats to come up with a list of factors that seem to protect girls from going off track. In essence, this is what girls need from adults to help them transform into powerful and influential women.

1)   Close relationships with their parents

Research by Mary Pipher, author of *Reviving Ophelia* and the *Shelter of Each Other*, determined three important factors that best predicted whether teens would get into drug and alcohol problems: a close relationship with parents, a strong attachment to school, and shared activities with family. It makes sense, right? In my book *Keeping Your Family Grounded When You're Flying By The Seat Of Your Pants*, I wrote a chapter on the importance of consistently adding deposits to the 'Good Will Account' (GWA) parents have with their children. If this GWA is full, kids feel loved, respected, heard, understood, accepted and connected. And when this happens, it's easy to be an influence in your child's life.

As girls grow into their adolescent years, parents often back off too far because they get mixed signals from their daughters. It feels like their sweet little girls are pushing them away. And in part, they are. But they still need a close, safe relationship with their parents.

They still need special one-on-one time with each parent. But as they get older, it needs to become more and more on their terms, on their time, and doing what interests them.

Marsha, the mother of 16-year-old Katie, told me a story that illustrates this point. She picked Katie up after school one day and told her in an excited voice, *"How about we go shopping for spring clothes at the mall, just you and me?"* Marsha expected her daughter to be excited and to jump at the chance to go shopping, even if it meant time with Mom. So she was disappointed and surprised when Katie answered by saying, sullenly, *"Do we have to?"* It hurt Marsha's feelings, but for once she stayed calm, and she asked Katie why she didn't want to go on a mom-daughter date. *"It's not that I don't want to do something with you, it's just ...well, you always want to go shopping, and I hate shopping!"* Katie said. *"We always have to do what you like to do, not what I like."* This was a revelation to Marsha. She'd just assumed a 16-year-old girl loved shopping. But what Katie proceeded to tell her was that she liked going to used bookstores and art galleries and plays—those were fun to her. From that conversation, Marsha and Katie started making dates that were more about Katie's interests, and their bond grew.

When I work with adolescent girls, I encourage them to teach their parents how they want to be supported. The ways their parents provided for them in third grade no longer feel right. They probably don't want Mommy and Daddy at their bus stop, and they don't want or need their parents to micromanage their lives or solve their problems. But they need to be specific with their parents about how they want to be taken care of. Girls can quickly rattle off all the stupid things their parents do that annoys them, but I have to push them to come up with concrete ways their parents can connect with them, spend time with them, and give them love and support. When that happens, it's a huge win-win for both sides.

Adolescent girls still need physical affection, but again parents need to be sensitive to the time and place and what their daughters desire. Many dads feel uncomfortable with their daughter's burgeoning curves, and aren't sure about hugs and having their girls sit on their laps like they did during the younger years. I think girls need it, want it, and aren't sure how to ask for it. They feel pressure from peers and the culture to be too grown up for that, so they often feel torn. Bring the subject out into the open, talk about, and get clear about what feels good to them. Don't stay quiet and avoid each other; this breeds resentment, hurt feelings and more disconnection.

2) Close Relationships with Relatives

I think it is so beneficial for all kids to know where they came from. Family stories provide rich lessons and modeling for girls. During our mother-daughter retreats, we usually have moms bring in pictures of the women in their and their husband's families. We encourage moms to tell stories about these women, i.e. aunts, grandmothers, great-grandmothers. Girls often can relate to these stories. They may not have gone through what an immigrant great-grandmother did, but they can connect with qualities these women exhibited, like courage, determination, or compassion. Knowing their family history, knowing on whose shoulders they stand, gives girls a sense of grounding and hope.

I especially like when moms share pictures of themselves at different stages of growing up and relate stories to these photos. Girls are incredibly hungry to know their mom's past, and especially what they were like and what they experienced at the girls' current age. These accounts tell them more deeply than anything else that their moms can understand them and what they are going through. So often parents don't realize the power their stories hold for their children.

Relatives like grandparents and aunts and uncles also hold a special place for girls in transition because they are able to see and value these girls for who they are. They don't view them through a lens of grades, accomplishments, and college scholarships like parents often do. Relatives can stay more in the moment and be wonderful, non-judgmental sounding boards for adolescent girls. Spending an afternoon or a weekend at your grandparents' house sometimes is just the respite girls need to relax and regain their equilibrium. Girls need these home-away-from-homes, and people who love them unconditionally. Sometimes parents just can't be there fully for their children, so having surrogates to step in is crucial. This is the it-takes-a-village concept we talk about so often. And for our 'sleeping beauties' it certainly holds true.

3)   Close Friends

Having at least one friend you can trust fully and know they can count on through thick and thin is immensely valuable for adolescent girls. They need peers with whom they can relax, let their hair down, and be themselves. Girls long for friends with whom they don't have to worry about looking good or being popular. This kind of friend accepts them for exactly who they are, without judgments or conditions. I was talking with 17-year-old Becca at a retreat recently, and asked her what she had done last weekend. The hardworking A/B student who was picked to be captain of the varsity lacrosse team as a junior and who is one of our CITs, (Counselors in Training), for summer camp, surprised me with her reply. *"I had my three best friends over Saturday night and we played old board games like Candy Land and Chutes and Ladders all night long. I haven't laughed so hard in a long time!"* It made my heart warm to hear that she could be a kid and play that way, but even more so that she had created friendships with girls who enjoyed having that kind of fun. That group of friends didn't care what other people thought; they were doing their thing and having a blast. I wish all girls had a friend or group of friends like Becca.

When girls feel overwhelmed by all the external pressures pounding them, it's nice to be able to escape and relax with like-minded friends who 'get you'. Ken Robinson, author of *The Element*, calls this finding your tribe. Robinson describes your tribe as people who see the world the way you do, who understand you and see your talents, and who can inspire and push you to be your best. When you are with your tribe, you feel most like yourself, most comfortable with yourself, and you act like your best self. Robinson says there are three main dynamics that a tribe provides: affirmation, inspiration, and the alchemy of synergy. Your tribe lets you know you are not alone, and that even though other people-- sometimes your parents included--don't understand you, your tribe will. Your tribe can inspire you to raise your bar of expectations and invest the 10,000 hours of practice author Malcolm Gladwell found that all the masters have put in (in his book *The Outliers*). The synergy the tribe provides allows for creative collaborations and dynamic teams that are often at the root of big philosophical movements: think Silicon Valley in the 1970s and the Civil Rights movement.

I have met so many girls who lacked such a tribe. Some had a hard time fitting in with girls their own age because they were more mature or 'old souls,' or because they had unique interests. They remind me of the women biographied in the book *Smart Girls Gifted Women*. Many of these present day girls are gifted and creative actresses, writers, poets, artists and musicians. They love deep conversations and diverse people, and they abhor drama and gossip. I encourage them to seek out their tribe, a group of people who are like-minded or share their passions. The sense of acceptance and affirmation they receive from such a group is priceless. And inappropriate labels like 'low self-esteem' or 'depression' quickly melts away when they have connections like this; they are at their best when they are in their element.

4)   Variety of Friends

Many of the emotionally healthiest adolescent girls I meet have a variety of friends. These girls can sit at different lunch tables and feel comfortable. And they often have friends who are older and/or younger. So if there is too much drama going on in one group, they can easily slide over to another table or crowd for a while until things blow over. In addition, with every additional person a girl befriends, she will learn something novel about herself. There is great value out in the real world of adults in being able to relate to diverse people, and these girls develop that skill at a young age.

I hear many parents worrying when their daughters hang out with older girls, so I have to remind them that when we were growing up, we spent a lot of time playing in the neighborhood with kids of all ages. And we turned out okay, right? Will they sometimes hear things you might not want them to hear? Probably, but older friends also can become positive mentors who show them that they, too, can make it through the middle and high school minefields--intact and alive. Older siblings once played this role, but with family sizes getting smaller, that doesn't happen nearly as often.

Hanging out with older kids also can cause girls to toughen up, become more resilient and determined, accelerate their verbal and social skills, learn to compete and push themselves, and help them develop collaborative and leadership skills. One of my favorite aspects of running summer camps for 23 years is seeing young campers who return year after year grow into the counselor-in-training role, and then become camp counselors who are incredible examples for younger girls. I love watching high school girls grab a shy 8 year old and pull her out onto the dance floor. The younger camper's face lights up at having been noticed by such a 'cool' older girl, and it gives them the courage to let go and dance the night away. And the camp counselor receives as much from the encounter as the 8-year-old.

5) Sacred Space

This important factor is discussed in detail in a previous chapter, but I'd like to mention a few Sacred Space details.

Sacred Spaces are protected arenas where girls can relax from all the pressures described in this book. They can feel free to be themselves without having to worry about what others think. They can let the little kid in them come out to play, and they can engage in activities that interest them without fear of being judged. In order for girls to enjoy these spaces, parents need to make them a priority. I talk to parents all the time who want their girls to come to one of my programs, but they complain that their daughters are too busy. They allow them to play on three soccer teams, but don't prioritize time for social-emotional learning. It's not just about my programs; it's the damaging pattern of scheduling girls so tightly that there is no down time and little time for them to pursue their other passions and interests. And these other interests often are more child-driven as opposed to parent-driven; the girls themselves initiate them and pursue them at their pace. Girls become really out of balance, and what gets left out are things like sacred space activities. These activities may not show up on their college resumes, so they get short shrift. But I hope parents understand the value once they read Chapter 10.

6)   Engaged in Their Passions

"There is a fine difference of perspective between getting involved and being committed. In ham and eggs, the chicken is involved but the pig is committed." John-Allen Price

Girls who have found an interest and are actively engaged in it are better able to manage their adolescent touchpoint than girls without such an interest. Pouring their heart and soul into something they love to do provides them with an incredible sense of fulfillment and value. This is especially true if they are the one who chose the interest versus being forced by their parents into it. As author Daniel Pink describes in his book, *Drive*, *"Control leads to compliance, or resistance. Autonomy leads to engagement. And only engagement leads to mastery."* It's only when you are fully engaged in an endeavor of your choosing that you are willing to put in the hours and discipline to become successful at it. It's also the prescription for getting girls to experience 'Flow.'

Flow means the experience of being so engrossed in something that your sense of time, place and self go away. You lose yourself, and performing the activity becomes its own reward. The book, *Flow: the Psychology of Optimal Experience*, by Mihaly Csikszentmihalyi, offers a much deeper understanding of this concept. Remember the eminent women I described at the beginning of this chapter? They were in flow, starting in childhood: Maya Angelou wrote poems and stories, Beverly Sills sang, and Georgia O'Keefe drew. It's through initiating, creating, action, and overcoming obstacles that self-esteem is acquired. I've met many, many girls and women who told me it was passions like creative writing, reading history, or raising money for a worthwhile cause that got them through the sometimes dark days of adolescence.

Sleeping Beauties, Awakened Women

Their friends might have betrayed them, their parents may have been distracted or absent, but their passion was always there for them. It was, for some girls, the only light they had in a world that felt dark. These activities sometimes became their career and life purpose, and sometimes they became a hobby during adulthood. No matter; what these endeavors did for them as adolescents is what is important.

When I talked about the 'sleeping' metaphor at the start of this book, I included in this the pursuit of activities that excite you. Part of the inward Heroine's Journey is discovering and embracing your strengths, talents and gifts. Girls who are focused on their interests learn valuable lessons and skills in self-discipline, self-motivation, self-efficacy, determination and courage. These endeavors offer the opportunity to take risks, learn from mistakes, overcome obstacles and challenges, and stretch them out of their comfort zones.

It was no accident that Dorothy, in the Wizard of Oz, attracted these particular friends on the yellow brick road. The Scarecrow represented her common sense, intuition and intelligence. The Tin Man represented her compassion and service orientation. And the Cowardly Lion represented her courage and ability to face and embrace her deepest fears. These weren't external qualities she had to buy or acquire. As the Wizard and Glinda the Good Witch explain to Dorothy at the end of the story, she had these abilities all along. But she needed to embrace them on her own before they could rise to the surface. That's what I mean when I say girls need to work on their inner resumes. And it's also why the athletes I've worked with who could no longer do their sport become so lost (see Chapter 8). They had been out-of-balance, with no time for getting to know themselves beyond their sport. Based on their life experiences, they were 'a soccer player' or 'a gymnast,' and that's it. They hadn't been given the time to develop any other interests, passions or callings.

Some parents complain to me that their adolescent daughters don't have a passion. They have a history of pursuing something for a while, becoming bored with them, and discarding it. What parents need to realize is that this is how some girls find 'their thing': by going through the buffet line of interests and opportunities and trying them one at a time until one clicks. They learn something about themselves with each one, so it's never a waste of time. They are right on schedule--their personal schedule.

So whether it is acting, singing, dancing, sports, science experiments, service projects, saving whales, rescuing stray dogs and cats, or reading stories, value passion where you find it. Support their pursuits even if they are not yours, or even if you judge the interest as not having much worth. And please don't discourage them from pursuing the 'arts' because 'you can't make a living doing it.' We discourage the creativity out of way too many children that way.

At a parenting workshop, we were discussing this concept of "value passion where you find it." One mom began complaining about her 16-year-old daughter. *"My daughter Angie is so lazy and unmotivated. Nothing motivates her except watching TV. She's so lazy, that if someone ever invents a remote control that can operate by blinking your eyes, she'll be first in line to buy it!"* "What is she into?" I asked. *"Nothing, she's a blob,"* she answered. *"I don't buy it,"* I responded. *"What does she enjoy doing?"* One of Brenda's friends interjected. *"Angie loves children. She's like the Pied Piper of our neighborhood. She's my kids' favorite babysitter."* At this, Brenda jumped back in. *"Yeah, and she told me she might want to be a preschool teacher, but I told her there's no money in that. She needs to get a business degree."* Yikes! Here's a mom who is missing the boat because she's not valuing her daughter's passion, working with children. And we find out why a moment later. *"I grew up in a small, coal-mining town in Pennsylvania. When I was 13 years old, the mine closed, and the whole town just dried up. We were extremely poor, and I vowed I would get out of that town. I got a college scholarship, worked my butt off, and got into law school. And I want to make sure my daughter gets a degree and a job so she can be independent and take care of herself and never have to go through what I did."* Wow! Now it makes sense. But it's unfair and unhealthy for her to make her story her daughter's story. Angie is not her!

7)   Service/Community Activities

"Help thy brother's boat across and lo! thine own has reached the shore." Hindu Proverb

It's easy for adolescent girls to get so caught up in the overwhelming dramas and stresses of their lives that they lose sight of 'the big picture,' i.e. what's really important. Our culture is driving them to become 'human doings' instead of human beings. Getting girls involved in community activities and organizations is a good antidote for this.

"We are most free to explore our identity in places outside of our normal life routines; places that are in some ways betwixt and between." Victor Turner, anthropologist

Out in the real world, working with people of all ages to impact the local, national or world community helps girls feel like they are part of something bigger than themselves. It encourages them to get out of themselves and into being of service to others. In doing this kind of work, girls will be valued for what they contribute, not for how they look or how popular they are. Peers and adults they work with will see them in a different light from the one they are judged by at school.

That's also why service projects and trips are so valuable. The reason for being together has nothing to do with who is cool or with attracting and competing for guys. The intention is to be helpful and kind, and to give of themselves. These kinds of groups and experiences have been the saving grace for many girls who struggled to fit in at school. On service trips, everyone is included and valuable. Gifts and talents that don't get much notice in the hallways at school are appreciated and valued. You may not be a good athlete or student, but everybody can be kind and loving and giving to others in some way.

8)   Non-Friend Related Competencies

As with the previous item, becoming involved in activities where you can shine or feel valuable and that don't involve your friends is helpful. It's good to get a break from friends sometimes. Girls need to know they can rely on themselves to be happy and fulfilled. This is what Cinderella story taught us. Girls need to know they are not their friends, just like they are not their gymnastics, soccer or any other activity they excel in.

My first year in college I performed in two plays and was a cheerleader for the basketball team. Both were new activities for me, a way to branch out and try out some new parts of myself. I became friends with people I never would have met otherwise. And I broadened my vision about who I was. That's what I want girls to experience. It means they might have to go against the grain. And the grain might be what's popular, what their friends think, or what their parents value.

"The nail that sticks up gets hammered down."

This old quote rings true, and the hammer is often teachers, schools, parents, siblings, friends, the media, religion and the culture. So it can be a big risk for girls to bust out and try activities or get involved in unpopular interests. But the girls who call up the courage to do so become empowered and confident. They truly are doing their thing, and that results in tremendous pride and fulfillment.

9) Spirituality

Some research shows that girls who know their values and consciously act consistently with them are happier and more grounded. I'm not talking about obediently going to a church or temple once a week because your parents make you. It's more about guiding girls to partake of their own spiritual journey. Girls need to understand concepts like integrity: doing the right thing not because you're getting rewarded for it or because it's a popular choice, but because internally you know it's the right thing to do.

I teach girls Laurence Kohlberg's stages of moral development, or in my words, the reason you would do the right thing. Here are these reasons or motivations, from lowest to highest.

(1) "I don't want to get in trouble." This level of motivation is based on fear, and is externally driven. If an authority figure is standing over you, you comply. If not, when the cat's away the mice will play. This is the reason why autocratic, authoritative teachers have to be present in their classroom at all times; otherwise the kids go crazy. They need external control because they never developed internal control. That's the adult's job.

(2) "I want a reward." Reward systems have become the bane of parents and teachers. We've created a generation of kids and young adults who constantly have their hands out, palms up, asking, "What will I get for it?" Whenever they are asked to do something, whether it is doing chores, completing homework or cleaning up the classroom, we've trained kids to need external motivators like rewards and praise. These kinds of rewards get in the way of a childs' own intrinsic motivations. Both of the above motivators make up our old-school carrot and stick approach to discipline. *Read Drive* by Daniel Pink, and *Punished by Rewards* by Alfie Kohn for decades' worth of good research explaining why this approach does not work.

(3) "I want to please you." This is doing something or making choices to gain someone's approval or to be liked. And girls are particularly vulnerable to getting stuck at this stage of moral development because of all the 'good girl' conditioning discussed in the chapter 3 on challenges. Girls are extremely sensitive to how other people are feeling, and they are also prehistorically wired for both connection and maintaining social harmony for survival. They've been taught to wait, avoid conflict and confrontation, smile, be nice to everyone, be obedient, make other people happy, and put other people's needs first (even to their own detriment). They are deathly afraid of hurting others' feelings and possibly losing friends. So it can be a challenge for girls to transcend this stage of moral development. In my retreats and camps, I help girls become aware of the costs to them when their primary motivation is to please others and be liked by everyone. This awareness can encourage them to do it differently.

(4) "I need to follow the rules!" This is a higher-level reason for doing the right thing, but it's still limiting. Sometimes rules aren't present, they're unclear, or they change. And strict rule-following doesn't allow much room for thinking outside the box or even thinking for yourself. I love to point out famous 'rule-breakers' like Rosa Parks, Eleanor Roosevelt, Mahatma Gandhi, and Martin Luther King Jr. All of them changed the world for the better because they did not follow the rules. All of the eminent women biographied in *Smart Girls Gifted Women* threw off the shackles society put on women of their era and refused to be held back by patriarchal constraints. They didn't care what other people or society thought about them; they forged ahead, marching to the beat of their own drum. And again, the world was far better for it.

(5) "I need to consider other people." This is higher yet in terms of reasons for doing the right thing and being in integrity. In our camps we call this Having Your Arrows Out. 'Arrows in' means

only thinking about yourself and what you want. 'Arrows out' means you also consider the needs of the whole community in your choices and decision-making. A quote by Atticus Finch in *To Kill a Mockingbird* fits well here. *"You never really understand a person until you consider things from his point of view, until you climb inside his skin and walk around in it."* Because girls are so sensitive to other people, they are good at being empathetic. At retreats, camps and in classrooms, I challenge them to start looking for examples of when their classmates exhibit arrows-out behaviors. When you are looking for these behaviors, you end up seeing more of them. And as the old saying goes, *"If you spot it, you got it!"*

(6) "I follow my own code of conduct." I'm going to refer again to one of my favorite literary characters, Atticus Finch, as someone who embodies this level of moral development. Level Six means you have developed your own personal code of behavior, and this code resides in your soul. You act from this code, oblivious to the behavior of other people, oblivious to whether your decisions are popular or sanctioned by your culture or religion, oblivious to whether you are pleasing other people. You act or make a choice because it is who you are, and you remain true to your code. Atticus Finch took on the case of defending a black man in the deep South of the 1930s when no other lawyer dared take the case. Why did he do it? Because it was the right thing to do. His decision wasn't based on fear or getting a reward. He did it because in his heart-of-hearts he knew it was the right thing to do. As part of their spiritual growth, I want girls to rise to the challenge of becoming level six moral thinkers and decision-makers. I want them making choices not because it's popular, not to fit in, not to be liked or please other people, not to blindly and obediently follow society's rules, but because in their heart and gut they know these decisions are right for them.

When they feel the friendship tensions and the mixed messages described in Chapter 3, I want them to go inward and find their truth, not outward. I want them to be more like salmon, swimming upstream and fighting through the unhealthy cultural messages and currents. I want them to become way more sensitive to their intuition, their gut sense, their inner voice. And I want them to develop the courage to act out of this place. Only then will they truly feel free.

When they are confronted with injustices at school, I want them to be leaders: by-players versus bystanders. I want them to have a moral framework anchored in kindness and to act each and every day out of that. Rachel Scott, the first student killed during the Columbine School shooting, was such a person. Read her story, as written by her father Darrell Scott, in two books: *Rachel's Team* and *Chain Reaction*. And keep showing your daughters stories that come out in the news periodically of courageous Level Six girls.

One example is the 14-year-old Pakistani girl Malala Yousa Fzai, wounded by a Taliban gunman for supporting education for girls in her country. Her bravery inspired the world. Another is Meghan Vogel, 17, an Ohio high school track star honored by the National Sportsmanship Awards in 2012 for an 'arrows out' action. She won the 1600-meter state title and an hour later competed in the 3200-meter race. She was exhausted and far back in the pack of runners when she saw another racer fall. And instinctively, she stopped. She draped the fallen girl's arm around her shoulder and guided her across the finish line, making sure the other girl finished before her. Vogel was surprised by all the media attention, because to her it was just the right thing to do. She told reporters, *"Sportsmanship is a much bigger deal than winning a race."* That is Level Six moral behavior! The kind of spirituality I think is protective for girls is the kind that encourages personal awareness and growth because it inspires girls be their best selves; authentic, loving, giving, and free.

10) Mentors

"People come into our lives for a reason, a season, or a lifetime."
Unknown Author

In most of the old fairy tales and myths, heroines experience the death of their mothers and absent or ineffectual fathers. In many of the tales, like Sleeping Beauty, Snow White and Rapunzel, there is a mean stepmother or witch who pushes them out of the comforts of home and into the real world. This starts their Heroine's Journey. But she needn't go on this journey alone. Our heroines need mentors for guidance along the way, people who can be mirrors for them. What do I mean by 'mirrors'?

These are people who see you for who you truly are, inside and out. A girl's first mirrors are her parents' eyes. If a young girl sees unconditional love and confidence there, she will feel confident to trust others, connect with others, and explore the world. If a young girl looks into her mother's eyes and sees fear and apprehension, she herself will begin to become anxious and insecure, because she interprets her mom's feelings as: *The world is unsafe, Be careful, and You need me to be there to protect you at all times.* This won't allow them to blossom into confident, assertive adolescents and women. They remain emotionally young and vulnerable. If a girl stays too attached and dependent on her mother, she may never branch out and create her own thoughts, feelings, or her own life. She will not undergo her evolution, her Heroine's Journey, because of fears or because she feels guilty for leaving her mother.

I've counseled many girls who have ended up taking on a caretaker role. For some, it was the death of a parent, a divorce, or a parent distracted by depression or addictions. These girls, like Cinderella, stepped in to fill the void, sacrificing their childhoods, their time with friends, their journey, and their happiness. These girls may have felt responsible for younger siblings or even a parent who emotionally or physically wasn't able to take on the parenting role. I find them incredibly mature for their age, self-sacrificing, and competent. But underneath these exterior layers, there often lies resentment, anger, bitterness, and unhappiness. They get tremendous value from being so needed, but they sense that they are missing out on being a kid. And they are. That's when a mentor can step in and help them sort out their feelings and needs. A mentor can help them become aware that their needs are important too, and that sometimes it's critical for them to put their needs first, not last.

When adolescence approaches, girls need advisors who are not their parents. In their eyes, mom has lost some of her 'magic.' Mentors, on the other hand, have the power, the keys, to unlock doors that lead to higher levels of consciousness and growth. Snow White's cruel stepmother actually becomes the force that pushes her out of her safe home and into the scary forest, which is symbolically the place where transformation occurs. Girls emerge from the forest more mature, self-aware and confident. These are the gifts she brings with her when she gets 'out of the woods.'

The mother-adolescent daughter dance is played out every day in our homes. They observe each other, criticize each other, admire and envy each other, imitate and repulse each other, all at the same time. Girls need enough space to undergo this touchpoint , and if moms hold on too tight, girls will create this space more aggressively. From the girl's side, she is experiencing a lot of fear and confusion about her new body and her sexuality, and about the dangers that lie ahead. If these feelings are not given a voice, she will often unconsciously take them out on her mom. Moms who take this personally will fight back and engage, and this creates the intense love-hate, push-pull so often experienced at this stage of development. This is where mentors can be so valuable. They don't become engaged in these power struggles like parents do. It is easier for them to remain detached, and thus safer for girls to talk to. They can see through an adolescent girl's acne, braces, awkwardness, and insecurities to find the queen within. Mentors can hold a vision of who the girl really is and what she can become at a time when the girl can't yet see it for herself. That's the mirroring girls need.

Snow White, like Eve in the Garden of Eden, bites into the poisoned apple and loses consciousness. Sleeping Beauty pricks her finger on the magic spinning wheel and does the same. They aren't ready to face their sexuality; as represented by the red apple and the blood. Snow White is encased in a glass coffin by the seven dwarfs, where all can see her, but she can't even see her own reflection yet. It's so hard for girls in middle and early high school to truly see themselves. In addition, our culture has depicted and conditioned them to see themselves as objects on display for men. And so they sleep.

It's often a mentor who shines the light of awareness on girls and awakens them. These guides can help a girl become aware of hidden aspects of her being and soul. They can help them see talents and gifts she's unaware of. They can nurture these gifts, give guidance and training, and direct girls about how to develop these talents. At this point in their lives, girls tend to take in this kind of coaching much more readily than from their parents. These confidants can be soccer coaches, art teachers, theater directors, vocal coaches, science teachers, camp counselors or therapists. They can look like bosses, grandparents, college-counselors, college professors, or your best friend's parents. These people fill a void at just the right time. As the old saying goes: *"The teacher appears when the student is ready."*

Cinderella has the memory of her dead mother, the birds and animals who befriend her, and the white dove perched on the Hazel tree at her mother's grave. Dorothy has Glinda, the good witch, the scarecrow, the tin man, the cowardly lion, and finally the Wizard of Oz himself.

Think back to your adolescent and young adult years and remember the mentors who guided you on your journey. For some fascinating stories, read *The Right Words at the Right Time* by Marlo Thomas. Most of us had this kind of guidance, and we wouldn't be where we are today without it. And mentors can be women or men-- it's less about gender and more about the needs of the girl fitting with the skill-set of the guide. I've received many letters over the years from my girl campers who tell me what a difference I made for them. But I also think that sometimes a circle of women elders is what girls need. This is similar to what adolescent boys obtain from male elders, to give them just the right male energy or magic needed at a certain point in their journey.

We do an exercise at our camps called 'the waterfall' in which all the females line up by groups; first the youngest campers, then the older campers, then the CIT's (counselors-in-training), then the older counselors. Starting with the youngest group, they share what they have learned from the group just above them. This might be being a good role model, being a good listener when they really needed to be heard, being a friend, being the older sister they always wanted etc. What they are describing is appreciation for the mentoring the older group has given to them. And in the case of our camps, it is a way for the elder counselors to be honored for their wisdom, the example they set, and for inspiring the younger girls. This process usually brings many tears of joy and appreciation.

Sleeping Beauties, Awakened Women

So mentors are there to value a girl for who she is, and to offer a larger vision for her at a time when she can't see it. Advisors like this hold the key to doors that contain girls' hidden talents, passions and desires. They offer understanding ears, guidance, and wisdom.

Mentors let girls know they are not alone, and that they will get through it, just as they themselves did. They come along at a time in the heroine's journey when girls need affirmation and inspiration. They help introduce her to the larger world, but only when she is ready. And that is magical.

CHAPTER 15

DADDY'S LITTLE GIRL

In Chapter 14 I discussed some of the more important factors that protect girls during these transformative years. In this chapter, I want to discuss some of the ways fathers can support their adolescent daughters.

It's important to remember that dads are not male mothers! We bring our own unique perspective and skills to parenting, ones that often get ignored or short shrift. And this, despite the studies that have shown again and again that having an involved father makes for a healthier daughter. I remember my mentor, Dr. T. Berry Brazelton, showing videos of moms and dads playing with 2- to 3-month-old infants. Moms would sit down quietly in front of the baby, gradually squeeze their legs and thighs, and make soft cooing sounds. The babies would reciprocate by smiling and cooing back, forming a beautiful back-and-forth dance of intimacy.

When a dad approached the infant, he immediately elicited what Dr. Brazelton called a 'pounce-look,' meaning the baby's eyes would widen, its heart and respiratory rates would accelerate, and its whole body would get keyed up. The infant was anticipating a different kind of interaction, even after just a few months of life. Dads would be louder, and they would poke at the baby, eliciting squeals of glee and joy. Which of course provoked Dad to poke some more, and the poking and laughter produced a different kind of dance. Moms waltzed, while dads rock and rolled!

Sleeping Beauties, Awakened Women

Research and experience has shown that playtime with dads is more physical, active, loud, and often more unpredictable. This kind of play elicits more creative and spontaneous interactions. Research has even shown that playtime with Dad was much more spontaneous and frequent when Mom was not around. Dad felt freer to parent when gatekeeper Mom wasn't there to calm things down.

I was sitting poolside last summer when a father and his probably 20-year-old daughter walked up. They both dived right into the water, and she immediately shrieked. Her dad asked what was wrong, and with a huge grin on her face, she laughed that her swimsuit bottoms had fallen down to her ankles. As they were both having a good laugh, the mom walked up and asked what had happened. I saw the girl shoot her dad a knowing look and then say, "Oh, nothing." I guess Mom wouldn't have approved. This kind of play helps girls stretch, take risks and push the envelope. Dads often are more likely to push the envelope as well, which gives their daughters permission to go outside the box.

In Louann Brizendine's book, *The Male Brain*, she cites research I found interesting about a study out of the University of Toronto that examined how moms and dads read nursery rhymes to their children.

Moms tended to sing the verses as they are written, whereas dads tended to change the verses each time, creating new and unpredictable rhymes. These kinds of interactions keep girls guessing and on their toes, making them more curious and open to learning. Dads also, in general, are liable to be more directive than moms. They are more matter-of-fact with their discipline and don't feel the need to explain their instructions. This too, when not an extreme, has value. Moms are predisposed to be a little more in-tune with their children's thoughts and emotions, probably because they spend more time with them and due to their female brain wiring. And as Louann Brizendine points out, a father's approach provides more of what kids will experience someday out in the real world of college and employment, where people won't be able or willing to read their minds and anticipate their every whim and need.

Dads are more apt to be comfortable with rough-and-tumble play. And studies have shown that kids whose dads play this way with them develop more self-assurance as they grow into their teen years. Dads also can coach daughters through this kind of play to be assertive, competitive, and appropriately aggressive. They also make girls feel more comfortable with rougher, more physical play, which will serve them in competitive sports. And this type of play is a healthy way for dads to be affectionate and stay close as their daughter's bodies change during puberty. Fathers also tend to be better at staying more emotionally detached when their daughters are revving up emotionally. They are less likely to take those feelings or disrespect as personally as moms, so they don't add to it.

If a girl comes home with reports of being bullied at school, it's imperative for both parents to listen empathetically. But then it becomes equally important to switch into problem-solving mode, and dads are good at this. Instead of rescuing your daughter, it's important to ask questions like: *So what will you do?* Dads do well at encouraging independent thinking and problem-solving skills. And researchers have found that girls who are aided by fathers to become more independent end up performing better as adults in the workplace.

Another way dads can play a role is in instructing their daughters to repress their emotions. Sometimes it's just not appropriate to cry or express feelings. And girls need to learn how to shut them off until a more appropriate time lends itself to being emotional.

In her book *The Male Brain*, Dr. Louann Brizendine describes how when a man's emotions are triggered, the emotional center in his brain activates just like for women, but some differences occur. These centers in males are smaller, and instead of the energy being channeled to their verbal circuits and pre-frontal cortex, like in the female brain, it gets channeled to the temporal parietal junction (TPJ). This part likes to analyze problems and search for solutions. That is why women complain that when they are upset and want to be heard and understood, all their husbands or boyfriends want to do is go right to their Mr. Fix-It role.

Historically speaking, this circuiting prevents men's thinking from being distracted by other people's emotions, strengthening their ability to find solutions analytically. If they were being attacked by wild animals or warring neighbors, they needed to be focused, in the moment, and not have judgment clouded by emotions. There are times when girls need that same focus and clear thinking, like when taking tests, playing in competitive sports, and performing at a recital. They can't, in those moments, become overwhelmed with feelings about an ongoing friend drama or girlfriend issue; thus, the need to learn to repress them. Many of the skills discussed in my chapter about redirecting stinking thinking apply here. So doing reality checks, repeating a calming mantra, breath work, and keeping in the present moment all can assist girls in controlling their feelings in those moments. This is one time when it is appropriate to distract yourself with positive, happy thoughts. Performing a quick visualization that focuses on happy memories can help. Talking to a friend, laughing, smiling or joking around works too.

As I described in Chapter 11, I want girls to do a much better job of expressing their emotions in healthy ways. But there are times when it's not appropriate, and because of Dad's brain wiring and abilities, he can be a big help in this area. Dads also tease their children much more than moms. This kind of bantering allows girls to develop a kind of internal BS monitor, and to be able to look below the surface of what other people say to them. I also find that it 'toughens girls up.' It's healthy for them to be a little sassy with their dads and to get away with it as part of their back-and-forth teasing. They learn not to take words and taunts so personally, and to let it roll off them much more easily. Girls learn to be more assertive, to shoot from the hip, and be bolder.

What is not healthy is when that is the only way a dad connects with his daughter. She also needs times when he can be more serious and vulnerable with her.

> *"Those who travel unworn paths find the rarest flowers."*
> Hindu Proverb

I have written articles and blogs on the need boys have for adventure in their lives. And girls need opportunities to experience and create their own exploits as well. Dads bring this sense of spontaneity and adventure to their children, inspiring and encouraging them to get out there and stretch and make something happen. Studies also have shown that girls who develop a sense of humor from joking with their dads end up becoming more independent, confident, and happier. So, these are some special gifts that fathers bring to their daughters.

Here are a few more ways dads can support girls during their adolescence:

1. Be a good listener.

Every father I work with wants his daughter to feel safe to talk with him about important issues. That is the No. 1 reason they bring their middle school- aged daughters to the father-daughter retreats my wife and I have been facilitating the past eight years. That's why it's incumbent on all dads to learn the mirroring skills I discussed in Chapter 6. If dads can stay composed, especially when their daughters are climbing up their emotional ladders, they will have a calming effect on their girls. And it's vital that dads don't switch right to the 'fix-the-problem' part of their brains when their daughters (or wives) come to them with stories and problems. Girls interpret dads who quickly offer solutions as not listening, not understanding them, and not caring. They complain to me all the time that: *My dad just doesn't get me!* And if dads aren't mirroring, they probably don't really understand.

Here's a quick review, or cheat sheet, for how to mirror someone when they are sharing with you: *So what I heard you say is ..., did I get that right?* This involves repeating back in your own words what you heard them say; it's paraphrasing. And it's done in the spirit of being truly curious about how your daughter sees the issue. It requires you to put their own opinions and facts aside for a moment, and to get into their shoes and see the issue from her perspective. That is when girls feel understood. You keep reflecting back until they have communicated all they need to share. If you mirror and they respond that you heard them right, ask for more information by saying: *Tell me more about that.* If you get a brain cramp and drift off and miss the point, ask them to repeat it until you hear it correctly. At this point, girls feel calmer, and they feel heard and understood. Their energy has been dissipated. Now is the point where you can guide them in problem solving. *So it sounds like you're having a tough time with your best friend Amy. What could you do about that?* Or you could ask her what she's already tried, and if it didn't help, why does she think it didn't? You can coach your daughter to get into the other person's shoes and see it from their perspective. Once she comes up with some new ideas, encourage her to try them out and report back to you about what happens.

In my Imago couples therapy training with Dr. Harville Hendrix, I learned an additional piece to this mirroring process. Once your daughter feels heard, you can add some validation and empathy such as, *it makes sense to me why you are feeling this way because... and I imagine it might make you feel....* You are showing her that her feelings are valid. But you aren't necessarily agreeing with her. What you are saying, in essence, is, *If I were in your shoes, and my best friend betrayed my trust, I might feel sad and hurt as well.*

And finally, this is the time when sharing a story from your past can be magical. Relate an example about something similar that happened to you around their age, and how you felt and reacted. Nothing lets a girl know you really understand her like an empathetic story of your own. Remember that the details of your narratives don't have to be the same. What connects you empathetically are the similar feelings you both felt. You are saying: *I know how you feel because I have felt that way before; I know you!*

Let me finish this section by giving you a list of reasons why girls tell me they don't feel safe to share their deepest feelings or their friendship issues with their dads.

(a) *"My dad hasn't been a good listener. He's been distracted, and not around much or interested in my life."* Or, *"All he does is cut me off and give me advice. He never really listens."*

(b) *"I don't want to disappoint him."* Girls may feel guilty or ashamed of their behaviors and not want their dads to negatively judge them.

(c) *"I feel like a failure."* If a girl has been bullied, excluded, is not popular, or feels like she is failing socially, she's more likely to put on a happy, 'good girl' face because she's embarrassed and ashamed of herself.

(d) *"I'm afraid he'll take my friends' side."* Girls don't want to be judged as being wrong or handling situations badly. It's easier to hide what's going on versus risk their dads being angry or critical.

(e) *"I don't want my dad judging my friends or thinking bad about them when I'm in the middle of some relationship dramas."* Girls want to heal relationships, not end them. They get tired of dads flippantly advising them to 'just ignore her,' or 'find some other friends.'

(f) *"My dad could never understand what I'm feeling or going through because he never went through something like this."* If I had a dollar for every time I've heard girls say this I'd be a very wealthy man. This occurs because dads haven't told their daughters accounts about themselves growing up as I described earlier. This is easy to remedy.

(g) *"I don't know what I'm feeling, so it's hard to talk about."* As I discussed in Chapters 5 and 11, girls haven't learned how to identify and express their emotions in healthy ways. Their confusion leads them to stay quiet about what's going on inside.

(h) Judgments: Mariah, 16, related this story about her dad to me. *"One night at the dinner table I told my parents that a girl in my class was pregnant and my dad immediately went off. He said it didn't surprise him; wasn't she considered kind of a slut because she'd had so many sketchy boyfriends? I couldn't believe he said that! I decided then and there that I could never talk to him about boys or sex. He is so close-minded and judgmental. He doesn't get it."* What Mariah's dad doesn't get is that his judgments have closed the door on his daughter's openness and honesty with him. His critical attitude has made it unsafe for Mariah to trust him with her deepest thoughts, feelings and questions.

Parents who are judgmental of their daughters or others don't create safety in their relationship. It's just that simple. Girls are feeling self-conscious and insecure at these ages, and they need parents who will love and accept them no matter what. Judgments interfere with that.

2.   Focus on their non-physical qualities.

Dads can be invaluable here in balancing out the toxic cultural messages that constantly tell girls, "*You are your body, What's most important is how you look*, and *You need to focus on being pretty and hot."* At my father-daughter retreats, I help dads become more aware of all the ways our culture and even well meaning parents and relatives keep this look-ism phenomenon going. I tell dads to notice what people say when they walk into a group with a daughter and son in tow. People immediately comment on how pretty or cute the girl is, or they complement her on her clothes, shoes, hairstyle, or accessories. Boys, on the other hand, primarily receive comments about how big they are, how strong they are getting, or how much they've grown. It's subtle, but sensitized dads will notice this conditioning everywhere and from a variety of people.

So it's crucial for dads to value and recognize other things, like their daughter's character, values, talents, and strengths. Dads can make a conscious effort to acknowledge qualities about who their daughter is versus what she's accomplished. Let her know you love her persistence, focus, dedication, honesty, sense of justice and fairness, her kindness and compassion, and her integrity. Remind girls of challenges and obstacles they have overcome, goals they have met, and intentions they have kept. Notice instances when they stood up for themselves or a friend, spoke their truth, took a risk, learned from a mistake, apologized when they were wrong, and showed courage in overcoming fears.

Girls are so much more than their bodies and their appearance. What dads focus on can allow girls to appreciate and embrace those aspects of themselves as well. Be sure, again, not to pay too much attention to achievements and ribbons. So many girls complain to me that the only connection they have with their dads is through their sports. And the time they spend together often is mostly about coaching them and critiquing performance.

Andrea, 12, was an intense and focused girl who was a top-level competitive swimmer. She practiced Monday through Friday from 3:30 to 6:30 p.m., Saturday mornings, and some mornings before school. And that didn't include all the meets and out-of-state travel for competitions. I was having dinner at her home one evening and asked Andrea what she liked about swimming. She came alive as she responded. *"I don't know. I think the best thing is the meets. I love the moment right before I perform, when all eyes are on me, and I get this kinda' rush feeling; it's hard to describe. I just love to perform in front of big groups!"* By this time, her face was lit up with the passion she felt from competing and performing. Then her dad cut in with this comment. *"Hey honey, go show Tim all your hardware."* Andrea lost some of her glow, and gave her dad a shrug as if to say: *Do I have to?* Her dad repeated his request. *"Take Tim up to your room and show him your hardware."* Andrea led me to her bedroom, and I discovered that 'hardware' meant all her ribbons and medals-- and she had a ton. All four walls and two bookcases were filled with blue ribbons and first-place trophies. But there was no more joy in Andrea's face, only resignation.

Her dad was missing the point. Medals and trophies didn't motivate her; it was the thrill of the competition and performance that drove her to practice and persist.

Remember to acknowledge your daughters as human beings instead of human 'doings.' Admire her courage, resilience, determination, stamina, strategies, athleticism, teamwork, leadership, sportsmanship, focus, and drive. Teach her through what you focus on that the process is what is most important, not the result; the journey versus the destination.

This does not mean that dads should not look for opportunities to commend their daughters. Girls need to know that their dads are proud of them, and that they believe in them. Fathers should tell their daughters that they will love and support them no matter what. It is invaluable for a girl to know that her dad believes that she has what it takes to get what she wants and to excel at whatever she puts her mind to.

So these are some of the distinctive ways fathers can support their daughters during this touchpoint. Of course, it is also beneficial for mothers to support girls with some of these means, especially by listening and acknowledging their qualities. The next chapter will take a look at unique ways moms can support their girls, and again there will be some crossover with my advice for dads.

But both parents, because of the different energy and qualities each brings to the table, have unique gifts to bequeath daughters.

CHAPTER 16

THE MOTHER-DAUGHTER DANCE

Let's spend a little time now looking at the unique role of moms in their daughters' transformative years. As mentioned earlier, many of the ideas in this chapter and the last one about the role of dads aren't really exclusive to one parent. But moms and dads are different, and they bring different and valuable energy and experiences to girls.

Here are some ideas about Mom's role during this touchpoint.

1.   Listening. The mirroring skills I've discussed in past chapters go for moms too, but with a few distinctive nuances. I've found that moms often have a harder time staying disengaged from their daughter's emotions. What girls bring to this stage is a roller coaster ride of emotions. They're up one minute, down the next. And they often don't even know why. I heard a great expression many years ago that goes like this: *Don't leap into your child's social pool and drown with them!* I may have heard it at a lecture given by author Michael Thompson. And moms everywhere need to heed that advice. When girls come home with stories about relationship aggression and girl dramas, listen empathetically, but stay detached. Don't bring your emotions into it. It's so imperative not to ride the roller coaster of emotions your daughter is on. When hers go up, yours need to go down. A switch in your head needs to turn on that reminds you: *Just relax, breathe, stay calm. She's starting to ramp up, so I need to ramp down.* A parent's calm presence really can help calm girls down. The

opposite is also true. If Mom starts getting upset, it triggers her daughter and here they go, spiraling out of control.

One reason moms get plugged into their daughters' social concerns is that they, themselves, haven't learned to handle friendship issues effectively. The pressures of being a 'good girl' have been around for a long time, and many moms have the same fears of conflict their daughters have. Most grade school teachers are women, and I believe that is one reason girls aren't being taught good conflict resolution skills in schools. Many female teachers never learned them, and it's hard to teach what you don't know and don't practice in your own life. Countless teachers I've encountered over the years are reluctant to sit in on the circle talks I do with girls. Part of it is the lack of training in practical class management skills by education programs. And there is also the lack of social-emotional learning experienced by female teachers themselves.

Another big reason moms can find it hard to stay detached when their daughters are upset involves the concept of Ghosts in the Nursery. For a more detailed account of how 'ghosts' can affect your parenting, read the chapter on it in my book, *Food Fights and Bedtime Battles*. But for now, let's see how it applies to moms and daughters.

Selma Fraiberg, an eminent psychiatrist, first talked about ghosts in the nursery in her thesis paper around 60 years ago. She was referring to moms who were having problems in their parenting as a result of old baggage they brought from their childhoods. Unresolved feelings and decisions from negative experiences in their past tended to resurface and 'haunt' their parenting, creating mischief; thus, the ghosts. Let me share an example from my counseling practice.

Brittany, 16, and her mom, Sandy, came in to see me because of intense power struggles and fights between them over the past year.

Brittany, a headstrong, intense girl, had always been a challenge for Sandy. But things intensified when Brittany started dating a guy two years older. Sandy had become stricter and more micromanaging of Brittany's social life, which, as expected, created more push-back from Brittany. When Brittany came home from a date half an hour late one Saturday night, Sandy grounded her for a month and took her phone away. Brittany responded by sneaking out the following Saturday night to meet her boyfriend. Mom found out, exploded, and they made the appointment to see me. I asked Sandy what her concerns were about Brittany dating this boy, and at first she gave me the standard litany of he's too old for her, and she wasn't sure if Brittany had good enough boundaries with boys. Brittany had no relationship with her dad, who had left the family when she was an infant. Mom worried about the effect of that on Brittany's need for a boyfriend. I kept pushing her to deeper layers of concern, until finally we hit home.

"I got pregnant with Brittany when I was 15 years old, and had her two weeks after my 16th birthday," Sandy said. *"I struggled to finish high school, ended up getting a GED, and now I have a hard time finding jobs that pay well. I don't want her getting pregnant and having to go through what I did. I want her to have a better life."*

I could see, hear, and feel the emotion in Sandy's voice as she spoke those last lines. She was scared. Brittany's dating had brought up a slew of old feelings about her teenage pregnancy and the resultant effects on her life. That's why she had a hard time keeping calm and detached with her parenting. That's why she had become too involved and micromanaging around Brittany's dating.

So anytime I see parents with problems remaining detached or reasonable in their parenting, my antenna goes up, looking for ghosts.

Let me share a few common ghosts that can affect the mother-daughter relationship.

(a) Friendship issues: If a mom had issues with relationship aggression or being excluded as a kid, you can bet she will be a tiger ready to defend her cubs. When a girl arrives home upset because someone teased or excluded her, these moms snap to attention and put on the full-court press. They get upset, take it personally and have a hard time not getting overly involved in the situation. These are the moms who will immediately call the 'mean girls' parents and demand action. They also may phone the teacher and demand action be taken immediately to punish the offending friend. And all of this before she does what I've advocated already in this book: listen, empathize, problem solve, and throw your children back out there to try to work it out themselves.

These are mothers who also can become guilty of 'mining for pain,' as I discussed earlier. Even if their daughter works things out with her friend the next day, Mom still harbors ill feelings toward the friend and may try to keep her daughter from playing with her.

(b) Shy girls: If a mom was shy growing up, and suffered because of it, she's more likely to over-parent if she ends up with a reserved daughter. I've seen moms with this ghost pushing their timid daughters too much, trying to make them more outgoing so they don't have to experience what they did. Power struggles and hurt feelings ensue.

(c) Weight: Moms who had issues with being overweight growing up often end up too invested in their daughter's eating habits. They care too much, restrict too much, and over-worry. This ghost can create intense power struggles around food, always a recipe for disaster during the teen years. Moms with a history of eating disorders, either their own or in a parent or sibling, also can become plugged into their daughter's nutrition, weight, and body issues.

(d) Absent parent: If a mom grew up with parents who were absent or neglectful, she often felt sad, hurt, alone, unimportant and unloved. If these feelings aren't expressed and resolved, they can become ghosts later on. Moms who are over-protective and over-involved in their daughters' lives often have this ghost. As kids, they told themselves, *When I have kids I will be there for them!* And boy, are they ever. They have a hard time staying out of their daughters' business, especially friendships. Girls feel smothered and angry, and struggles result.

So you get the picture. If you have problems staying detached from your daughter's life, issues, or emotions, you may indeed have a ghost in the nursery haunting your parenting. These feelings from the past are normal, they just need to be handled and made conscious. It's when they are subconscious that they can cause mischief. In order to be a good listener, and to do a good job of mirroring, you have to be able to get out of your own position and into your child's shoes, to see things through her eyes. Any ghosts in the nursery need to be exorcised in order to pull this off.

Another impediment to being the safe, non-judgmental listener all girls need and deserve is when a daughter is 'just like me.' If a mom sees herself in her daughter's qualities or behaviors, it has the potential to cause problems. Let me explain. An exercise that works well here is having the mom picture that daughter and complete the sentence: *What I see in my daughter that I see in myself is...*

As I wrote about previously, people who get under our skin are usually mirrors for us; they show us something about ourselves. There's an unconscious reason a certain daughter gets to us more than our other children. Sometimes moms see a trait they also see and judge negatively in themselves.

"What I see in my daughter Kim that I judge and try to change all the time is how bossy she is with her friends," Carol said. *"She always has to have things her way. How does that fit for me? Well, I know I have a problem being too controlling. I wish I could let go more and be more flexible. I think I've pushed some friends away over the years because of it, and I don't want that for Kim."* Instead of Carol being more aware of and working on her own issues with control, it's been easier to criticize it and try to change it in Kim. Kim, in essence, is Carol's mirror for this issue.

At other times, the mirror can be about Mom wishing she were more like her daughter. *"I get on my daughter Christy all the time because she seems too selfish,"* Elizabeth told me. *"She has no problem asking for what she wants, and I get afraid she's becoming too entitled. There's a part of me that wishes I was more like her. I grew up being told to stay quiet, and not ask for things unless they're offered. A 'good girl' shouldn't speak up for herself like that. I really admire how assertive Christy is."* Elizabeth's criticism of Christy is really reflecting her self criticism that she's not assertive enough. But, again, it's easier to point the finger outward than it is to take a good, hard look at ourselves and take responsibility for changes we need to make.

When a mom is willing to face her own demons and make the changes for herself, her judgments about her daughter fade away. It wasn't really about them; their daughter was just mirroring an aspect of themselves that needed some attention. In this way, your daughter can be your greatest teacher.

Finally, in order to be a good listener, moms need to remember not to parent out of fear. Looking at a present behavior of your daughter's and then imagining the worst-case scenario outcome of the behavior is a prescription for disaster. And I see moms do this a lot. A teenage girl's messy bedroom means she'll be a disorganized mother someday. Being quiet or shy in first grade means she'll be a follower as a teen and vulnerable to peer pressures about drugs, alcohol and sex. Being a 'tom-boy' in fourth grade means she may become a lesbian. Preferring to hang out with guys in middle school instead of girls means she may become 'easy' and promiscuous.

Making those mental leaps causes extreme worrying and ruminating, and as a result moms parent out of fear versus being in the moment and taking every situation as it presents itself. Scared parents are often overprotective, over-controlling, too restrictive, and too micromanaging--all of which can damage their relationship with their daughter.

2.   Body Image:. Moms also have a special role to play here with girls. As puberty approaches, girls oftentimes feel more comfortable talking to their moms about the changes they are undergoing with their bodies. So moms need to provide the information I discussed in chapter 4 about the female brain, hormones, and the menstrual cycle. It's important to reassure girls about the normal changes in the shape of their bodies and their weight. If their point of reference is the models in magazine ads, girls will end up miserable and feeling fat and less-than. Discuss what beauty means, and who defines it.

I wrote an article recently in *Town and Style Saint Louis* magazine about the sexualized and provocative commercials shown during the Super Bowl. A mom wrote me a kind and thoughtful response.

"I was thrilled to read Dr. Jordan's article about the Super Bowl commercials. I'm not that old, but I've shuddered at these ads. Being thin and drinking is not sexy, nor what women strive to be. We want to be pursued and cared for, but wearing miniskirts and being sultry

doesn't beget this. Why isn't a woman who listens, loves and laughs touted as glamorous? Thin, sexy and drinking is not the epitome."

As I mentioned in the chapter about dad roles, moms too need to value and acknowledge who their daughter is way more than how she looks. Over-focusing on their weight, figure, hair, and clothes does girls a disservice.

There is good research showing the value of being with your daughter while she is watching television and movies. *Huffington Post Parents* published an article on October 17, 2012 about "6-year old girls wanting to be sexy." Sixty-eight percent of 6- to 9-year-old girls chose a sexy doll dressed in tight, revealing clothes over a doll dressed in a trendy but covered-up loose outfit. And 77 percent of these girls said the sexy doll was more popular. But moms who reported watching TV and movies with their daughters and using those experiences as teaching moments about good behaviors and unrealistic scenarios were much less likely to have girls who said they looked like or preferred the sexy doll. There is great power when moms guide girls through media images. Their instruction can act as protection from the sexualization and objectification of girls so rampant in our culture.

By the way, in the study, moms who reported their own self-objectifying behaviors (like worrying about their appearance and clothes many times throughout the day) had daughters who were more likely to say the sexy doll was popular.

When I facilitate mother-daughter retreats, I'll ask the moms, in front of their daughters, how many of them talk negatively about their bodies. You know, negative comments about wrinkles, cellulite, sagging breasts, putting on weight, and aging. Out of a group of 25 moms, I typically get about five hands raised. When I then ask the girls how many of *them* have heard their moms talk this way, nearly all, if not all, the girls raise their hands. When their moms try to argue the point, the girls quickly rattle off their mom's negative mantras, and the moms get quiet.

Oftentimes, moms aren't aware of the little negative comments they make about their appearance that daughters pick up on and register within. So we strongly encourage them to become super-aware of this, and to make more positive observations. Their example in this area is critical in how girls come to look at and judge themselves. Modeling contentment with your body and accepting the normal changes incurred through pregnancies and aging will create a template for how girls can embrace and accept the changes occurring in their bodies during adolescence and puberty.

3. "You can have it all!" I believe moms can also play a unique role in making sense of the mixed messages discussed in chapter 3. Balance to me is a key component to a healthy daughter and a happy life. It's true that women today have many more opportunities to work in any field they choose. They can "be whatever you want to be." And the more archetypal male energy components of ambition, competition, and aggression that girls are internalizing and acting upon have broken a lot of those glass ceilings.

What may have been lost is how to find the right balance between career and personal life, between CEO and motherhood, between success at work and a successful marriage. I'll discuss this more in a later chapter, but mom's role here might be to help keep girls' lives balanced right from the start. Keep away from the perfectionism-in-all-places mentality gripping our culture. Say no to too many activities, too-intense coaches, and schools too focused on getting every girl into an Ivy League college. Don't allow your daughters to play the same sport 12 months of the year. Make sure she has enough down time to play, relax, and spend time with her family.

Sleeping Beauties, Awakened Women

In the 1950s, we talked about keeping up with the Joneses, which meant having the need to compete with your neighbors in acquiring the latest new appliances or automobiles. But today, everyone has flat-screen TVs, three-figure sneakers, and cell phones. Our present-day mantra is, 'keeping up with the Joneses children. This means if your daughter's friend is going to three soccer camps this summer, you'd better get on the stick, otherwise your daughter is going to fall behind!

And that, to me, is the biggest fear driving this phenomenon of over-scheduling kids today: our fear that our kids are going to fall behind the other kids and not keep up. Getting behind for a 7-year-old girl might mean later not being able to make your high school sports team or get a scholarship to an elite university. Remind yourself that these are just fears and not reality.

So moms, put up your dukes and go to battle to fight these temptations to over-push your daughters. Keep everything in balance, and do what's right for your daughter and your family. Resist the urge to give your kids a leg-up or push them too hard in order to 'give them an edge.'

As my grandmother used to say, *"Everything in moderation!"*

CHAPTER 17

A BAKER'S DOZEN WAYS TO SUPPORT YOUR DAUGHTERS

There are countless ways both moms and dads support girls. Below are some valuable tools to help guide daughters through the adolescent touchpoint.

1. Handle conflicts. Provide plenty of opportunities at home for girls to resolve their conflicts peacefully and effectively. This could involve siblings, parents, or friends. Use the framework for conflict resolution I described in Chapter 6. Teach your kids the words to ask for what they want, to mirror each other, and to create win-win solutions. Let them know by your actions that they are responsible for solving their fights, not you. Instruct them how, and then step aside and let them work things out. In this way, you become an unbiased mediator, not the judge, juror and executioner. If girls can learn to voice their needs directly to another person and successfully work out problems, they will take this skill to school and friendships. And it won't be as scary and foreign to confront people and handle disagreements.

2. Problem solve. There are daily opportunities for you to allow your daughter to think for herself and solve her own problems. A teaching moment can derive from something as simple as misplaced soccer shoes:

Girl: *"Dad, I can't find my soccer shoes!"*

Dad: *"Well, how could you figure out where you left them?"*
Girl: *"I don't know."*
Dad: *"Well, think about it. I'm sure you can figure it out."*

This kind, but firm, approach puts the onus on girls to come up with their own solutions. And when they are successful, it brings a sense of confidence and competence. *"So, what will you do?"* is a terrific question to keep in your tool box. It's a more respectful way of saying, "So why is that my problem!" Eventually, girls learn to be more independent and responsible, and they involve their parents only in the bigger issues.

Start young. I hear stories from college professors about parents calling them on behalf of their adult children, complaining about grades and asking what classes they should sign up for! And parents tell me their 20-year-olds text them 10 times a day asking questions about things like where a classroom is located or what to do about parking fines. These parents are still solving their children's problems, and keeping them young, dependent and irresponsible.

3. Have a voice. Look for opportunities to ask your daughter's opinion about a variety of topics. Allow free-for-all discussions around the dinner table, where all opinions and perspectives are heard and welcomed. Coach girls to question everything, and not to be afraid to disagree or stir the pot. This will give a daughter the confidence to raise her hand at school and to put her thoughts out there with confidence and authority. Break down the constraints of being a quiet, obedient, 'good girl.' Let her know it's okay to ruffle some feathers and have a different opinion. Encourage her to read biographies of both women and men who spoke up for what was right, even if it went against the grain. The eminent women mentioned in Chapter 14 make a good starting point.

And let girls know that, even today, powerful women may get judged and criticized as being 'aggressive bitches.' Women are hard on each other in the workplace, as they struggle with the mixed messages of being all you can be--but not too much. Give girls feedback about times when they are being strong, powerful and assertive versus times when they become overly aggressive. They need to understand the difference. I use role playing to demonstrate it. Look for examples of both in the news, books, or movies.

4. They are in charge of their feelings. I discussed the concepts of tomato words and not giving power away in Chapter 12. My experience leads me to believe that dads have an easier time not taking things personally and not getting engaged in friendship drama, but moms can step up to the plate here too. If your daughter comes home from school with a story about being teased or called names, listen and mirror her until she feels heard and understood. At that point she will be calmer, less emotional and more open to thinking about the situation in a different way. Remind her that she always has a choice when someone calls her names. She can choose path A, where she allows this to make her feel sad and hurt, and think about it all day long. Or she can choose path B, where she coaches herself to keep her power and not let any words bother her. Play the push game from Chapter 12 with her, and role-play effective ways to deal with these situations. This type of guidance can mean the difference between creating a victim versus a powerful girl who doesn't care about what others think of her. That girl knows true freedom. Make girls aware of the language they use in describing situations. Help them catch themselves when they use victim language like: *"She made me feel..."*, and have them switch it to: *"Suzie did _____, and I allowed myself to feel _____"*. Our thoughts and words are powerful. Educate girls to be careful about how they talk about situations.

5. Opportunities to lead, initiate and create. My children loved being the leaders at our weekly family meetings. It gave them a tremendous sense of authority and independence. Kids who are given appropriate ways of having a voice don't need to engage adults in power struggles, because they already feel a sense of control. So don't do everything for your daughters. Have them do research about summer camps, buying a car, or family vacations. Do not take responsibility for their boredom by becoming their entertainment directors. Go old school with them. Remember that as kids, most of us were sent outside to play unsupervised, so we needed to make our fun happen. We created our own adventures and games out in the neighborhood. We built tree houses, forts, and bike ramps, and created our own worlds through imaginary play. We initiated these games, and created fun out of very little. We learned to do more with less. Buy toys that encourage more creativity. Too many toys today have self-prescribed actions; these take the imagination out of playing. Put girls in charge of events in your home. Whether it's running family meetings, organizing a movie night, cooking a meal, or creating a chore list, these are opportunities where girls can step up and lead what may be their toughest group of critics; their family!

6. Protected space. Encourage and support your girls' need for the sacred spaces discussed in Chapter 10. For many, this involves just giving them 'space' to have quiet alone time. Right after school is often one of those occasions. Girls often don't want to talk about their day on the car ride home or when they walk in the door from their bus ride. And they especially hate when their moms barrage them with 50 questions. They need some time to decompress. They've been working hard at school, absorbing a day's worth of social politics and dramas, and they need to sort things out. Some girls like to exercise to blow off steam and

relieve tension. Others do want to talk with someone; it's their way to let things go and download what they've taken in all day. Some girls require quiet time because they are sensorally over-stimulated. They need a quiet, calm space to refill their empty tank of tolerance. Refueling can look like reading, doing art, dancing, singing, or writing. Journaling is a constructive way for them to put their thoughts and feeling onto the pages so they can better process through them. Remember, too, that sacred space also means a place to let your hair down, be silly, let your 'kid' out to play. It's an opportunity for rough-and-tumble activities, shooting hoops, or putting on some loud music and dancing crazy. It is invaluable for girls to have a home where they can act in these ways without being judged.

Parents have told me that the times they see daughters the most uninhibited and relaxed is on vacation in a place where they can run free. Playing at the beach or having the run of their grandparents' farm allows girls to relax and play and feel the freedom and grounding of nature.

7. Service and activism. Help your daughters find opportunities to be of service, to give of themselves. It takes them out of the perfectionism/look-ism/sexualization/ popularity loop for a while and puts their focus on being helpful and valuable. Some of the happiest and most powerful girls I know are the ones who find passion for a cause and try to do something about it. Activism gives girls chances to initiate, create, lead, and be part of groups of people of all ages. It can connect them to the bigger communities of this world, which is exciting and gratifying. The more this comes from them, the better. It becomes their thing, their cause, their passion, their purpose. They own the process and the results, and that is where growth and fulfillment occur best.

Another benefit is that it provides opportunities where the reason for getting together has a 'higher purpose'--something other than looking good, being popular, attracting boys and competing to be the best. In these settings, there is usually little to no relationship aggression drama. On the contrary, girls tend to be kinder, more inclusive and more relaxed. There tends to be a feeling of closeness and trust lacking at school. There is a higher sense of community and camaraderie.

8. Media savvy. Parents have an important role to play in educating their daughters about the images and messages they constantly see and hear in the media. And by media, I mean TV, movies, magazines, advertising on billboards, mall windows, grocery store check-out lines, and anywhere else companies can push their products, including the Internet and phone apps.

At the mother-daughter and father-daughter retreats my wife and I facilitate, we spend time instructing both girls and parents about these images. We oftentimes show them two short videos produced by the Dove Company that can be found at Dove.com. One is called *Evolution*, and it's extremely powerful. The two-minute video begins with a normal-looking girl of about 18 who looks like she just got out of bed. She sits on a stool, some bright lights are turned on her, and then the transformation happens. Over about a 60-second timespan, they work on her in extreme fast-forward mode. They blow dry and poof up her hair. They apply a ton of makeup. And then the Photoshopping begins. They raise her eyebrows, thicken her lips, hollow out her cheekbones, lengthen and thin her neck. They add color and tone here and there. Finally they stop, and the camera pulls away slowly to reveal her face on a billboard. And what is fascinating is that almost none of the girls makes the connection that the girl on the billboard is the same as the one from the beginning of the video. Once we replay it, there are a lot of oohs and ahhs as they get it.

This leads into a discussion about the value of examining every image they see in the media. The girls and their parents come up with questions they could ask themselves when they see pictures of 'beautiful' women in magazines or on TV. Here is a partial list our girls have come up with:

- Why would she dress like that?
- Is she really happy?
- What does the girl think about how she really looks since they work on her for hours?
- What does she think of her image?
- What did it take for her to look like that?
- Do I really need that product?
- Will it make me happy?
- Why would I want to be the same as everyone else?
- Why do I want this product?
- Will it really change me?
- Does the product really work?
- Can you really buy beauty and happiness?
- Do most or any girls and woman really look like that image? If not, why then would they put it in a magazine?
- Do you have to follow the latest trends and have the latest products to be popular? Happy? Accepted? Liked?
- Who decides what 'beauty' is?

And here are my two favorites:
- What are they trying to sell me?
- What are they saying to me about me? Am I too fat, or is my hair too wavy, etcetera?

Sleeping Beauties, Awakened Women

I want girls to be skeptical about every image and message they receive. Girls who do that won't be as easily swayed by the culture. They'll have a deeper understanding of what advertising and images are inherently about.

The truth is these companies are not really selling products; they are selling some very harmful messages:

- In order to be happy you need this product.
- More is better.
- Happiness can be bought.
- The way to feel better is to buy our products.
- If you want to be popular and have cool friends, buy our products and you'll be just like these scantily clad, hot people in the ad.

They are selling a lie, but it's hard to resist because it is everywhere, 24/7. That's why studies have shown that watching TV and movies with your girls, and discussing what you see there protects girls from these ideas.

I love sitting with middle and high school girls flipping through magazines they bring to camp. We laugh and talk about what's on the pages. Girls don't understand until we tell and show them that no one looks like those girls in the magazines, not even the girls in the pictures! I love showing them the before and after photos of women at photo shoots. They are amazed at all the air-brushing and Photoshopping that went into the final pictures. It's a real revelation to them. And it's freeing. They won't waste as much time comparing themselves unfavorably with these fake images. They now understand what those companies are selling. Girls and their parents need to become more sensitized to all of these images: notice them, discuss them, question them, and put them into their proper context.

9. What are you really saying? When you have concerns or frustrations with your daughters, get really clear about what's really going on for you before you talk with them. Let me illustrate this point with an example. Gail was in my office complaining about her daughter Jackie, 17, who was seated across from her on the couch. *"For the past year, she walks in the door after school, barely says hi, goes right up to her room and closes her door. And she spends hours up there texting her friends and talking to people on Facebook."* I mirrored Gail back, and then asked her what her concern was about Jackie being in her room talking to her friends. *"Well, the rest of the family is downstairs doing something together. We'll be playing a board game or watching a movie together, but she's holed up in her room and doesn't want to come down and join us."* I reflected that back, and pushed Gail to go a little deeper by asking her what her fear was about that. *"Well, she's never spending time with the family anymore. It's always about her friends!"* At this point, Gail sounded less angry and more sad. I mirrored her back, and asked her what her concern was about Jackie spending time only with her friends. Before she answered, Gail paused, looked a little deeper within, got tears in her eyes, and then replied to my question. *"I miss my daughter."*

That was the pay dirt. All of the stuff about being in her room and not playing board games that Gail had been harping about to Jackie was just the foam on top of her root beer feelings. Much more important than Gail's frustration was her sadness; she was grieving the loss of the relationship she'd had with Jackie when she was younger. I always suggest that parents do this un-layering process before they bring complaints to daughters. If all Gail does is complain about how much time Jackie is spending in her room, all she'll get back is arguing and resistance.

But if Gail started a heart-to-heart conversation showing her root beer feelings, i.e. "Jackie, I've been feeling really sad lately because I miss you,", there is a much better chance of Jackie listening. She loves her mom and doesn't want to hurt her, so she'll tune in better and be less defensive. Thus, the conversation will bear more fruit.

10. The Birds and the Bees: I am often asked by parents when to talk to girls about sex. Because girls today start puberty at earlier and earlier ages, it's hard for them to know when it's appropriate. I have a different take on sex-education. I think it should start in the toddler years! You heard right. I say this because most of this discussion should not be about the actual physical act.

    The following are key points in educating girls about sexuality, starting as young girls.

    a) Don't talk about boyfriends. I cringe every time I hear adults asking 5-year-old girls if they have a boyfriend. Girls in grade school hear this far too often from well-meaning but misguided parents and relatives. And many start to wonder if they are abnormal because they not only don't have one but also have zero interest in boys. It's another example of how adults unwittingly start nudging girls to grow up too fast. And in a sense it's part of the early sexualization of our girls.

    b) Don't over-focus on looks. As I described in previously in chapter 15, girls constantly get noticed and acknowledged by adults for being 'cute,' 'pretty,' and for the clothes they wear. But these comments reinforce the lie that girls are their looks. If they buy into this belief system, they will become too sensitive to what boys think of them, and too invested in being pretty, thin, attractive, and hot. Conversely, parents who value a girl's character and qualities will teach them to value themselves from the inside-out, versus the opposite.

c) Sibling rivalry. The relationship girls have with their siblings is an important template for future relationships, so it's important for parents to provide good guidance in this area. Teach girls to take responsibility for their conflicts with older and younger siblings. If girls can become skilled at asking for what they need in relationships at home, and also listen to their sibling's needs, then they'll have the ability to create good win-win solutions. They will then become well-prepared to do the same with same-sex friends in grade school and middle school, and with boys down the road. Girls can be encouraged to develop the courage to speak their truth with their siblings and parents. They can practice expressing their needs and wants with authority in a way that gets them results. Again, this is great training for doing the same with friends and boys later on.

d) Strengthen friendship skills. Healthy sexuality should begin and end with healthy intimacy. And intimacy requires accomplished relationship skills. After 'practice' on siblings, these tools need to be sharpened in friendships before adolescence, usually with same-sex friends. In my retreats, camps, and school programs, I help girls to become proficient at listening, like the mirroring discussed previously. I teach them the conflict resolution process, and encourage them to handle their disagreements and relationship needs directly with the other person. And most important I give them opportunities to practice this expertise with real-life situations they are experiencing. Girls need practice.

During gatherings with girls, I don't really hope for relationship dramas, but if some occur, they become great opportunities to practice these skills. I worry that schools are falling behind in the area of relationship-building. With so much emphasis on test scores and competing with other countries in the three R's, there is no time allocated to instruct and practice these important skills. And when relationship aggression or drama occurs, it often brings punishments and lectures, but no hands-on-teaching. What a waste!

e) Engaged in their passions. I've shared stories previously about girls who had poor boundaries with their friends or in their dating relationships. One way to prevent this pattern is for girls to fully engage themselves in a passion of theirs, be it sports, art, theater, music, or writing. These activities bring girls a sense of fulfillment and accomplishment, and it raises their self-esteem. In this state of mind, they know they deserve to be treated respectfully, so they take better care of themselves.

f) Connect in non-sexual ways. Teens today have bought another lie propagated by the media and the culture: the myth that intimacy means sexuality, and that the way to be close to someone lies in the bedroom. As a result, many of their dating relationships start with the physical, with sexual hookups. And, too often, the boys move on and the relationship never grows in friendship or intimacy. Part of the reason girls are willing to conform to this pattern is because we haven't taught them non-sexual ways to connect. TV sitcoms, reality shows, and movies are chock-full of stories that show little or no true intimacy--just sex and more sex.

At my co-ed camps, we try to provide opportunities for girls to connect with guys in non-sexual ways. Lying down near each other on the tarps talking as they star gaze is one way. We have some really deep, open discussions about God, death, sexuality, religion, war--you name it and we've discussed it. This is a healthy form of closeness. Giving back rubs, holding hands as they walk the steep hill from the lake, giving each other piggy-back rides; these are examples of a different kind of intimacy. We also talk to teens a lot about their intentions in these situations. You can act the same way physically, i.e. give someone a back rub, but it will be received differently depending on your intention. If a boy's intention is sexual, then a girl will sense a different kind of energy than if the intention is platonic. We teach teens to check in with themselves when they are with each other and get clear about their intention.

We also discuss, on the first day of weekend retreats and summer camps, the issue of 'pairing-off.' And I usually have one of our college-aged staff lead this discussion rather than me, from whom it might sound too much like a lecture from their parents. Pairing-off means focusing on one person. These are hot-blooded teenagers at camp, not robots. And they have sexual feelings and desires. It's not wrong to be attracted romantically to someone at camp. But for the camp week, we ask them not to go there. Returning campers usually understand why we ask this. If you're interested in a guy at camp, it's easy only to focus on them and miss out on making a lot of new friends. You also will be more self-conscious about what you share during our learning time, and past campers have verified they did indeed hold back because of what a particular person might think of them. Also, boyfriend/girlfriend behaviors often elicit jealousies and drama, which distract everyone from being present and open.

If they can keep their intention on deepening friendships and learning about the opposite sex in a platonic way, they leave camp with huge lessons. They have also been able to experience intimacy non-sexually, through deep conversations, shared laughter, star gazing on the tarp, and doing our service project together. Teens really enjoy experiencing this different kind of closeness. It feels better, more right. Work to provide opportunities like this for girls.

g) Modeling. When my daughter Kelly was turning 16 years old, I decided to take her on a father-daughter trip. She chose Chicago, and off we went for a weekend. Before we left, I decided one of my goals for the trip was to show her how a guy should treat her. I held doors open for her, I had her share what she wanted to do on the trip, I listened to her intently during conversations. I treated her like a lady. At the end of the weekend I told her she should never expect to be treated less than the way I had treated her; she deserved the best. You don't have to travel to Chicago to deliver this message. Your behavior toward your daughter speaks volumes each and every day. Do you allow her to have a voice? Do you value her opinion? Do you encourage her interests, whether they are girly or 'tom-boyish'? Do you treat her with respect? Do you listen to her? Do you spend quality time with her? Do you respect and encourage her decisions and choices? Do you acknowledge all her qualities and character? Do you allow her to disagree with you and speak her truth? Do you respect her boundaries and allow her to say no?

For dads, can you answer "yes" to the above questions in the way you treat your wife? Girls are watching and learning a lot about relationships through their parents' marriage. Even if parents are divorced, girls still take in how their parents treat each other. All six of the ideas above educate girls about sexuality, which is really learning about relationships and taking care of yourself. This kind of training starts in the preschool years.

As I have discussed in a previous chapter, girls need good information also about the female brain, female hormones, and the changes that occur with puberty and their monthly cycles. This type of education can happen around the fifth grade, earlier if your daughter starts showing signs of the onset of puberty. I personally don't think girls need to know the details of physical sexuality until later in middle school. Some girls in middle school are really innocent and have no interest in boys; they may not be ready for this conversation until eighth grade. For the more socially precocious girls, sixth or seventh grade is probably a better time to talk about sex, before they are sexually active. Use your intuition and what you know about your daughter to decide when to have this discussion with them.

11. Stories. The power of our stories is tremendous. Girls love to hear accounts about our experiences growing up. They are hungry to know we understand. I think girls oftentimes look at their parents and believe they never struggled. They see us as the finished product; we've found our mate, have successful jobs and close friends. What they didn't see was seeing us in middle and high school. They missed seeing us during our awkward stages: resplendent with pimples and braces, our struggles with homework, friendship dramas, dating, decisions about college, majors, and careers. Teenage girls tell me their parents could never understand what they are going through because their parents never went through what they are experiencing. Really? But then how would they know unless you tell them your stories?

At the end of our retreats and camps we have a parent program to describe the week and what their kids learned. Sometimes we do a fishbowl exercise where the parents sit on the carpet and the campers sit on chairs surrounding them. The campers have to just quietly listen and observe, like looking at fish in a fishbowl. It's the parents' time to share.

We'll ask them to share their experiences about questions like:

- How did you feel different when you were your daughter's age?
- Did you ever feel like you didn't fit in?
- Any friendship troubles or dramas?
- What was your relationship like with your parents at this age?
- Talk about your first crushes.
- Did you ever struggle in school? Did you try your hardest?
- What did you do for fun with your friends?
- What were you worried or stressed about?
- Describe the social scene at your school.
- Did you feel pressure about your clothes?
- Did you judge your body or appearance?
- Your first dating relationship? First kiss?
- What was the naughtiest thing you did?
- What were your dreams at my age?
- Did you have the same problems and stresses as us?
- Where your parents over-protective?
- Biggest pet peeve with your parents?

These questions were all brought up by the girls at camps and retreats. And I promise you the girls sit spellbound as their parents share. Most have never heard their parents talk about these issues. And that's a shame. Don't make the mistake of withholding your stories. Girls interpret the disclosures as: *"My mom does understand me!" "My dad did go through something like I am, therefore he gets it, he can relate."* And that's a gift.

12. Your presence. You have to be there, which means having enough time with them. It means you are present and available in case they need to talk. It means there is enough down time in your home where girls know that if they need to share there is time for it. And it means being fully present, not distracted. Too many parents today are externally distracted with cell phones, iPads, and other such devices that cause them to be half there, and half not there. Girls can tell whether they have your full attention or not. Parents, as much as kids, are addicted to their electronics. Parents are also often internally distracted. This looks like worrying about work issues or finances. Parents who have marital issues are oftentimes emotionally shut down, except for showing anger.

A dad told me at a father-daughter retreat that when he walked in the front door after work, his two young daughters would rush up to him for hugs. They were so excited to see him. But at some point that welcome stopped. And he realized it was because he had gotten into the habit of walking in the door still talking to clients on the phone, thus not giving his girls his full attention. That's why they stopped rushing up to greet him. So he made a decision to finish his phone calls before he walked into the house. Many days that meant sitting in the driveway completing a call. But then he turned his phone off, and when he came through the door he was ready to play, fully present. His daughters started greeting him again with their old enthusiasm.

Another dad related an interesting story. He and his wife and now teenaged children were watching old home movies one night. And he became aware that he didn't remember most of the events depicted on the tapes. He was actually the person who had taped the events, but still he had no recollection of being there. He realized it was because he hadn't really been there. He'd been so focused on building a successful business that he was constantly distracted with it; it had taken up all his time, energy, and attention. So he had missed out on his children growing up.

I believe it was Jesse Jackson who said once, *"Your children need your presence, not your presents."* They need you to be fully present, not distracted. Make this a strong priority.

13. Advocate. Schools need to take a more proactive role in teaching girls the social-emotional skills discussed in this book. Teachers need permission to take the time necessary to work through the relationship aggression issues girls are experiencing, and to manage any other current social-emotional concerns that are impacting student's ability to learn. Girls also need to take an active role in creating the kind of community they want to exist at their school. For this to happen, parents need to take on a much stronger role. They need to advocate for programs like *Strong Girls Strong World* to be instituted in the school. Schools have a higher chance of adopting these programs if parents demand them. Parents need to tell the principal at their school and the teacher in their daughter's classroom that they want time allocated for social-emotional learning and community building. Parents need to tell schools they value these kinds of life skills as much as reading, writing and arithmetic.

There has been a lot of good research on the effects of social-emotional learning programs in schools. Outcomes include better sense of community, more positive attitudes toward school and learning, higher academic motivation, improved coping with school stressors, more pro-social behaviors, reductions in aggression and disruptions, more classroom participation and higher engagement, improved grades and higher test scores, and better problem solving.

To me, it's a no-brainer. This is not some experimental nonsense that is going to negatively affect learning time. It helps out in *all* areas of performance and behavior at school.

So make sure your school knows that you value these types of programs for girls.

CHAPTER 18

A MODERN FAIRY TALE

*"At any age, if we get a taste of who we are, if we fall in love
with life in whatever form we find it and choose to embrace it, we
can fairly call that moment "the prince's kiss."*
Joan Gould, from *Spinning Straw into Gold*

Now let me tell you a more modern fairy tale, with a different
theme and ending.

Ever since Gail was a young girl, she looked for the next mountain
to climb. She had a strong spirit of adventure and competition, and
was always willing to do whatever it took to win. Gymnastics was the
first dragon she attempted to slay. And slay it she did, becoming
successful enough to get her picture in the *New York Times*. Her next
challenge was school, and she poured herself into not only making the
grade, but getting the best grades. The golden chalice was an A+
transcript, because that would get her to her next quest, Harvard
University.

Did she take the time to 'sleep,' like her fairy tale counterparts?
No way! Gail didn't have the time or patience for 'sleep': too many
mountains to climb. She attacked Harvard University with her typical
gusto, and returned home magna cum laude.

But she passed through home only on her way to her next battle, NYU Law School, which was successfully slain in no time. She was on a roll, and she steamed across town to her next adventure, Wall Street. Her drive, brains, fearlessness, and tenacity quickly won over the giants she encountered there. And she became known across the land as 'The Golden Girl.' She worked night and day, day and night to climb to the pinnacle of this career path, CFO. She was totally focused on her challenge, consumed by the fires of ambition, willing to sacrifice herself and everything--to beat the giants at their own game. She married a prince along the way, but he couldn't compete with the kingdoms she was after. He slowly slid from view, devoured by Gail's relentless striving. Gail didn't even glance up to notice: too many fires to put out, giants to slay, obstacles to overcome.

But eventually her demons caught up with her, and then they betrayed her. The golden rings she had been so desperately grasping for turned to stone. They lost their luster. She was thrown out into the wilderness, alone and lost. She was a climber and an adventurer--but there were no more hills to climb, and no other giants to slay.

Gail was confused.

"Who am I", she asked, *"if I'm not killing dragons and scaling mountain peaks? If I am no longer doing these things, then who am I, and what's to become of me."*

Maybe now it was time for her to rest. And so she began her sleeping period. Gail walked out of town one day and entered a dark, foreboding forest. Our heroine wandered in the forest for what seemed like days or even weeks; she totally lost track of time and place. She was tired and lonely, but for the first time in a long time, she also felt calmer. Some days she hiked, other days she slept all day. One evening, she sat down atop a large, flat, white stone on the edge of a babbling brook. The sun was setting and the sky was awash with beautiful hues of orange and purple. She put her bare feet into the water, and enjoyed the cooling and relaxing effect it had on her.

She listened intently to the sounds around her: the music of the crickets, the songs of the whip-o-will, the hooting of an owl and the cooing of morning doves. She heard the wind as it rustled through the leaves of trees overhanging the brook. And best of all was the peaceful, continuous babbling of the brook. It was mesmerizing. Gail also noticed the strong scent of nearby pine trees, and it reminded her of the Christmases of her youth. And this reminded her of the loss of her husband and the lack of children in her life. She began to cry, large crocodile tears streaming down her face and into the stream. Suddenly, slaying dragons didn't seem so important any more. She felt alone, confused, and lost. And that's when the child appeared.

To Gail's surprise, a young girl walked into the clearing and headed toward her. She was holding a beautiful red rose, the kind Gail's father used to grow at their house when she was growing up. The girl was surrounded by a warm white light, and she had the most gentle and kind smile Gail had ever seen. She immediately felt safe and loved just being in the presence of this child. But Gail wondered why the girl was alone in the forest.

"What are you doing here in the forest?" Gail asked. *"Are you lost? Can I help you?"* The child's smile widened, and her voice was soothing to Gail's ears. *"I'm not lost. I've been looking for you for a long time; you're the one who was lost. But now you're found."* Gail didn't understand. *"I don't even know you, so why would you be looking for me?"* The child smiled. *"Oh, I think you do know me. But in all of your busyness you've forgotten me. But it's okay, I'm here now."* Gail paused, and then asked, *"Am I dreaming? Am I just imagining this?"* The child smiled again. *"Actually, I am more real than all the dragons you've slain. Think about it: were you really wide awake and happy during those times?"* Gail thought about the

child's words before she answered. *"Not really; I was in a kind of fog. I was so busy there was barely time to breathe. It's all just a blur now, and I have nothing to show for it."* The child responded. *"Well, all you experienced has brought you here, and this moment right now feels pretty good, doesn't it?"* Gail nodded. *"I can't remember the last time I felt so calm and peaceful. It's the feeling I used to have when I came home after a sleepover or a week of camp. It just feels like home. I guess that sounds kind of crazy."* The child shook her head. *"Not at all, because for you, I am home. Look at me closely and tell me, what do you see?"* Gail stared intently at the young girl, as if for the first time. The girl seemed so natural, so happy, so genuine. *That's how I used to feel too*, thought Gail.

And then it hit her: the little girl was her. It was Gail when she was young, carefree and innocent. *"You're me, aren't you?"* she asked. *"Yes, I'm a part of you; the part that got forgotten when you set out on your adventures. You used to love to sing all day and dance down the street. You loved to draw funny animals on the sidewalk with chalk. You didn't have a care in the world."* Gail smiled at the child. *"It's been so long since I felt that way; it's hard to remember."* Gail said. *"Why did I turn my back on you?"* *"You started looking for something one day that you thought you were missing, something that would make you feel better about yourself,"* the child responded. *"So for a long time you searched for more trophies, more victories, hoping that would make you feel right. Sometimes it did for a few hours, but then you'd feel empty and restless again, and off you'd go after the next challenge."* Gail nodded again, this time with a slight grimace on her face. *"I noticed that the good feelings from the victories went away sooner and sooner, and it took bigger and more exciting dragons to pull me out of my funks,"* Gail said. *"But that's why you're here,"* responded the child. *"What you needed to feel good about yourself wasn't out there; it was within you all along. You just weren't ready to see it yet. But now you are, and I'm right here in front of you."*

It slowly dawned on Gail that what the young girl was saying was spot on. She looked at the child, stared straight into her eyes, and for a moment she felt the kind of joy and love she'd experienced as a young girl. Her eyes slowly shut, and she fell into a deep sleep.

She awoke to the sounds of the stream and the birds perched on branches overhead. It was morning. Gail felt more refreshed and rested than she had in years. And she felt different too. She was no longer feeling afraid and confused. She felt at peace. In her right hand was the lovely red rose the young girl had been holding. Just the sight of it made her smile.

Gail started walking down a new path, and after a few twists and turns she found herself at the edge of the forest. In front of her were rows and rows of apple trees, stretching as far as the eye could see. She picked a bright red apple and bit into it. She couldn't remember ever tasting such sweet fruit in her life. She laid the rose at the foot of the tree in gratitude, and she started walking in the direction of the morning sun. It was a beautiful new day, and Gail felt confident that there would be many more like it.

And there were….

This modern fairy tale illustrates what I see happening for girls in the years stretching from their teens through their 30s. It's a new story, with few good models to delineate the proper paths along this journey. Which explains why so many young women today feel a little lost and empty. The striving and relentless pushing starts in grade school with the pressures to achieve straight A's, national championships in sports and cheerleading or dancing, being popular, and attracting a hot boyfriend. Girls tell me all the time about these pressures to be perfect in everything they do.

Sleeping Beauties, Awakened Women

By high school, they already feel like hamsters on a treadmill, grinding out grades and activities to pad their college transcripts. The love of learning and playing sports just for fun takes a backseat to performing for adults and giving parents, coaches, and teachers what they want. If they go on to college, which is the ideal they've heard about since grade school, some troubles can await them. Recent articles from university presidents and health specialists point to an alarming increase in mental health problems in American and Canadian college students.

A 2011 national college health assessment survey of 1,600 University of Alberta students uncovered some scary statistics:

- 51.3% felt things were hopeless
- 87.5% felt overwhelmed by all they had to do
- 66.6% felt very lonely and very sad
- 34.4% felt so depressed that it was difficult to function
- 52% felt overwhelming anxiety
- 41% felt overwhelming anger
- 57% experienced more than average stress
- 7% considered suicide while 1.2% attempted suicide

Wow! The usage of mental health services at U.S. colleges reflects these statistics, as these service centers have been overrun with needy students in recent years. Girls have been told since they were young that their choices and futures were limitless; they could aim for the stars and be whatever they wanted to be. The glass ceilings restricting women's career choices have been shattered, freeing girls to pursue opportunities that in the past were unavailable to women.

But what I question is how women are making these choices.

Sheryl Sandberg, Facebook COO, illustrated her beliefs about this topic in her commencement address at Barnard College. *"Don't lean back, lean in! Put your foot on that gas pedal and keep it there until the day you have to make a decision--and then make a decision. That's the only way, when the day comes, you'll even have a decision to make."* What Sandberg seems to be telling women is to put their heads down and drive themselves to the top of their career ladder, and don't look up until you reach home plate. I believe that the majority of girls and women who pursue this path are running in the dark, half asleep. They are blindly following a course laid out for them by the culture, without ever having taken the time to really know themselves and what's right for them.

Girls start on the treadmill in grade school and they just keep running, like Forrest Gump. It's what a good girl 'should' do. Don't think about it; don't reflect or soul search. Just go! Lean in! More is better! Faster is better! More money, more accolades, bigger house, more expensive car, more prestige: *these are* what will make you happy. I hear and read about women in their 20s, 30s and 40s who are experiencing what men often complain of in their 50s, the so-called 'mid-life crisis.' *"Is this all there is?" "I've reached the top and I have all the toys, but I'm still not happy." "I've slaved and sacrificed myself for years, but it's still not enough. I'm exhausted and unfulfilled."*

What I want for girls and women is similar to what Sheryl Sandberg relates in her book *Lean In*. I hope women will move into more leadership positions throughout society, and to not be afraid to 'sit at the table'. It is high time they dropped their 'good girl' fears of standing out or people not liking them and plow forward with courage and determination. But I do not want women to do this because it is the cultural or feminist imperative to do so. I don't want them to be motivated by 'shoulds'. What I mean is that young girls are getting the message early on that to be successful, you need to be at the top of the class, on the best teams, attending only elite universities, and rising to the top of your career ladder. And anything else is considered a failure. Talking to girls as often as I do reminds me that this is not an exaggeration.

I want girls starting in grade school to learn how to go inward and to know themselves. They can discover what they need, what they desire, what turns them on, and what they have a passion for. And I do not want girls and women to base their choices and decisions on what the culture, the media, peers, parents, teachers, coaches, or anyone says is right and proper for them. It needs to be their journey, their destiny. Glass ceilings have been broken through. But excessive pressures as I described above can lead to a different kind of box, where women still feel it is not their life they are living. The ceiling is gone, but the sides of the box are still constricting.

The queens and princesses in past fairy tales knew how to work hard and fully engage themselves in their passions. They just did it with more balance and forethought than our modern day heroines.

When I hear of women and men who are working 80 hours a week and pushing themselves to be more successful, I wonder what is driving them. Is it coming from a belief of not feeling good enough? Are there some 'ghosts' from their past that make them feel like they don't measure up? Did they decide because of experiences growing up that in order to be loved, they had to be the best or to be perfect?

I have found that these sorts of belief systems do drive many of the highest achievers. It's not wrong to be motivated in these ways. But in many cases it results in people becoming out of balance in their lives. It's just never enough. I have met many entrepreneurs who work like crazy for years to build up a hugely successful company, feel burned out because of the lack of life balance and because they realize they have neglected their spouse and children. So they sell their business, make enough money to retire 10 times-fold, and lo and behold, within 6 months they have started a new business venture and they are off to the races once again. That is the pattern I want our princesses to avoid.

Erin Callan, former CFO of Lehman Brothers, and the model for my fairy tale, had some words of advice for young women based on her experiences. *"I was consumed! I worked all day and was completely available for my company. You don't suddenly wake up one day and make a decision that you want to live that way; it just sort of happens over time. I refer to it as 'the new normal.'"*

She plunged into her career path in a half asleep, unconscious way. She lacked awareness, self knowledge, and balance. *"It was when I got later on in my career that I started to realize maybe this isn't all there is. Maybe this isn't where I want to take the rest of my life. I missed out on a lot of things, including having children."*

This was her moment of truth, when she finally started questioning what she was doing. *"Don't let someone tell you what to do or make you feel bad. Follow your heart. I will no longer wake up every day with anxiety about doing the next big thing. I'm finally okay with who I am."*

I believe that women can truly 'have it all', but only if they consciously decide what that means for them as an individual, free of any constraints and 'shoulds', and not due to some past unhealthy beliefs about themselves. For some women this might look like becoming CEO of a Fortune 50 company, for others it might look like being a stay-at-home mom. The key is that their choice is what they really want, not what they should achieve. This kind of self-awareness can only be obtained if girls receive the kinds of supports I have described in this book, and if they are guided to more consciously undergo the crucial touchpoint of adolescence.

The marriage of the princess and prince, or the queen and king represents the union of the female and male energies I discussed back in chapter 2. I want girls and young women to have the qualities of assertiveness, ambition, boldness, and being willing to stretch themselves and take risks. If they so choose, I want them to step with confidence and authority up to the tables that Sheryl Sandberg speaks of.

"Being tender and open is beautiful. As a woman, I feel continually shhh'ed. Too sensitive. Too mushy. Too wishy washy. Blah. Blah. Don't let someone steal your tenderness. Don't allow the coldness and fear of others to tarnish your perfectly vulnerable beating heart. Nothing is more powerful than allowing yourself to truly be affected by things. Whether it's a song, a stranger, a mountain, a rain drop, a tea kettle, an article, a sentence, a footstep, feel it all. Look around you. All of this is for you. Take it and have gratitude. Give it and feel love." Zooey Deschanel

And, I want them to also bring with them the archetypal female qualities of collaboration, creativity, appreciation for the value of relationship-building, intuition, a win-win mentality, and yes… love. Our culture and world have been driven for far too long by male, patriarchal values without the balance of the matriarchal energies. And we have suffered for it. This has become true as well for girls and women individually and as a collective.

So I think it is much healthier to 'lean back' before you start out on a path. Do what the Runaway Bride did: take the time for self-discovery and self-awareness. Follow the examples laid out by our fairy tale heroines and withdraw from the world and 'sleep.' The heroines awaken from these periods of 'sleep' wiser and more grounded. And they know how to proceed along their journey with a healthy balance between feminine and masculine qualities.

CHAPTER 19

HAPPILY EVER AFTER...

"I know who I am, yesterday, today and tomorrow. The world may be hard, it may be full of loss, but I believe in myself and what I am doing. And that belief can carry me through the hard times, can allow me both a sense of purpose and a sense of joy."
Victor Frankl, from Stephen Hinshaw's book, *The Triple Bind.*

I wish every adolescent girl had this much confidence in herself that it could carry her effortlessly through this touchpoint. But our fairy tales and myths and experiences have taught us that the Heroine's Journey often requires solitude, suffering, overcoming challenges, pain, struggle and periods of darkness. This journey, with its ups and downs, is normal and necessary for the successful transformation all girls undergo in adolescence. So as a culture we need to redirect our focus from pathology to normal touchpoint; from depression, cutting and mood swings to the root causes of these symptoms; from fears about girls' struggles to the hope that springs from growth and evolution.

As a culture, we need to reframe what adolescent girls experience, while girls at the same time need to redefine their experiences and make healthy new decisions about themselves and life. They need to create their own stories about who they are, what they have experienced and who they will grow into. Cinderella experienced the death of her mother, a neglectful father, years of servitude and sacrifice, and social isolation. She easily could have decided she couldn't trust anyone (*"people I get close to go away"*) or she could have concluded, *"I'm not important or good enough or lovable"* (thanks to a neglectful father). She also could have decided, *"I don't fit in, I'm weird and not pretty enough"* (because of step-sisters who harassed and excluded her). Fortunately, she used her teen years instead to grow in confidence, wisdom and self reliance. She didn't slink into the prince's ball; she walked in with the heart of a princess: powerful and radiant. Her years of 'sleeping' were well-spent.

The ugly duckling, shunned by her duck family, could have decided she was unattractive, no good, and so different that no one would ever love her. Her travels ('sleep') allowed her to discover herself and to find a family she could connect with.

I hope after reading this book that you have a much clearer understanding of the pressures and challenges girls are facing today, and what will help them overcome these.

If our frame of reference is the Touchpoints model, we'll begin from a perspective of normalcy instead of pathology. We'll be able to see friendship dramas, negative self-talk and emotional overload for what they are: the out-of-sorts behaviors that arise from an impending leap in development. We can offer information, understanding, tools and guidance instead of worries, labels and medications. But if we continue to allow girls to be driven by externals like straight A's, national championships, college scholarships, materialism, and being rich and famous, we will keep them distracted from what's really important: the Heroine's Journey.

"And the day came when the risk to remain tight in a bud was more painful than the risk it took to blossom." Anais Nin

I want us to disregard labels like 'poor self-esteem,' 'mean girls,' and 'those moody teenage girls.' Instead, let's keep the focus of our discussion on concepts like self discovery, solitude, soul-searching, evolution, growing edges, incubation and renewal, rebirth, change from the inside-out, metaphorical sleeping and waking up, and transformation. These aren't just words; they are a frame of mind, an attitude, and the prism through which we will perceive our girls.

It pains me to hear most adult parents expressing fear and judgments about raising teenage girls. They start loathing this stage when their daughters are toddlers. *"Boys are **so** much easier to raise than girls. I am **so** not looking forward to her teenage years."* Sound familiar?

If someone tells you they are a middle school teacher, a common refrain is, *"Oh my God, you must be a saint!"* That is so disrespectful to those kids, and most often the negativity is directed at the girls. We've all heard about 'mean girls,' and 'queen bees' and friendship dramas. The shame here isn't that there is no truth to these perceptions; it's that this is all people seem to see!

Probably my favorite kind of group work is with middle school girls, sitting on the floor in a circle and hearing them share their world. They are so alive and in the moment. I love that they are riding a rollercoaster of emotions and thoughts. As long as I don't go up and down with them, I can see through the rattling to who they really are. I see the forest and the trees. Parents can do the same if they know what to focus on and are more aware of what girls require.

Awareness is at the top of the list. Be aware of the significance of this touchpoint. Understand the normal falling apart that accompanies every large leap in development, including this stage. Understand the Heroine's Journey, and the need for 'sleep,' protected space and quiet times during which they can gather themselves. Stay focused on the long term, big picture of transformation. Don't fret and worry about suffering, mistakes, obstacles or regressions. These are signs of growth and evolution, and with support, girls will move through them all to a higher level of consciousness.

Information is also crucial. Girls need knowledge of the female brain and hormones, and about the effects of the hormonal changes they experience with their monthly cycles. They need to know about the normal physical changes all females undergo so they don't get stuck with negative body image and unnecessary judgments about their changing appearance.

Emotional Intelligence is critical as well. Girls need to be able to slow down and check in with themselves so they know what they are feeling. They need better language to talk about **all** their emotions, and they need practice expressing them in healthy ways. And at times they need to be able to suppress emotions when it's not appropriate to convey them.

Self-quieting is another important skill. I want them to be exposed to lots of means to get calm and to be given the opportunities to practice these. I want girls to become proficient at journaling, writing stories, poems and songs, and expressing themselves through singing, dancing and musical instruments. Artistic girls need to find their preferred medium for self-quieting, be it drawing, painting, sculpting or knitting. In response to girls telling me they'd love to do these activities but, *"There's just no time,"* I say to parents: You've got to make this a priority! If solitude and reflection are last on to-do lists, they won't get done at all. Girls have to make it important, and in order to do that, parents have to model and value it as well.

Girls need to understand the costs to them of being electronically plugged in 24/7 or busy and distracted in other ways as well. They need more slow time, and they need times when they are unreachable.

They require this down time to keep themselves grounded and in balance.

Understanding relationship aggression is necessary to preventing it. I want every girls to understand the reasons behind these behaviors and dramas, and to have the tools to prevent and handle whatever friendship issues come their way. School and team dynamics would be different and better beasts if girls learned to deal with their disagreements and friendship problems directly and effectively. A classroom with a ton of drama and hurt feelings is not normal. Playing with social power, disagreements and misunderstandings are normal. If not dealt with effectively, they fester and build up to dramas and exclusions. Girls need guidance and skills in social-emotional learning, and they need opportunities to take more responsibility for their learning environments.

As girls traverse through grade school, middle and high school, they need to become aware of any negative beliefs and decisions they are making about their experiences. Girls need help to redirect their propensity for negative rumination and making detrimental assumptions. They can learn to catch and redirect any negative self talk, and to focus on reality and what's true about them.

Practice. Practice. Practice. Learning these skills is no different than becoming proficient at a sport like soccer. Soccer players are expected to go through lots of repetition in order to develop muscle memory. The exercises build up muscle groups and strengthens your core. After running a drill a thousand times, it becomes second nature. Social-Emotional learning is just a different set of muscles. Just like in soccer, you have to learn these behaviors and tools, practice them with real-life examples, and carry those lessons forward to the next experience. You can't expect kids to hear these principles one time at an assembly and then be able to live them out. It doesn't work that way, same as soccer, math, or anything else.

Having a lot of tools in your toolbox to draw on in moments of crisis helps girls feel more in control of situations, and thus more confident. So parents, teachers, coaches, and any other adult who works with girls must give this part of their education as much weight, validity and time as the rest of their instruction. Making it important means you will allow girls the time, practice and attention this deserves.

> *"Why is everyone here so happy except me?"*
> *"Because they have learned to see goodness and beauty everywhere," said the Master.*
> *"Why don't I see goodness and beauty everywhere?"*
> *"Because you cannot see outside of you what you fail to see inside."*
>
> Anthony deMello

In *The Wizard of Oz*, Dorothy runs away from home to start her adventure, gets scared when she looks at her future in Professor Marvel's crystal ball, and tries to return home as the storm of puberty approaches. She falls asleep, and her Heroine's Journey begins. Her 'sleep' involves integrating all the parts within herself. She must embrace her intuition, street smarts, her inner 'knowing,' and her decision-making abilities (Scarecrow). She also must embrace her compassion, emotions, and the ability for closeness and love (Tin Man). Dorothy then embraces her courage, determination and the ability to manage her fears (Cowardly Lion). She embraces her spirituality (Glinda the Good Witch) and her wisdom (Wizard). And she must even embrace her dark side, her shadow, her inner demons like anger, jealousy, apathy and aggression (Wicked Witch).

This is how Dorothy works on her 'inner resume.' The yellow brick road is her path of self-discovery, and along the way she gathers the inner resources she'll need as a woman. At the end of the movie,

Dorothy asks Glinda to help her get home. Glinda responds, *"You don't need my help any longer; you've always had the power to go back to Kansas."* *"I have?"* asks Dorothy. *"Then why didn't you tell her before?"* the Scarecrow interjects. *"Because she wouldn't have believed me,"* Glinda says. *"She had to learn it for herself."* *"What have you learned, Dorothy?"* asks the Tin Man. Dorothy thinks and then says, *"I think it wasn't enough just to want to see Uncle Henry and Auntie Em, and it's that....if I ever go looking for my heart's desire again, I won't look any further than my own backyard; because if it isn't there, I never really lost it to begin with. Is that right?"* Glinda smiles. *"That's it. And she had to find it out for herself."* Dorothy taps her heels three times and repeats, *"There's no place like home"* and... she wakes up!

Her home is the same, but Dorothy isn't; she's grown up. She has transformed, and from now on she'll see and experience the world differently. She brought all her resources back with her and she now has the wisdom, courage and confidence to meet the world. That movie is the perfect metaphor for the touchpoint adolescent girls must pass through. Girls themselves are the agents of change. They have the ability to make their story as they wish. It's their path, their destiny. And they need our guidance and support as I've outlined throughout this book.

Armed with this awareness, knowledge, skills and support, girls will be able, in beneficial ways, to lose consciousness for a while in order to incubate, germinate and eventually blossom into their true authentic selves. With a healthy balance of female and male energies, they can step into their magnificence and lead the lives they were meant to live. And they will pursue their passions and purpose, fully engaged and with the balance they choose for themselves. Then, and only then, will our daughters be able to live 'happily ever after!'

About the Author

Tim Jordan, M.D. is a Developmental and Behavioral Pediatrician, Author, International Speaker, Media Consultant and a leading expert on girl's issues. Dr. Tim has worked with girls in his counseling practice, weekend retreats, summer camps and schools for more than 30 years.

He is the creator of the Strong Girls, Strong World programs in schools teaching social-emotional intelligence skills to girls.

Dr. Tim resides in St. Louis, Missouri, with his wife, Anne, and their dog Scout. The Jordan's have 3 adult children.

Please visit his website at www.drtimjordan.com and his blog at drjordansblog.wordpress.com.

Resources About Girls

Jordan, Tim. *Food Fights and Bedtime Battles: A Working Parent's Guide to Negotiating Daily Power Struggles* (Berkley Publishing Group 2001).

Jordan, Tim. *Keeping Your Family Grounded When You Are Flying by the Seat of Your Pants* (Children and Families Inc. 2005).

Gould, Joan. *Spinning Straw Into Gold: What Fairy Tales Reveal about the Transformations in a Women's Life* (Random House New York 2005).

Johnson, Robert. *She: Understanding Feminine Psychology* (Harper 1989).

Johnson, Robert. *He: Understanding Masculine Psychology* (Harper Perennial 1989).

Johnson, Robert. *We: Understanding the Psychology of Romantic Love* (Harper San Francisco 1983).

Manheim, Ralph. *Grimms' Tales for Young and Old* (Anchor Books 1977).

Murdock, Maureen. *The Heroine's Journey* (Shambhala 1990).

Ragan, Kathleen. *Fearless Girls, Wise Women and Beloved Sisters* (W.W. Norton & Company 1998).

Estes, Clarissa Pinkola. *Women Who Run With the Wolves: Myths and Stories of the Wild Woman Archetype* (Ballantine Books 1992).

Von Franz, Marie-Louise. *The Interpretation of Fairy Tales* (Shambhala 1996).

Frankel, Valerie Estelle. *From Girl to Goddess: The Heroine's Journey through Myth and Legend* (McFarland & Company 2010).

Cashdan, Sheldon. *The Witch Must Die: How Fairy Tales Shape Our Lives* (Basic Books 1999).

Brazelton, T. Berry. *Touchpoints: Your Child's Emotional and Behavioral Development Birth to 3* (Da Capo Lifelong Books 1992).

Hinshaw, Stephen. *The Triple Bind: Saving Our Teenage Girls from Today's Pressures* (Ballantine Books 2009).

Simmons, Rachel. *Odd Girl Out: The Hidden Culture of Aggression in Girls* (Harcourt Inc. 2002).

Simmons, Rachel. *The Curse of the Good Girl* (The Penguin Press 2009

Brown, Lyn Mikel and Gilligan, Carol. *Meeting at the Crossroads: The Landmark Book about the Turning points in Girls' and Women's Lives* (Ballantine Books 1992).

Gilligan, Carol. *In a Different Voice: Psychological Theory and Women's Development* (Harvard University Press 1993).

Brizendine, Louann. *The Female Brain* (Morgan Road Books 2006).

Brizendine, Louann. *The Male Brain* (Broadway Books 2010).

Gurian, Michael. *The Wonder of Girls: Understanding the Hidden Nature of Our Daughters* (Pocket Books 2002).

Pipher, Mary. *Reviving Ophelia: Saving the Selves of Adolescent Girls* (Ballantine Books 1994).

Hersch, Patricia. *A Tribe Apart: A Journey Into the Heart of American Adolescence* (Fawcett Columbine 1998).

Wiseman, Rosalind. *Queen Bees and Wannabes* (Crown Publishers 2002).

Stepp, Laura Sessions. *Our Last Best Shot: Guiding Our Children Through Early Adolescence* (Riverhead Books 2000).

Cohen-Sandler, Roni. *Stressed Out Girls* (Viking 2005).

Kilbourne, Jean. *Deadly Persuasion: Why Women and Girls Must Fight the Addictive Power of Advertising* (The Free Press 1999).

Durham, M. Gigi. *The Lolita Effect: The Media Sexualization of Young Girls and What We Can Do About It* (The Overlook Press 2008).

Kilbourne, Jean and Levin, Diane. *So Sexy So Soon: The New Sexualized Childhood and What Parents Can Do to Protect Their Kids* (Ballantine Books 2008).

Maine, Margo. *Body Wars: Making Peace With Women's Bodies* (Gurze Books 2000).

Stearns, Peter. *Fat History: Bodies and Beauty in the Modern World* (NYU Press 2002).

Orenstein, Peggy. *School Girls: Young Women, Self-Esteem, and the Confidence Gap* (Anchor Books 1994).

Snyderman, Nancy. *Girl in the Mirror: Mothers and Daughters in the Years of Adolescence* (Hyperion 2002).

Eagle, Carol and Colman, Carol. *All That She Can Be: Helping Your Daughter Achieve Her Full Potential* (Simon and Schuster 1993).

Sessions Stepp, Laura. *Unhooked: How Young Women Pursue Sex, Delay Love and Lose at Both* (Riverhead Books 2007).

Belenky, McVicker Clinchy, Rule Goldberger, Mattuck Tarule. *Women's Ways of Knowing: The Development of Self, Voice, and Mind* (Basic Books 1986).

Silver-Stock, Carrie. *Secrets Girls Keep: What Girls Hide(& Why) and How to Break the Stress of Silence* (Health Communications, Inc. 2009).

Lamb, Sharon. *The Secret Lives of Girls* (The Free Press 2001).

Ponton, Lynn. *The Sex Lives of Teenagers* (Dutton 2000).

Holmes, Melissa & Hutchison, Trish. *Girlology: A Girl's Guide to Stuff That Matters* (Health Communications Inc. 2005).

Apter, Terri and Josselson, Ruthellen. *Best Friends: The Pleasures and Perils of Girls' and Women's Friendships* (Three Rivers Press 1998).

Thompson, Michael. *Best Friends, Worst Enemies: Understanding the Social Lives of Children* (Ballantine Books 2001).

Covey, Stephen. *The 8ᵗʰ Habit: From Effectiveness to Greatness* (Free Press 2004).

Anthony, Michelle and Lindert, Reyna. *Little Girls Can Be Mean: Four Steps to Bully-Proof Girls in the Early Grades* (St. Martin's Griffin 2010).

Cooper, Scott. *Sticks and Stones: 7 Ways Your Child Can Deal With Teasing, Conflict, and Other Hard Times* (Times Books 2000).

Dellasega, Cheryl and Nixon, Charisse. *Girl Wars: 12 Strategies That Will End Female Bullying* (Fireside 2003).

Berg, Barbara. *Sexism in America: Alive, Well, and Ruining Our Future* (Lawrence Hill Books 2009).

Sandberg, Sheryl. *Lean In: Women, Work, and the Will To Lead* (Alfred A. Knopf 2013).

Settersten, Richard and Ray, Barbara. *Not Quite Adults: Why 20-Somethings Are Choosing a Slower Path to Adulthood, and Why It's Good for Everyone* (Bantam Books 2010).

Hine, Thomas. *The Rise & Fall of the American Teenager* (Avon Books 1999).

Csikszentmihalyi, Mihaly. *Flow: The Psychology of Optimal Experience* (Quality Paperback Book Club 2001).

Wilber, Jessica. *Totally Private & Personal: Journalling Ideas for Girls and Young Women* (Free Spirit Publishing Inc. 1996). Devries Sokol, Dawn. *Doodle Diary: Art Journaling for Girls* (Gibbs Smith 2010)

Beck, Martha. *Finding Your Own North Star Journal* (Potter Style 2009).

Reber, Deborah. *Chicken Soup for the Teenage Soul: The Real Deal, Friends* (Scholastic Inc.2005).

Ford, Amanda. *Be True To Yourself: A Daily Guide for Teenage Girls* (Conari Press 2000).

Kirberger, Kimberly. *Chicken Soup for the Teenage Soul Journal* (Health Communications Inc. 1998).

Gadeberg, Jeanette. *Brave New Girls: Creative Ideas to Help Girls Be Confident, Healthy, & Happy* (Fairview Press 1997).

Dellasega, Cheryl. *The Girl's Friendship Journal* (Champion Press 2006).

My Favorite Books For Girls

Be Yourself:

Stand Tall, Molly Lou Melon, Patty Lovell - be confident in yourself

Odd Velvet, Mary Whitcomb - love and believe in yourself, accept differences

The Boy Who Grew Flowers, Jen Wojtowicz - accept and embrace differences

Stephanie's Ponytail, Robert Munsch - march to your own drum- not compare self

Brontorina, James Howe - love yourself

I Wish I Were a Butterfly, James Howe - love and accept yourself

The Rough-Face Girl, Rafe Martin - inner beauty, believe in yourself

The Ugly Duckling, Monique Peterson - believe in yourself

Freckleface Strawberry, Julianne Moore - accept yourself as you are

Makeup Mess, Robert Munsch - girls are more beautiful without makeup

Chrysanthemum, Kevin Henkes - love yourself, supportive adults

Smelly Socks, Robert Munsch - okay to be unique and not worry about what others think

Kiss Me I'm Perfect, Robert Munsch - not care what others think, dress for yourself

Pete the Cat: I Love My White Shoes, Eric Litwin - you are in charge of your story

So Few of Me, Peter Reynolds - too busy and stressed, simplify

I Like Myself, Karen Beaumont - love yourself

Friendships:

The Sandwich Swap, Queen Rania - accept differences

Farfallina and Marcel, Holly Keller- best friends forever

Help!, Holly Keller - don't judge friends

The Hating Book, Charlotte Zolotow -

misunderstandings/assumptions hurt friendships

Snail Started It!, Katja Reide - negativity spreads

Lilly's Purple Plastic Purse, Kevin Henkes - misunderstandings

Rosie's Story, Martine Gogoll - how everyone feels different, story

writing to express self

Little Mouse's Painting, Diane Wolkstein- see things from other's

point of view

One Smile, Cindy McKinley – kindness, pay-it-forward

Ribbon Rescue, Robert Munsch - kindness/giving brings fulfillment

King Looie Katz, Dr. Seuss - don't just do what everyone else does,

be yourself vs. copy-cat

The Sneetches, Dr. Seuss - competition/ comparing self to others, include others

The Butter Battle Book, Dr. Seuss - power struggles lead to wars

The Zax, Dr. Seuss - power struggle because try to be right and best vs. win-win

We Share Everything, Robert Munsch - sharing with friends, setting boundaries

Enemy Pie, Derek Munson - befriending your enemies

Strong Girls:

Princess Pigsty, Cornelia Funke - be true to yourself

The Princess Knight, Cornelia Funke - go for what you want

Princess Hyacinth, Florence Parry Heide - be true to yourself

The Princess and the Pig, Jonathan Emmett - go for what you want

The Paper Bag Princess, Robert Munsch - brave girls don't need boys!

Princess Smartypants, Babette Cole - go for what you want

Sheila Rae, The Brave, Kevin Henkes - overcome your fears

Where is Gah-Ning?, Robert Munsch - go for what you want-

persistence

Creativity:

The Dot, Peter Reynolds - not judge yourself, find your passions

Ish, Peter Reynolds - follow passions, not be hard on yourself

Purple, Green and Yellow, Robert Munsch - be creative!

Bridget's Beret, Tom Lichtenheld - overcoming artist's block

Parents:

Mars Needs Moms, Berkeley Breathed - appreciating mothers

Something Good, Robert Munsch - girl wants to be valued by dad

Fairy Tale Books:

The Barefoot Book of Princesses, Caitlin Matthews

The Barefoot Book of Fairy Tales, Malachy Doyle

Not One Damsel in Distress, Jane Yolen

Don't Kiss the Frog, Fiona Waters

Anderson's Fairy Tales, Hans Christian Andersen

CPSIA information can be obtained
at www.ICGtesting.com
Printed in the USA
FFOW01n2300250814
7035FF